Reviewer Praise for Other Best-selling Books By Douglas Gray

THE COMPLETE CANADIAN SMALL BUSINESS GUIDE (with Diana Gray)

"This guide is truly a gold mine ... taps into the authors' extensive expertise ... an encyclopedic compendium ... the bible of Canadian small business ..."

Profit magazine

"...Thorough and wide-ranging ... bursts with practical tips and explanations ..."

Vancouver Sun

"The ultimate in small-biz aid—if I ever quit my day job this is one of the first books I'd rush out and buy."

Linda A. Fox, *The Toronto Sun*

HOME INC.: THE CANADIAN HOME-BASED BUSINESS GUIDE (with Diana Gray)

"...Should be required reading for all potential home-basers ... authoritative, current and comprehensive ..."

Edmonton Journal

"An absolute necessity for your bookshelf ... crammed with useful information ... will pay for itself in short order."

Victoria Times-Colonist

THE CANADIAN SNOWBIRD GUIDE

"...an invaluable guide to worry-free part-time living in the U.S. ... by one of Canada's best-selling authors of business and personal finance books ..."

Globe & Mail

"... the book is a complete how-to written in his characteristically thorough style ... If you or someone close to you winters in the U.S., you should have this book ..."

Business in Vancouver

THE CANADIAN GUIDE TO WILL AND ESTATE PLANNING (with John Budd)

"A bargain for its price, it should be part of every family's library."

The Globe and Mail

"The 80 pages of sources and forms are almost as valuable as the tips in the rest of *The Canadian Guide to Will and Estate Planning.*

Mike Grenby, *Money Matters*

"This is an informative, practical guide to some of the issues, challenges and vocabulary of estate planning. The authors—a lawyer and a chartered accountant—cover all the bases, from the importance of preparing a will, to powers of attorney, trusts, tax planning and funerals."

The National Post

Best-selling Books by Douglas Gray

SMALL BUSINESS TITLES
- *The Complete Canadian Small Business Guide* (with Diana Gray), 3rd edition
- *So You Want To Buy a Franchise* (with Norm Friend)
- *Home Inc.: The Canadian Home-Based Business Guide* (with Diana Gray), 2nd edition
- *Start and Run a Profitable Consulting Business*, 5th edition
- *Have You Got What It Takes?: The Entrepreneur's Complete Self-Assessment Guide*, 3rd edition
- *Marketing Your Product* (with Donald Cyr), 3rd edition

REAL ESTATE TITLES
- *Mortgages Made Easy: The Canadian Guide to Home Financing*
- *Canadian Home Buying Made Easy: The Streetsmart Guide for First-Time Home Buyers*, 2nd edition
- *Condo Buying Made Easy: The Canadian Guide to Apartment and Townhouse Condos, Co-ops and Timeshares*, 2nd edition

PERSONAL FINANCE / RETIREMENT PLANNING TITLES
- *The Canadian Guide to Will and Estate Planning* (with John Budd)
- *The Canadian Snowbird Guide: Everything You Need to Know About Living Part-time in the USA and Mexico*, 3rd edition

The Canadian Small Business

LEGAL ADVISOR

Douglas Gray, LL.B.

McGraw-Hill Ryerson

Toronto   Montréal   Boston   Burr Ridge, IL   Dubuque, IA   Madison, WI
New York   San Francisco   St. Louis   Bangkok   Bogotá   Caracas   Kuala Lumpur
Lisbon   London   Madrid   Mexico City   Milan   New Delhi   Santiago   Seoul
Singapore   Sydney   Taipei

McGraw-Hill
Ryerson Limited
A Subsidiary of The McGraw-Hill Companies

Care has been taken to trace ownership of copyright material contained in this text; however, the publisher will welcome any information that enables them to rectify any reference or credit for subsequent editions.

The material in this publication is provided for information purposes only. Laws, regulations and procedures are constantly changing, and the examples given are intended to be general guidelines only. This book is sold with the understanding that neither the author nor the publisher is engaged in rendering professional advice. It is recommended that legal, accounting, tax, and other advice or assistance be obtained before acting on any information contained in this book. Personal services of a competent professional should be sought.

ISBN: 0-07-551734-5

1234567890 WEB 0987654321
Printed and bound in Canada.

National Library of Canada Cataloguing in Publication Data

Gray, Douglas A.
   The Canadian small business legal advisor

Includes index.
ISBN 0-07-551734-5

1. Small business—Law and legislation—Canada—Popular.   I. Title.

KE1658.G73   2001   346.71'0652   C2001-901464-3

Publisher: **Joan Homewood**
Editorial Co-ordinator: **Catherine Leek**
Production Co-ordinator: **Susanne Penny**
Editor: **Tita Zierer**
Interior Design and Electronic Page
   Composition: **Heidy Lawrance and Associates**
Cover Design: **Sharon Lucas**

Table of Contents

Preface

Every business decision involves a legal implication. Every stage of your business involves legal issues. And, every business is different with different potential legal problems. Legal issues need to be understood as much as possible in advance, so problems can be pre-empted by the early warning signs and timely streetsmart legal advice. You owe it to yourself to be pro-active about anticipating and avoiding legal difficulties.

This book was written out of a desire to help Canadian small business owners avoid the common legal pitfalls. With over 25 years offering services to small business as a lawyer or consultant, it was frustrating to see how many business owners repeatedly fell into the classic legal traps. The unfortunate reality is that all these problems could have been anticipated and avoided in many cases, from a lawyer's perspective. The implications of these legal traps can be very onerous. In the more serious cases, the business could go under with the business owner losing a lot of money, or all the money he or she has. The implications on one's personal and marital health and well being are often most unpleasant. This is not the type of life learning curve you want to experience.

The basic premise of this book is that you can run your business with less legal hassle and expense if you spend a small amount of time in the beginning to understand the relevant laws, what you must do, should do and don't have to do.

A word of caution. Although this book explores the many types of pitfalls and legal issues you are likely to encounter, don't make the mistake of thinking that a book can replace your lawyer. Only your lawyer can give you customized advice on the tactics and strategies to follow in your specific situation. Provincial laws impacting on your business can vary from province to province and from municipality to municipality. Federal laws may or may not be applicable to your business, depending on the nature of your business. This book is therefore simply a guide. It is intended to enhance your general level of awareness, so you will have a better understanding of the legal issues involved. The contents of this book will provide you with more knowledge to make your legal advisory meetings more productive and relevant. This will save you time, money and stress.

Although the book chapters are mutually exclusive, the contents and issues are frequently interrelated. As in any business operation, every decision has to be viewed in the context of the effect it will have on the other areas of the business.

The 17 chapters cover the range of key issues you need to know when starting or operating a business. Chapters cover legal and other advisors; types of business structures; creditor proofing your business; regulations, zoning and licencing; estate planning; tax strategies; and raising money. Also covered are leases; hiring and firing staff; insurance; credit and collection; buying a business; buying a franchise; and buying real estate. The final chapters discuss intellectual property; litigation and the ADR process; and bankruptcy and insolvency. An extensive glossary will help you understand the jargon. You will find a section at the end of the book (page 269) inviting reader input, as well as contact information.

I hope you enjoy this book and find the information and insights practical and helpful. Best wishes for a long, enjoyable and successful small business career.

Douglas Gray, LL.B.
Vancouver, B.C.
June, 2001

Acknowledgements

I am indebted to the thousands of Canadian small business entrepreneurs who have shared their experiences with me over the past 25 years, through my seminars, or business consulting and legal practices.

I am also grateful to the many individuals who have given generously of their time and expertise in the preparation of this book.

Many thanks to Lloyd Murphy, C.A., of BDO Dunwoody in Vancouver, for his input on insolvency and bankruptcy. Thanks also to Stephen Lim, C.A., in Vancouver, for his review of the section on tax. I appreciate all the assistance from John Budd, C.A., of Toronto, for his expert guidance on tax and estate planning issues and strategies. Many thanks to Gary Arkin, LL.B., of Moffat and Company in Ottawa, for his assistance on intellectual property.

I would like to thank my dedicated assistant, Laurie Chappell, who helped keep the project on track by effectively meeting deadlines, and whose proofreading, editing and technical skills were invaluable.

Last, but not least, I would like to thank the staff at McGraw-Hill Ryerson for their consistent patience, encouragement, assistance and professionalism.

One

Legal and
Other Advisors

Introduction

Professional advisors are essential to protect your tax and estate planning interests. They can provide knowledge, expertise and objective advice in areas in which you have little experience.

It is important to recognize when it is necessary to call in an expert to assist you. Because of the costs associated with hiring a lawyer, accountant, or financial planner, some people are inclined to try the do-it-yourself approach. This can be a short-sighted, detrimental approach. For instance, the person who processes his or her own income tax return rather than hiring a professional tax accountant may miss out on tax exemptions that could save much more than the cost of the accountant's time. Or a person who does his or her own will or power of attorney could end up having the will or power of attorney deemed invalid due to a technicality.

Professional advisors serve different functions, and you have to be very selective in your screening process. The right selection will enhance your peace of mind and protect your legal and financial health. The wrong selection will be costly in terms of time, money, and stress and could leave your estate unnecessarily depleted.

General Factors to Consider

When selecting professional advisors, consider the person's professional qualifications and experience in your specific area of need. Prepare a list of questions, to pose to each prospective advisor. Prioritize the questions in case you run out of time. You want to control the agenda but also determine if the advisor is proactive and asks you questions. Some people may feel awkward discussing fees and areas of expertise, but it is important to establish these matters before you make a decision to use that person's services.

Qualifications

Before you entrust an advisor with your affairs, ensure that he or she has the appropriate qualifications to do the job. This may include a lawyer's or accountant's professional degree, or professional accreditation and related experience. An active member of a professional association or institute usually indicates ongoing interest and current professional training.

Experience

Factors such as the degree of expertise, the number of years' experience as an advisor, and percentage of time spent practising in that area are critically important when choosing an advisor. The fact that a lawyer has practised law for ten years does not necessarily indicate a high degree of expertise in the area in which you are seeking advice, for example, will preparation. Perhaps only 10% of the practice has been spent in that specific area.

An accountant with 15 years' experience in small business accounting is not likely to have expertise on tax and estate planning strategies. You may require specialized expertise on Canada/US cross-border tax and estate planning, if you have assets in the US. If you don't ask about the degree of expertise and length of experience in your specific need area, it may make the difference between selecting the right or wrong advisor.

Compatible Personality

Make certain that you feel comfortable with the individual's personality in terms of the communication, attitude, sincere approach, candour and commitment to your needs. A healthy respect and rapport will increase your comfort level and enhance understanding of the issues. If you don't feel comfortable with the chemistry, don't continue the relationship. If you don't like someone, you'll resist contacting that person, possibly compromising your best interests.

Good Communication Skills

You want an advisor who is a good listener, who elicits your responses and provides feedback in understandable layperson's terms. Any issues and options should be fully disclosed, with pros, cons and recommendations.

Your advisor should return your phone calls promptly and keep you regularly informed in writing. Some people and situations require more frequent communication than others do.

Accessibility

If your advisor become too busy for you, reconsider the relationship. Your needs should be a priority. If you are shunted to a junior advisor against your wishes, your original advisor may be culling clientele to concentrate on more lucrative clients.

Objectivity

If advice is tainted in any way by bias or personal financial benefit, obviously it is unreliable and self-serving. Get a minimum of three opinions on your personal situation, before carefully deciding which professionals to select.

Trust

Whether the person is a lawyer, accountant, financial planner or other advisor, if you don't intuitively trust the advice as being solely in your best interests, never use that person again. You have far too much to lose, in terms of your financial security and peace of mind, to have any doubts whatsoever. You cannot risk the chance that advice is governed primarily by the advisor's financial self-interest, with your interests as a secondary consideration.

Integrity

Your advisor should display a high standard of personal and professional integrity. The advisor's reputation with other professional colleagues is one reference point. Keeping confidential information confidential is another.

Depending on the nature of the advisory relationship, you may disclose your personal needs, wants, hopes and dreams, as well as concerns. This puts you in a potentially vulnerable position.

Confidence

You must have confidence in your advisor if you are going to rely on his or her advice. After considering the person's qualifications, experience, personality and style, you may feel a strong degree of confidence and trust in the individual. If you do not, don't use the person as an advisor.

Fees

Are the fees and payment terms fair, competitive and affordable? Do they match the person's qualifications and experience? The saying "you get what you pay for" can be true of fees charged by lawyers, accountants, financial planners and other professionals. For instance, if you need a good tax accountant, you may have to pay a high hourly rate for quality advice. On the other hand, if you only require the preparation of annual financial statements, then perhaps a junior accountant can do the job competently at a more affordable rate. Be certain the rate is within your budget, or you may not fully use the advisor because of the expense.

Most initial meetings with a lawyer, accountant or financial planner are free or a nominal fee. Both parties can evaluate the advisory relationship for a good fit.

References

References and word-of-mouth referrals are particularly important for any advisor taking an overall holistic approach to your financial affairs. Ask for professional references and then contact those professionals and ask about the advisor's strong attributes and any professional weak points. Also, ask how long they have been dealing with each other. Don't feel embarrassed to ask the tough questions—candid feedback can provide you with a telling reality check.

Don't ask for or expect an advisor to provide you with a list of clients as this would normally breach confidentiality

Comparison

See a minimum of three advisors before deciding which advisor is right for you. Seeing how each respond to your questions will be an effective benchmark in making a qualitative comparison.

Selecting a Lawyer

A lawyer is recommended when drafting a will, living will, or powers of attorney, when creating a trust, planning your estate, buying or selling real estate, and when negotiating leases, contracts, insurance or accident claims or legal disputes. Every business decision has legal implications. Although your lawyer will give you legal advice as to your rights, remedies and options, you must decide on the action to be taken.

Protect Yourself from the Beginning!

David and Monique were starting a software development business. With their limited budget, they did not feel they could afford a lawyer. However, a friend suggested they phone the lawyer referral service in their province, and obtain a free initial consultation. They interviewed three business lawyers through this service and the advice they received convinced them to change their original plans to minimize the risk. They decided to set up their business structure as a corporation to reduce personal exposure; subcontract with consultants rather than hire employees; request substantial deposits and progress payments for software development; develop standardized client contracts; and sign a partnership agreement with each other. If they had not obtained legal advice, they would not have thought of these issues at the outset, any of which could have caused harm to the business.

Qualifications

Lawyers generally have a Bachelor of Laws degree (LL.B.) from a recognized Canadian university, and have to be licensed to practice by the provincial law society in the province they are practising. A lawyer in Canada is called both a barrister and a solicitor, but depending upon that individual's preference, the lawyer may act as a barrister or solicitor or both. A barrister practises courtroom law and deals in civil and/or criminal legal matters. A solicitor generally does not attend court, but can draft or review legal agreements, including wills, leases, mortgages or contracts, estate or trust matters, or real estate conveyancing.

How to Find a Lawyer

Lawyer Referral Services

Most provinces have a lawyer referral program, usually coordinated through the Canadian Bar Association. Simply look in the telephone directory under Lawyer Referral Service or contact the provincial Law Society or Canadian Bar Association branch in your province.

When you call, explain briefly the specific problem you have, or the type of law on which you want a lawyer's opinion. The lawyer referral service will give you the name of a lawyer in your geographic area with whom you can meet for up to 30 minutes for free or at a nominal fee (generally around $10). At the end of the interview the lawyer will estimate the cost of your legal requirements and how long it would take. Most lawyer referral services programs will only give you one lawyer's name per day, so keep phoning back to get the three names for comparison purposes. However, be careful because lawyers can have their names associated with up to three different areas of law. Ask what percentage of time is spent in your area of interest. As a guideline, use a minimum of 50%. There is a direct correlation between the percentage of time spent in a particular field and the quality of expertise, interest and related advice.

Referral by Friends, Banker, Accountant or Other Professional Advisor

Asking friends or other advisors for referral can be helpful but a friend or relative may suggest a lawyer whose speciality has nothing to do with your area of need. Ask what that person's personal experience has been with that lawyer. Maybe the person is just a next-door neighbour or friend. Always do your own comparisons.

Yellow Pages and Newspaper Advertisements

In the Yellow Pages telephone directory under the heading "Lawyers," you may note that some lawyers have a preferred interest or designated speciality. Offers of free initial consultation are common. With the removal of restrictions on advertising in most provinces, some law firms are now using newspaper ads. Free initial consultations are also an effective "loss leader" marketing technique.

Preparing for the Meeting

Since you are buying your lawyer's time, the less you use, the less it will cost. On the other hand, it is important that you clearly understand the advice and options. Before going to see your lawyer, get all your papers and documents in order—assuming that you wish to get advice on existing facts. Then, write out all the issues that you want advice on, and the associated questions. Deal with critical matters first. It may be helpful to give a copy of your questions to the lawyer, who could use them as an agenda. Compiling your questions will force you to focus on the reasons for seeing the lawyer. Stick to the facts, good and bad. Ask questions if you don't understand, and keep informed of developments if you are retaining the lawyer on an ongoing basis.

Understanding Fees and Costs

Following are the most common fee arrangements and the types of costs you might encounter.

Hourly Fee

A lawyer bills out on a fixed rate per hour for all work done. The fee could range between $100 and $400 per hour.

Fixed Fee

If you hire a lawyer to provide a routine service such as a conveyance (transfer of property to your name), or a will, the lawyer may be able to quote a flat fee, regardless of how much work might be involved. For example, a simple will may cost from $200 to $250.

Percentage Fee

Sometimes fees are calculated as a percentage of the value of the subject matter. This approach is often used when probating an estate. Most provinces have legislation that limits the maximum percentage that can be charged, regardless of the time spent.

Contingency Fee

Many provinces allow lawyers to charge on a contingency fee basis, that is, for a percentage of the total amount awarded if the case is won. For example, let's say that you have a strong case, but do not have the funds to pay your lawyer at the outset. Your lawyer may agree to act for you and charge a percentage of the amount that you eventually receive, either at trial or settlement. If you lose or the matter is not settled, the lawyer gets nothing for the time spent. You would be responsible for paying the lawyer's disbursements, however.

Resolving Disputes

Misunderstandings on fees or other matters should be immediately clarified to avoid allowing them to become serious problems. You may decide at any time to have the working file transferred to a new lawyer. If you seriously question a lawyer's invoice, you can have it "taxed" or reviewed by a court registrar. This is an informal procedure and results in the fee being upheld or reduced. Your local court office will be able to provide further information.

If you feel that the lawyer acted improperly or incompetently, you have other forms of recourse. All provincial law societies require their members to have a certain minimum coverage for professional liability insurance for negligent or incompetent advice. Individual law firms could have additional coverage. If trust funds are missing, the Law Society allocates funds to cover that situation. Suing your lawyer is an option, but certainly the last resort.

If you have complaints such as possible conflict of interest, poor advice or other forms of professional misconduct or incompetence, you can file a formal complaint with the provincial law society. The complaints committee has many forms of discipline.

Selecting an Accountant

Many accountants are generalists who can provide basic advice on tax and estate planning issues. Others have branched out into financial planning, have obtained their CFP (Certified Financial Planner) designation. They can develop a full financial plan and assist you in implementing it. Some accountants specialize in international tax and estate planning.

Qualifications

Anyone can call himself or herself an accountant without any qualifications, experience, regulations, or accountability to a professional association. There are two main designations of qualified professional accountants in Canada that could provide tax and estate planning advice—Chartered Accountant (CA), and Certified General Accountant (CGA). A Certified Management Accountant (CMA) does not normally get involved in individual tax or estate planning. Provincial statutes govern accountants with the above designations.

How to Find an Accountant

Again, "the rule of three" applies to seeking an accountant, in terms of speaking to three different tax experts. Ensure that the accountant specializes in tax and estate planning matters. Most initial meetings are free, without any further obligation, but clarify this in advance. Remember that some professional tax experts are very conservative in their advice while others are the opposite. Some enjoy the professional and intellectual challenge of toeing the fine line, and adopt an aggressive approach to tax planning strategies. Others are more reluctant to do this. In all instances, use only accredited professional accountants. They have too much to lose, in terms of their career and reputation, to advise you improperly.

Professional Associations

You can telephone or write the professional institute or association which governs CAs or CGAs to obtain the names of three accountants who provide service to small businesses within your geographic area. Most initial consultations will be free of charge.

Referral by Friends, Banker, Lawyer or Other Financial Advisor

Friends or a banker, lawyer or financial advisor may be able to give you names of people they personally deal with or know.

Yellow Pages and Newspaper Ads
In the Yellow Pages under the heading "Accountants," you will generally find listings under the categories "chartered" and "certified general." Occasionally you will see ads in newspapers or other publications placed by accounting firms offering services in your area.

Preparing for the Meeting
Prior to your first meeting, prepare a prioritized list of your questions and concerns in writing. Ask about fees, which will vary, depending upon experience, speciality, service provided and size of firm. The fee can range between $150 and $250 or more per hour for specified tax and estate planning advice.

Resolving Disputes
If you have complaints about fees, service or conduct, attempt to resolve the dispute directly with the accountant concerned. If that doesn't work, complain to the manager of the firm. Depending on the issues, you can also complain to the provincial professional accounting association. The association can investigate and discipline members. In addition, these provincial professional associations will have a basic insurance package to cover professional liability for negligence or incompetence, as well as missing trust funds. Individual accounting firms may have supplemental professional liability insurance coverage.

Selecting a Financial Planner
Everyone's financial planning needs are different. The process should take into account all the psychological and financial factors that impact on your financial goals and objectives and provide a long-term strategy. Some financial planners liaise with other professionals to make sure that the overall plan is integrated.

Qualifications
Anyone can call himself or herself a financial planner; no federal, provincial, or local laws require certain qualifications (except Quebec), such as those imposed upon lawyers. However, several associations grant credentials that signify a planner's level of education, although criteria can change from time to time, so check with the association. Some of the most commonly recognized designations follow.

Registered Financial Planner (RFP)
This designation is awarded to members of the Canadian Association of Financial Planners (CAFP) who have engaged in the practice of financial planning for a minimum of two years and who have fulfilled satisfactory educational requirements. An individual with an RFP must take ongoing professional development courses and be covered by professional liability insurance, generally a minimum of $1,000,000. An RFP is also governed by a professional code of ethics and can be

disciplined for breaching that code of ethics. Many financial planners with an RFP also have a CFP designation (see below) and other designations.

Certified Financial Planner (CFP)

CFP is an internationally recognized designation first introduced into Canada by the Financial Planners Standards Council of Canada (FPSCC) (their Web site is *www.cfp-ca.org*).

To obtain a CFP, one must take one of three approved financial planning programs, each taking an average of two years to complete. A six-hour, two-part exam is written. Candidates must also satisfy a work requirement of at least two years in the industry. After the licence is granted, it is renewed annually, as long as the planner follows the code of ethics and completes 30 hours of continuing education each year. If complaints are received by the FPSCC about a planner, and if they prove to be valid and serious, FPSCC has the authority to revoke the CFP designation.

Chartered Financial Consultant (CHFC)

The CHFC designation is conferred by the Life Underwriters Association of Canada (LUAC), which deals with life and health insurance agents. CHFCs may assist with wealth accumulation and retirement planning, and may sell mutual fund products and segregated funds. To earn the designation, the financial planner must pass various courses, possess industry experience and adhere to strict ethical standards. These individuals may also have a CLU, or Chartered Life Underwriter designation, also awarded by the LUAC. This latter designation deals primarily with life and disability insurance products and group benefits for employees.

Chartered Financial Analyst (CFA)

This designation is awarded to those who pass a test administered by the Financial Analysts Federation and demonstrate expertise in investing in mutual funds, stocks, bonds and other investments. Many CFAs have also branched out into full-service financial planning as investment counsellors. CFAs would normally be used if you have a lot of money to invest and require the assistance of an investment professional. They frequently use a team approach with lawyers, tax accountants and insurance brokers to co-ordinate and integrate information and strategies.

How to Find a Financial Planner

Referral by Friend, Accountant or Lawyer

If using word-of-mouth referral, ask why a particular person is being recommended. Does the person making the referral currently use the planner's services? How long have they known the person professionally?

Professional Associations

There is one national financial planning association in Canada, with provincial chapters, who will provide you with names and other educational information.

Canadian Association of Financial Planners (CAFP)
1 St. Clair Avenue East, Suite 700
Toronto, ON M4T 2V7
Tel: 416-593-6592 or
1-800-346-CAFP (2237)
Web site: *www.cafp.org*

By contacting the CAFP, you will be sent a free publication called *A Consumer Guide to Financial Planning* and given a contact phone number for your provincial chapter. You will also be sent a roster of Registered Financial Planners (RFP) in your province. This list shows experience, credentials, services provided, lists any financial products sold, and outlines the method of payment, e.g. fee for service, commission, or both.

Yellow Pages and Newspapers Ads

Check the Yellow Pages under "Financial Planning Consultants." For investing advice only, look under "Investment Advisory Services." You will also frequently see ads in specialty publications or in the finance section of the newspaper.

Consumer Shows

In the fall and spring of each year, two- and three-day financial and money shows for consumers are offered in major cities in Canada. You can speak to exhibitors, pick up information, and listen to seminars. The major national producer for these types of shows is the Financial Forum. Check the dates on their Web site at *www.financialforum.ca*.

How to Select a Financial Planner

Once you've made the decision to seek the services of a financial planner, you may have many more questions: Which professional is right for me? How do I identify a competent financial planner who can coordinate all aspects of my financial life?

Just as you select a lawyer or accountant, base your decision on a number of factors—education, qualifications, experience and reputation.

When selecting your financial planner, choose one you can work with confidently. It is your responsibility and right to fully inquire about the practitioner's background, numbers of years in practice, credentials, client references and other relevant information. Meet with the practitioner to determine compatibility and financial planning style. Meet with at least three planners before you make your final selection. To work effectively, it's important to find someone with whom you feel completely comfortable.

How a Financial Planner is Compensated

It is important to understand, and be comfortable with, the way your financial planner gets paid. Financial advisors are compensated in one of four ways—solely by fees, a combination of fees and commissions, solely by commissions, or through a salary paid by an organization that receives fees. In some cases, financial advisors may offer more than one payment option. Here's how these different methods work.

Fee-only

Many lawyers, accountants and fee-only financial planners charge an hourly rate, including time in research, reviewing the plan with you and discussing implementation options. Others just charge a flat amount, but usually offer a no-cost, no-obligation initial consultation. Some will do a computerized profile and assessment of your situation for a fee that can range from $200 to $500 or more.

Fee-only financial advisors typically advise you on investments, insurance and other financial vehicles, but do not benefit from commissions. The planner has no vested interest in having you buy one product over another. Some fee-only financial planners will help you follow through on their recommendations using mutual funds and other investments. Otherwise, you will have to take your own initiative.

Commission-only

Some financial advisors are compensated solely through commissions earned by selling investments and insurance including life insurance, annuities or mutual funds. A commission-only advisor will develop recommendations for your situation and goals, review the recommendations with you and discuss implementation.

In some cases, commissions are clearly disclosed, for example, a percentage front-end load commission on a mutual fund. In other cases, the fees are lumped into the general expenses of the product, as with life insurance, so you won't know how much your planner makes unless you ask. When you interview your potential planners, ask about the relative percentages of commission revenues from annuities, insurance products, mutual funds, stocks and bonds and other products. The planner's answers will give you a sense of the kind of advice the firm usually gives.

You could also pay ongoing charges that apply as long as you hold an investment. Some insurance companies pay planners trailer fees for each year a client pays premiums. In other situations, you must pay a fee if you sell a product before a set period of time has elapsed. These surrender charges, a percentage of your investment, reimburse the insurer for the commissions it has paid your planner. Some mutual funds require a back-end load fee, on early sale. These usually are applied on a sliding scale. After the set time period, you will not be charged. Some companies entice commission-motivated planners with free travel, merchandise, or investment research if their sales of a particular product reach a target level. Your planner might not like your questioning of his or her cash payment and perks. However, it is your right to know whether the products you buy generate direct fees and indirect benefits for the planner in order to decide whether the advice is self-serving or objective.

Fee Plus Commission
Some planners charge a fee for assessing your financial situation and making recommendations, and also earn a commission on the sale of some of those products.

Some planners are "captives" of one company, so they recommend only its product line. Others are independent and can recommend the mutual funds or insurance policies of any company with which they affiliate.

Another form of compensation, called fee offset, involves a reduction in fees for every product purchased. If you buy so many products that your entire fee is covered, request a refund of the fee you paid for your basic plan.

Salary
In most instances, the staff financial advisors at many banks, trust companies and credit unions are paid by salary, and earn neither fees nor commissions. Of course, there could be other monetary incentives based on the volume and value of the business done or quotas. Career advancement could also be tied to sales performance.

If an advisor helps you select and monitor the purchase of investments or insurance, there will be some cost to you and/or payment to the advisor. This could be in the form of a commission, redemption fees, trailer fees, or asset management fees.

Additionally, many investments charge annual management and transaction fees. For example, if you open an RRSP, the company that serves as trustee may charge an annual custodial fee for the service. Weekly comparisons of the management expense ratios of various funds are available in newspapers. These costs will be in addition to the fee for advice.

What to Know about a Financial Planner
Compensation is just one important element that should figure into your decision about hiring a financial advisor. Be sure that the planner you choose uses the financial planning process, including addressing your current situation, setting goals, identifying alternatives, selecting and implementing a course of action, and periodically reviewing. It should be a client-centred process. Education, credentials, references, trust and rapport are also important.

Choose the compensation method which best meets your needs. As a smart consumer, you want to know what you're buying and how much you're paying for it and you're entitled to that information. Do not consider hiring a financial planner who is reluctant to disclose how he or she is compensated.

Research shows that consumers rate "trust" and "ethics" as the most important elements in their relationship with financial advisors. In fact, survey respondents gave this response twice as often as they mentioned good advice and expertise.

Resolving Disputes

If you have any complaints about fees, service or conduct, first attempt to deal directly with the person concerned. If that does not resolve the matter, you can complain to management, the professional association that the advisor may belong to, the national industry association, the provincial regulatory association and the provincial securities commission with which the advisor is registered. If your company is a member of an organization that offers mediation services, be aware of your rights and obligations before you agree to mediation. You could have a claim against the Canadian Investor Protection Fund if the company is covered by that fund, in case of insolvency or bankruptcy. Litigation is the last resort, as the process is lengthy, expensive and unpredictable. Avoid potential advisory problems by pre-empting them through careful selection.

Selecting an Insurance Broker

An experienced insurance broker can help you by:

- Assessing your insurance needs
- Determining the type of policy
- Recommending the amount of coverage that you should have
- Obtaining competitive quotes, preparing comparative analysis, and making a recommendation
- Helping you with the policy application and arranging for any medical examinations that may be required and
- Providing ongoing advice and reviewing your insurance needs with you on a regular basis.

Qualifications

Insurance agents are licensed and regulated by the provincial governments. Some agents are tied to a particular insurance company, and will sell only the insurance products offered by that company. However, it has become far more common for life insurance agents to operate as "brokers" and to deal with any number of insurance companies, although officially licensed by one company. Agents who hold the designation "Chartered Life Underwriter" (CLU) have studied several areas of insurance and personal financial planning. Other professional designations, such as Chartered Financial Consultant (CH.F.C.) and Certified Financial Planner (CFP) may also attest to the agent's knowledge and experience.

How to Find an Insurance Broker

There are several ways to find an insurance broker:

- Look in the Yellow Pages under "insurance brokers."
- Ask your accountant, lawyer, business associates and friends for a recommendation.
- Ask your business, trade or professional association who they would recommend.

How to Select an Insurance Broker

Choose an agent you can trust, and who will take the time to listen to you and understand your needs. Ask the agent how long he or she has been in the business, and consider asking for references or a recommendation from one of the agent's other clients.

Ask if the agent has experience in dealing with business owners and their estate planning needs. Life insurance can be used in the family business succession planning, such as to provide funding for a shareholder buy-out arrangement, or to cover capital gains taxes arising on death.

Your insurance agent should be willing to work with your accountant, lawyer, investment advisor and tax advisor in order to develop the optimum estate planning strategy. Check with your business association, local Chamber of Commerce and provincial retail merchants association for special rates.

How Insurance Brokers are Compensated

Insurance agents earn their income in commissions on the insurance policies they sell. Commission rates vary from company to company, and from one life insurance product to another and recommendations should be evaluated as objectively as possible.

However, despite this apparent built-in lack of objectivity, the vast majority of life insurance agents are people of integrity who will not recommend the purchase of life insurance unless it is clearly warranted under the particular circumstances. They know that their recommendations must be able to withstand scrutiny by the client's accountant or financial advisor, and their reputations are at stake.

Resolving Disputes

If you have a problem with an insurance broker, deal with it directly, assertively and candidly. Put your concerns in writing so that there is a "paper trail." If this approach does not work, talk to their manager, then the regional or provincial manager, and even the national head office. You can also speak to the regulatory agency that licences insurance agents in your province (in the blue pages of your phone book). Always keep copies of your correspondence.

Selecting a Realtor

When buying or selling real estate relating to your business, the right realtor will make all the difference in ensuring a positive purchase or sale experience.

Qualifications

Real estate agents are regulated by provincial government real estate legislation. Agents have to successfully complete an approved real estate agent licensing course and re-new their licence annually.

As of 1995, a new relationship structure sometimes referred to as agency disclosure replaced the old system. Many people assumed that if they found a realtor and the house was listed on the MLS system for example, the realtor would represent their interests exclusively when an offer was presented and through negotiation.

The new system spells out the respective roles and responsibilities of each realtor involved. The seller still pays the real estate commission, which is shared with any other realtor involved. All disclosures of who is acting for whom is spelled out in the agreement of purchase and sale. Some agents working with the buyer may also enter into a Buyer Agency Contract. In other words, each realtor is acting exclusively for the benefit of the buyer or seller. However, if the listing realtor is also the selling realtor (double-end deal), the agent has to enter into a Limited Dual Agency Agreement. This is agreed upon and signed by both the buyer and seller. The agent modifies his or her exclusive obligations to both the buyer and the seller by limiting it primarily to confidentiality as to each party's motivation and personal information.

You can get more information from any real estate agent, real estate company, or your local real estate board.

How to Find a Realtor

There are a number of approaches to finding a good real estate agent:

- Friends, neighbours, and relatives can give you recommendations.
- Open houses provide an opportunity to meet realtors.
- Newspaper ads list the names and phone numbers of agents who are active in your area.
- "For Sale" signs provide an agent's name and phone number.
- Real estate firms in your area can be contacted.

How to Select a Realtor

Consider the following suggestions when choosing a realtor:

- Choose an agent familiar with the neighbourhood you are interested in. Such an agent will be on top of the available listings, will know comparable market prices, and can target the types of commercial properties that meet your needs.
- Choose an agent who is particularly familiar with the buying and selling of residential or commercial properties, depending on your needs. Choose an agent who is experienced and knowledgeable in the real estate industry. Look for an agent who is prepared to pre-screen properties so that you see only those that conform to your guidelines.
- Look for an agent who is familiar with the various conventional and creative methods of financing, including the effective use of mortgage brokers.
- Choose an agent who is knowledgeable on background such as length of time on the market, reason for sale, and price comparisons among similar properties. An agent familiar with the Multiple Listing System (MLS) computer can find a lot of information in a short time. Choose an agent who will be candid with you in suggesting an offer and explaining the reasons for the recommendation.

- Look for agent who has effective negotiating skills to ensure that your wishes are presented as clearly and persuasively as possible.
- Look for an agent who is working full-time.
- Look for an agent who attempts to upgrade professional skills and expertise.
- Look for an agent who is familiar with financial calculations.

How Realtors are Compensated

Traditionally the vendor pays the realtor on commission. Commissions are negotiable. Some are fixed percentages and some are variable, depending on the price involved. Some commissions are a negotiated flat rate, regardless of the sale price. Different commission structures exist for residential or commercial properties.

If there is more than one realtor involved, for example, a listing broker and a selling broker, then the commission is split based on an agreed formula, eg. 55% listing broker (because they incur more expenses to sell the property) and 45% to the selling broker.

Resolving Disputes

If you have a dispute with a realtor, keep a record of all your correspondence outlining the complaint. Speak to the realtor first, followed by their manager, then regional, provincial and national manager. If the complaint is more serious, complain to the local real estate board or provincial agency licencing realtors.

Summary

You need to have a minimum benchmark comparison of three advisors in each area of your interest, before you can make a reasonable decision which one to select, if any. As good advice is critical to your business and personal well being, the selection process has to be thorough. This process will also greatly accelerate your learning curve, confidence level and quality of decision-making.

Two

Business Structures

Introduction

One of your first considerations when starting a small business is the form of legal structure you should choose. This decision will be necessary before you set up a company bank account, apply for a business licence, or register your company name. Your main choices will include sole proprietorship, partnership, or corporation. If you are going into business with others, you need to have a shareholder or partnership agreement.

Types of Legal Structure

The type of legal structure you decide on will depend upon the type of business you are in, your potential risk and liability, and the amount of money you need to start and expect to earn. If your potential risk and liability are high, the incorporation process will provide protection from possible disasters. Become familiar with the differences between legal structures, and consult a lawyer and tax accountant.

Accountants might say there is no tax benefit to incorporating until you are earning a certain amount of money. However if there is any risk, incorporating for personal liability protection is the priority whether you are working at your home or outside your home. Refer to the chapter on Creditor Proofing Your Business.

Sole Proprietorship

A sole proprietorship owns a business in his or her personal name, or operates through a trade name. The business income and the owner's personal income are the same for tax purposes; business profits are reported on the owner's personal income tax return, based on federal and provincial income tax schedules. Business expenses and losses are deductible. It is advisable though, to keep personal and business bank accounts separate so that Canada Customs and Revenue Agency does not deem both accounts as business accounts. Pay yourself a salary from your business account and deposit it into your personal account for your personal needs (food, clothing, lodging, personal savings). A proprietor is personally responsible for all debts or liabilities of the business.

Partnership

A partnership is a proprietorship with two or more owners. The owners may not necessarily be 50-50 partners; the percentage may reflect their investment and contribution to the partnership. Each partner shares profits and losses in proportion to his or her respective percentage interest. The partnership business itself does not pay any tax. Instead, the individual partners pay tax based on their portion of the net profit or loss, shown on their personal tax return. Each partner is personally liable for the full amount of the debts and liabilities of the business. Each of the individuals is authorized to act on behalf of the company, and can bind the partnership legally, except if stated otherwise in a partnership agreement. Don't enter any partnership agreement without a written agreement between the partners regarding responsibilities for financing, sharing the profits and losses, specific duties, and other important considerations.

In a proprietorship or partnership, the company continues until the owner ceases to carry on the business or dies. If the business uses a name different from the owner's personal name, the company name (a "trade style" name) should be registered with the appropriate provincial registry. Your provincial government business name registration department will provide the necessary forms and a copy of the *Partnership Act*, which governs sole proprietorships and partnerships.

Advantages of a Sole Proprietorship or Partnership

- Sole proprietorships and partnerships are easy to form. In most provinces, there is a nominal one-time fee for registering the company.
- The personal tax rate is lower than the rate for corporations in certain situations. During the early phases of the business, it may be more tax advantageous to remain a sole proprietorship or partnership. Once the business is earning about $30,000 annually, the company could be rolled over into a corporation.
- Business losses can be offset against the owner's other income, thereby reducing the owner's overall personal marginal tax rate. Check with your accountant regarding current tax legislation.

Disadvantages of a Sole Proprietorship or Partnership

- The owner is personally liable for all debts and obligations of the business.
- It is frequently difficult to raise capital, apart from conventional loans, because of the potential liability and risk.
- Customers and creditors may perceive the proprietorship as having a low level of business sophistication. It may be perceived to be in business for a short term rather than long term.

- Some government loan, subsidy, or guarantee programs are available only to limited companies (corporations).
- Sale of the business could involve having to disclose owner's personal tax return.
- If the business fails, the owner(s) are not eligible to collect Employment Insurance benefits unless they have accrued enough employment time elsewhere or before pursuing the business.

Corporation (Limited Company)

A corporation is a legal entity separate from the owner or owners of the business. After being incorporated with the provincial or federal registry, the corporation must file annual reports, regular tax returns and pay tax on the profits of the business. The owners of the business are called shareholders and have no personal liability for the company's debts, unless they have signed a personal guarantee. The liability of the company is limited to the assets of the company. The shareholders elect directors who are responsible for managing the business affairs of the corporation. Directors are usually shareholders. Directors are personally liable in certain situations, primarily based on federal and provincial legislation for debts of the business covered later in this chapter. Also, refer to Chapter 12 on "Creditor Proofing Your Business."

The profits of the corporation may be retained for reinvestment or distributed to the shareholders in the form of dividends, at the discretion of the directors.

Obtain legal and tax advice to assist with the preparation of the incorporation documents and shareholders' agreements.

Advantages of Incorporation

- The shareholders are only responsible for debts or obligations if they have signed a personal guarantee. Always use the full corporate legal name in legal documents and ensure that you are signing as an "authorized signatory" of the company.
- A corporation is eligible for government financing incentive programs that may be unavailable to unincorporated businesses. It can attract investors and provide better security to lenders through debentures, common shares, convertible shares, and other structures.
- The corporation continues regardless of whether a shareholder dies or retires.
- In general terms, a corporation can imply a higher prestige, more stability, and greater resources in terms of capital and expertise.
- There is increased stability in that shareholders can come and go but the business continues uninterrupted and all contracts of the corporation remain valid.
- A corporation can convert itself to a public corporation by meeting the requirements of the provincial Securities Commission and other government regulatory departments, thereby raising money on the stock exchange.

Disadvantages of Incorporation

- Directors could be held personally liable for provincial and federal government debts owing by the company.
- Incorporating costs more money: legal costs are approximately $300 to $500 plus the lawyer's out-of-pocket disbursements, which are $300 or more. Disbursements include provincial filing fees, search and reservation fees for the name, long-distance phone calls, costs of the corporate seal and minute book and photocopies. This monetary outlay is simply another cost of doing business if the reasons for incorporating a business are appropriate.
- The operating losses and tax credits are not available to individual shareholders even if the corporation is unable to utilize them.

In many cases, however, the advantages of incorporation are compelling. Simply put, don't operate a business without incorporating, if there is any risk of being sued.

Steps to Incorporation

The complexity of the incorporation process will depend on whether there is one or a number of shareholders; whether it is strictly a provincial corporation; or whether it must be federally or extraprovincially registered as well. A lawyer can incorporate your company, you may do your own incorporation, or you can hire an incorporation service. Ideally, you should have a lawyer do your incorporation so that you can obtain important legal advice relating to the corporate structure, shareholder agreements and other issues. If you are planning for more than one shareholder, you will require a lawyer to prepare a shareholders' agreement.

Choosing a Name

There are three main parts to the corporate name—a distinctive word, a descriptive word and the suffix, or corporate label. For example, the distinctive word could be "Superior;" the descriptive word could be "Investments;" and the suffix could be "Ltd." Your choice for a suffix would include: "Ltd." or "Limited;" "Corp." or "Corporation;" "Inc." or "Incorporated;" "Ltée" or "Limitée." Before selecting a name, contact your provincial consumer ministry or Industry Canada in the case of a federal incorporation. You can obtain a brochure describing the government's guidelines.

You may have a trade style name by which you are known to the public and which you use on your business cards, letterhead and invoices, rather than using the incorporated name. Normally this latter reference is in small print on your stationery, but it has the legal benefit of telling the public that you are an incorporated company behind the trade style name. All trade style names should be filed in the appropriate provincial proprietor or partnership registry, for a nominal fee.

Numbered Company

A numbered corporation uses a number instead of a name; for example, 157894 Alberta Ltd. The number is assigned (it cannot be requested) by the ministry from a consecutive series

People use numbered companies when they cannot get their preferred name accepted by the corporate registry or when they simply want a private holding company. Some people incorporate under a numbered company and operate under a trade style name. The company's stationery would show the trade style name as a division of the numbered company.

People use numbered companies to incorporate a company quickly. The numbered company can be obtained the same day, whereas it takes weeks for the registration of a corporate name. At some future point, you can change the number to a name. Some businesses are not attempting to establish goodwill under the corporate name. For example, if you were buying real estate properties for investment, a numbered company could be sufficient for your needs.

Who Makes Up the Corporation?

The owners of the corporation are its shareholders. Shareholders elect or appoint the directors to direct policies for corporate management. In larger corporations, the directors have to be approved through re-election at the annual meeting of the company. In a small business, the procedure is more informal. Meetings may not actually be held, but decisions are made instead by resolutions. The responsibilities of elected or appointed officers including president, secretary and treasurer are governed by the provincial legislation affecting corporations. The officers can be hired or fired by the directors at any time. In a small business, the shareholders, directors and officers are frequently the same people.

Shareholder Agreements

Shareholder agreements can be used in a number of situations including the following.

Potential Conflicts if More than One Shareholder

Some businesses are essentially partnerships, owned 50/50 by unrelated individuals. Second and third generation family businesses are often owned by a number of siblings and cousins. Sometimes they own equal shares, even though only one is actively involved in running the company. This often leads to serious conflicts. For example, those not actively involved in the business may want to maximize their shares' dividend income each year. On the other hand, the family member running the company may want the company's profits reinvested in the business (e.g. to reduce bank loans or acquire new equipment). Remuneration of employed family members may also be a bone of contention.

Utilizing a Buy/Sell Agreement

Where there is more than one shareholder of a private corporation, it is extremely useful for all parties to enter into a comprehensive shareholders' agreement. Such an agreement can deal with issues such as:

- The policy regarding the reinvestment of annual earnings in the business or payment of dividends
- The remuneration of officers and directors
- What happens in the event that an owner/manager becomes seriously ill or permanently disabled, or what happens to his or her shares in the company after the death of a shareholder.

Some shareholder agreements deal primarily with the last point, and are referred to as "buy/sell agreements." The typical buy/sell agreement sets out the terms and conditions under which the surviving shareholder, or the company itself, is to acquire the deceased's shares. This agreement is especially useful in situations where conflicts are likely to arise after the death of a shareholder. Some buy/sell agreements call for a compulsory purchase by the surviving shareholder(s). The purchase price may be stated in the agreement itself (and revised from time to time by an addendum to the agreement). Another approach is to set out a formula for determining the purchase price (e.g. a formula based on a certain multiple of earnings or book value). Alternatively, the buy/sell agreement may require an independent third-party valuation of the company by a major accounting firm or firm that specializes in business valuations.

If you are not the sole owner, a shareholders agreement is a must, regardless of what approach you take regarding the purchase price after a shareholder's death. A shareholders agreement is almost as important as your will and could impose a binding legal obligation on the survivor(s) to acquire your shares from your estate. In that way, your spouse or children would not find themselves in the position after your death, where they cannot find any interested third-party buyer. Furthermore, in the absence of a binding buy/sell agreement, the other surviving shareholder(s) might be content to carry on with your spouse or children as their fellow shareholders. This might not be what you had in mind. Your spouse or children might feel very financially insecure in the years following your demise.

Funding a Buy/Sell Agreement with Life Insurance

If you already have or are thinking about a buy/sell agreement, consider how the purchase of shares after a shareholder's death will be funded. Will the surviving shareholder(s) have to obtain a bank loan? What if the person has trouble obtaining a loan? Alternatively, should the company itself buy back the shares from your estate, using "excess cash"? What if the company is not able to do this, and is also unable to borrow any additional money? Are there other sources of funds (e.g. selling off part of the business)?

Of all the funding alternatives, life insurance can offer significant income tax advantages and provide the future funding for buying back a deceased's shareholder's stake in the company. Talk to an experienced life insurance agent and refer to Chapter 9, "Insurance."

Preparing Shareholder and Partnership Agreements

The casualty rate of business partnership or shareholder relationships is very high. Conflicts occur due to differences of priorities, personalities, or philosophies. In addition, there could be differing expectations by each of the individuals in terms of the contribution of time, money and talent. Issues of ego and power are frequently the undoing of business relationships.

Business conflict usually arises when extremes occur. For example, when the business is doing very well, some partners or shareholders become greedy and would like to get rid of the other partners. Conversely, when the business is doing poorly it is human nature for one partner or shareholder to blame the other for the difficulties. Many people get tired of the time, energy and commitment involved in a business operation and want to go into another business or otherwise free up their invested money. Marital or health problems can also cause a person to lose interest or create conflict within the business.

For these reasons, a shareholder's agreement should be prepared prior to incorporation, or in the case of a partnership, prior to commencing business during the "honeymoon phase" of the business relationship. Also consider a management contract, even if the manager is one of the shareholders and directors.

If you don't have an agreement, there is no framework for resolving disagreements. Each partner plus the corporation will have to retain their own lawyer. Legal fees can go up exponentially, and a resolution, if one can be attained, can be expensive, protracted, stressful and uncertain.

Frank and Jim Forgo Preventive Measures—and Regret It

Frank and Jim decided to start a pet care business, as a partnership. Because they had known each other for years, they did not even think of having a partnership agreement setting out the terms of the relationship. Eventually, disagreements occurred over the operation of the business, causing a serious falling-out. Both parties went to different lawyers and ran up large bills fighting with each other. Eventually, the business went under. Frank and Jim lost about $50,000 each that was owing to various suppliers.

In hindsight, the partners should have incorporated the business and signed a shareholders agreement, setting out what happens if one party wants out or wants to buy the other out. This would have provided a formal structure to deal with disputes. Also, by incorporating a company, Frank and Jim would not have had to pay back the creditors personally, as long as they did not sign personal guarantees or owed money to statutory (e.g. government) creditors.

Clauses to Consider

The agreement sets out methods of resolving potential disputes and other issues including:

- Division of duties and responsibilities
- Life insurance on partners
- Powers of directors
- Selling the business
- Share sales and transfers
- Shareholder investment, loans or guarantees
- Division of profits and losses.

Some additional provisions include:

- Banking arrangements including signing authorities
- Financial restrictions on partners
- Attention and time paid to business
- Management including powers of partners and limitations
- Drawing arrangements and benefits
- Buy/sell obligations
- Borrowing powers of the company.

One of the key provisions in a shareholders agreement is a buy/sell provision in the event of a disagreement or a change of priorities. This is a voluntary buy/sell formula, in that any partner could use that clause. A compulsory buy/sell clause, in the event of death, mental or physical incapacity, bankruptcy, termination of employment or default of terms of the agreement is also possible.

Drafting an Agreement

If you don't have an agreement, list the key factors that you would like included, after discussion with your partners. Make sure that every partner has independent legal advice, as the corporate lawyer drafting the agreement cannot also advise the individual partners. This would be a conflict of interest. Review the agreement at least once a year, as well as when any significant issues face the company or shareholders.

The legal costs for preparing a shareholders agreement ultimately depends on the time expended, the complexity of the agreement, the number of shareholders involved, and the number of meetings that might be held going over the various terms of the agreement. Retain a lawyer who has expertise with shareholder agreements; even an experienced lawyer will spend a minimum of five to ten hours on a basic shareholders agreement, a tax deductible business expense for you.

Directors

Although generally, shareholders are not personally liable for debts or liabilities of the corporation unless the shareholder signed a personal guarantee, directors and officers could still be liable. Many small business owner-operators have their spouses as directors of the company, a potential disadvantage when borrowing money. Lenders may request that all the directors of the company sign personal guarantees for loans, which would mean that your spouse would be asked to sign.

Directors can be individually and collectively liable for the full amount of the debt or liability under most of these statutory federal and provincial regulations. As a director of a company, you are deemed to know or should know of the obligations of the company to meet its legislative commitments. Some of the common areas of potential director liability are as follows:

Employee Deductions
When deductions are taken off an employee's salary for income tax, CPP and EI, they are to be remitted every month to Canada Customs and Revenue Agency (formerly Revenue Canada). If the funds are not remitted, you can be sued for the amounts outstanding, in your capacity as director, under the *Income Tax Act, Pension Plan Act* and *Employment Insurance Act.*

Sales Tax
If you are operating a business that is responsible for collecting and remitting provincial sales tax, and the company fails to do so, you could be held responsible as a director.

Corporate Income Tax and GST/HST
If your company owes money to Canada Customs and Revenue Agency and fails to pay it, you could be responsible as a director.

Employment Standards
If your company has not paid employees for past services rendered or for holiday pay, then employees can formally complain to the appropriate employment standards department, which could then sue you.

Workers' Compensation Board
If your company fails to make Workers' Compensation Board payments, the WCB could sue the company and, depending on the provincial legislation, could also make a claim against the directors.

Extraprovincial Business Activity
If you are doing business in another province, and have not registered your corporation in that province, you could be personally liable as a director if someone sues your company in that other province. Doing business usually means having a telephone number and listing, office address, business licence and staff. Mail-order marketing across Canada does not constitute doing business in another province.

Environmental Damage
Both the federal and provincial governments have legislation holding directors liable for environmental damage caused by their company.

Builder's Lien
If you are doing any building or renovating and fail to pay for the labour and supplies, you could be liable as a director under the builder's lien legislation in most provinces.

Bankruptcy
If your company goes into bankruptcy or insolvency and it was shown that the directors acted in a way contrary to the federal *Bankruptcy and Insolvency Act,* directors could be liable. Under provincial legislation, directors could be liable for any fraudulent conveyance or preference to defeat creditors, if the company was insolvent at the time.

Securities Act
To protect yourself from personal liability exposure as a director be duly diligent in terms of monitoring the company's operation. If you do not make the time, or you are unable to obtain the information because of poorly managed systems or lack of cooperation from management, consider resigning as a director and protect yourself by clearly writing out the reasons for the resignation. Keep copies of any correspondence.

Shares
The company offering shares can be a public or private one. A public company is listed on a stock exchange, whereas a private company is not. When an incorporation is formed, various types of shares can be used for investment purposes.

Common Shares
Owning common shares represents part ownership in a company, and provides potential return on the investment. If the corporation should fail, though, all other creditors and preferred shareholders are repaid before holders of common shares.

Preferred Shares
Owners of preferred shares can claim on the company's earnings before payment can be made on the common shares, if the company liquidates. Preferred shares are usually entitled to dividends at a specified rate when declared by the board of directors, and before payment of a dividend on the common shares. Preferred shareholders generally do not have voting privileges. Because preferred shares offer a smaller potential return than common shares, convertible preferred shares allow shareholders to exchange preferred shares for common shares when the company's future looks more promising.

Convertible Debentures
This is a long-term debt in which all or a portion of the debenture may be converted into common shares instead of being repaid.

Debt with Warrants
Similar to the convertible debenture, but this debt allows a creditor/investor to purchase a specified number of shares at a set price, even after the business has paid the debt but before the expiration of the warrant (e.g. one year or two years afterward). Debentures and debt must generally be repaid before holders of common and preferred shares are paid, or shareholders' loans are repaid.

Provincial or Federal Incorporations
There are advantages and disadvantages to incorporating federally or provincially; obtain competent legal and tax advice on the relative benefits for your company. A federal incorporation has to be registered in the province in which it is actually doing business. A provincial corporation can carry on business only in the province in which it is incorporated. The right to register in the province does not automatically mean the right to do business, whether provincial or federal, if the business does not conform with provincial or local government licensing requirements, or if its name is the same as an existing business.

A federal corporation has more reporting requirements and restrictions on meetings than most provincial corporations. If you extraprovincially register your federal corporation in another province you can have two reporting requirements— one federally and one for the province you have extraprovincially registered in.

Depending on your business, you may be required to incorporate federally. For example, if you have a business that involves interprovincial transport, or you have a radio station, then you are required by law to federally incorporate.

Extraprovincial Companies
When you incorporate, consider your long-range objectives. If it is your intention to do business in other provinces across Canada, you can either incorporate in your own province and register extraprovincially, or you can incorporate federally. If you incorporate federally, you still have to extraprovincially register your federal corporation in each province that you are doing business. The legal fees for an extraprovincial corporation will be at least as much as when you incorporated your provincial corporation or federal corporation. The *Company Act* in your province sets out the rules and regulations to do with extraprovincial corporation.

Summary
When considering your business structure, do an objective and thorough risk assessment in terms of the company being sued by creditors, clients, customers or others. If in doubt, incorporate. In addition, there are numerous tax benefits of incorporation. If you have a partner in your business, insist on a signed shareholder/partnership agreement. Use the services of a business lawyer to protect your interests.

Three

Buying a Business

Introduction

While there are obvious advantages to buying an existing business, buying a small business is a complicated and potentially risky transaction. You have to carefully assess the available opportunities, evaluate the business for your needs, negotiate the purchase price, and then sign the necessary legal documents. It is essential that you have a lawyer and accountant to protect your interests before you even start your search, and certainly before you sign an offer.

Advantages and Disadvantages of Buying a Business

Advantages

- Buying a business allows you to get into business without the cost, energy, time and risk in starting your own business and going through the first hazardous year or two growth stage.
- You can examine the track record and financial statements showing revenue, expenses and cash flow. It is easier to project potential revenue and profit, thereby minimizing the cost in starting from scratch.
- After you have negotiated a purchase price, you know the fixed amount you are dealing with. When starting from scratch, you would have no idea of how much money you might have to expend.
- You may obtain a return on your investment much sooner than if you start from scratch.
- A distressed business may be purchased at a low price and then turned around for attractive profits. The distress may result from a partnership split, health or marital problems, to burnout or poor management. Financing will be easier because the lender can assess the history.
- You might be able to obtain seller-backed financing for a portion of the purchase price. There could be tax advantages to the seller to do this, and the buyer can use the cash flow from the business to pay the seller.

- A trade creditor would also be more likely to extend more credit and more favourable terms than if you started from scratch.
- You might be able to purchase leasehold improvements that are already in place, at a considerable saving.
- The buyer can usually draw on the knowledge of the seller regarding the business, merchandise and community.
- You may also inherit intangible assets such as production techniques, inventory control, credit and collection or other administrative systems, licences, secret formulas and a non-competition covenant from the seller.
- Trained personnel may stay with the new owner.
- A great deal of the time-consuming guesswork is eliminated. The store size, location, type of leaseholds or equipment to install, how many employees to hire and what training is required—all these questions are answered when you buy an existing business.
- An existing business might have an excellent location with high traffic volume and public familiarity and acceptance. It could take a considerable time for somebody starting from scratch to either find a similar location or reach the same point in terms of sales volume, reputation, and customer loyalty.

Disadvantages

- The existing location of the business may not be as attractive as it was originally, due to changing traffic flow, nearby competition or declining population.
- You could be locked into the layout and location because the lease comes as part of the purchase price, a potential problem if you want to expand or make alterations.
- You could be assuming an older building that will cost more in heating, maintenance or improvements.
- You may be required to pay for the present owner's goodwill (the value placed on the established customer base, business reputation and net profit) which may be difficult to assess and agree upon.
- It could take some considerable adjustment to retrain the customers from a poor credit and collection system; some may be lost in the process.
- Some of the equipment might be obsolete or defective and therefore require early repair or replacement.
- The previous owner's employees may be accustomed to sloppy procedures or lack of systems. Employees might quit quickly if they do not like your style and this could create difficulties.
- You could inherit customer ill will, which could impair your growth.
- You may be temporarily locked into the management or operation policies of the seller as well as the pricing structure for the services or products. Although you should be able to change these over time, they could result in customer resistance and therefore a decline in revenue.

- You may want to alter merchandise lines creating customer resistance.
- Your business could have inherently serious problems that you were unaware of before you purchased.
- If you are buying shares, you could be exposed to a lawsuit for actions or debts of the previous owner.

Risky Businesses

Buying the wrong business could result in financial disaster so watch for these common warning signs.

High Pressure to Buy Business

If the seller or an agent of the seller is putting high pressure on you to buy the business, be wary. Possibly the business is about to go under or the agent feels that their listing is going to run out. Never make a quick decision on something as critical as buying a business.

Unfamiliar Business

The dangers in running a new enterprise are accentuated by inexperience and unfamiliarity. You could be buying a business totally unsuited to your personality, talents or interest and would be at a considerable disadvantage with your competitors. Avoid any businesses that are overly hyped.

Partner Wanted Business

Business partnerships based on sound economic data may be worthy of your consideration. On the other hand, many business partnerships do not survive because of conflicts of personality, philosophy, policy, priorities, or contribution of money, time, or skill into the business. Be cautious of any business partnerships that promise a disproportionate return on investment of money or time.

Businesses Requiring Skills that the Buyer Lacks

If a particular business requires one-on-one contact with customers, and the owner does not feel comfortable interacting with the public, the existing customer base could drain away quickly.

Buyback Business

A seller may attempt to induce a prospective purchaser to buy by promising to buy back the business if the buyer is not satisfied. Once the money has been obtained, the seller could renege on the commitment or disappear. Although you would have recourse to sue, you could be wasting further money.

Owner Claiming Skimming

A business owner may try to induce a sale by claiming that the financial statements do not accurately record the amount of cash coming into the business. In other words, the seller would be stating (discreetly and obviously not in writing) that half of the cash was pocketed without recording it or paying tax on it. Don't purchase such a business—you cannot rely on the financial records, placing you at high risk. If the seller has evaded taxes, he or she is not credible and consequently nor is the business.

Andy's Short-term Gain Leads to Long-term Pain

Andy decided to buy a deli business that he saw advertised in the paper. The vendor told him that the business was a "cash" business and that he skimmed a lot of money. In fact, the true revenue was twice what the financial statements showed. Impressed, Andy decided he would save money on a lawyer and accountant and negotiate the deal himself.

After a month operating the business, Andy found that the revenue was not even what the statements showed, let alone twice that amount. Also, to his surprise, the former owner opened up a new deli a block away, draining most of his clientele. Andy had been duped.

If Andy had consulted experts, the accountant would have advised Andy of the folly of relying on the "skimming" ploy, quite apart from the CCRA (formerly Revenue Canada) taking a dim view of that type of activity. The accountant would have advised Andy to walk from the "deal." The lawyer would have prepared proper legal documentation, including a "non-competition" clause, restricting the vendor from being involved directly or indirectly in a competing business within 20 blocks for a period of three years.

Businesses which Use up All Investment Capital

If all of your financial resources are required to purchase a business, you are starting off undercapitalized, without working capital or reserve for future needs. If there is a decline in profit during the transition phase, you won't have any resources to buffer the financial crunch.

Personal Service Business

If you are considering a personal service business (for example, an architectural, engineering, dental or legal practice), ask about the goodwill or one-to-one relationship between clients and the professional. Once the business is purchased, much of the clientele could go to other professionals because of a difference in style and operation. Build in contractual protection (paying over a few years for example) because of the high risk that the goodwill may not necessarily endure when the vendor leaves.

Declining Neighbourhood

If you are considering a business that is in an area that is changing rapidly in population base, reconsider. Maybe the location is becoming more commercialized and older residential buildings are being torn down for office buildings. If your target market is the homeowner this could result in enough lost income that your business would not survive.

Emotionally Based Interest

If your very positive emotional feelings for a business tend to dominate your decisions, rather than a focus on the business aspects, don't proceed any further. Emotional and unrealistic expectations can very quickly turn into financial disaster.

Failing or Distressed Business

Unless you are an expert in businesses going through serious financial problems, avoid such companies. Some people buy businesses with a turnaround strategy in mind, and skilfully negotiate an attractive purchase package. This can be done effectively only if the buyer is sophisticated in this type of distress purchase.

Evaluation of a Business

After you have decided on a specific business, the next issue is determining its worth. Although you want the business with as little financial outlay as possible, the seller is considering his or her "sweat equity"—the years of time, energy, and stress and the small returns during the first years of growth. Most business owners have an inflated assessment of the value of goodwill, which may have little or no bearing on the business or market value.

Use professionals to help you evaluate the business including the business broker, the realtor, a professional commercial business appraiser and a professional accountant. Depending on the "experts" experience and vested interest, the assessment of the business could vary considerably. Rely on your accountant's advice plus your own judgement. Ultimately the price of the business is really determined by the buyer, not the seller.

Why the Business is being Sold

One of the first steps in the evaluation is determining why the business is being sold. Some reasons may not have any impact, while others could cause you to lose your investment completely. Here are some of the possibilities:

- Facilities are obsolete or too expensive to upgrade
- Lease is about to expire and the landlord does not want to renew it or wants to renew it at a much higher price
- The product line is poor and the owner is having difficulty getting a new product line
- Sales are declining, possibly due to changing economic or market factors, poor location, or unmarketable services or products
- Competition has just come into the area or will be coming soon and the owner wants to sell before that factor makes the business unattractive

- Owner is having partnership problems
- Owner is having marital or health problems, or wants to retire
- Owner has lost enthusiasm for the business after many years of hard work
- Owner wants to sell to purchase another, more attractive business opportunity
- Government regulations (federal, provincial, or municipal) have just come in or will be coming in which would require the business to expend monies
- Location of the business is no longer attractive because of changing zoning bylaws, traffic patterns, or transportation services
- Owner is concerned about potential lawsuits and wants to sell before they commence
- Due to a poor credit and collection policy, the business is unable to collect receivables, is suffering serious cash flow problems and is unable to obtain further financing
- Business has lost one or more key employees
- Business has lost one or more major contracts, without which it is no longer financially viable.

Factors that Affect a Business Evaluation

Value is in the eyes of the beholder. For example, the seller frequently sees value in relationship to cost, but in reality, cost is not necessarily an important element of value. The business that may have cost the owner $40,000 to equip four years ago may be worth anywhere from $10,000 to $100,000 today.

At the outset, obtain income statements (profit-and-loss statements), tax returns and balance sheets for the past three years, lists of accounts payable and accounts receivable, all other liabilities of the company and the books of the business. Get a copy of the current lease, any contracts the company has with employees, suppliers or others, and other documentation that your lawyer and accountant may request.

Here are the most common considerations in establishing a selling price.

Accounts Receivable

If these are to be included in the purchase price, they should be examined closely. Accounts under 30 days have a higher incidence of reliability, while those between 30 and 60 days are higher risk. Any receivables over 60 days may be uncollectible. Before purchasing, contact the customers to make sure that they agree with the outstanding balances. You may want to arrange that you will defer payment or partial payment to the seller until you have received the accounts receivable.

Fixed Assets

The building, fixtures and leasehold improvements may not have maintained their market value. The improvements traditionally stay with the landlord at the end of the lease.

Movable Assets
The value of the equipment, furniture and furnishings may be based on its original value, its replacement value, its auction-sale value as used equipment, or depreciated value.

Inventory
Use an independent, qualified appraiser to determine the dollar value of the inventory, including finished goods, work in process and raw materials. Personally inspect the inventory for style, condition, saleability, quality, age, freshness and balance. Some might be outdated and would be difficult to sell. If possible, purchase inventory at a discounted price. Normally inventory is paid for separately from the business purchase price, as of the day that the business is taken over. Take into account:

- Is the inventory in character with your target market?
- Is the inventory in accord with what you would like to sell?
- How much would have to be cleared out at a loss and what would that loss be?
- Does the inventory list contain items that have been sold and paid for but not yet shipped?
- How does the average industry ratio of inventory to sales compare with the business for sale?
- Has the seller kept adequate records of inventory and for how long?
- Are all the items owned by the business or are some on consignment?
- Does a lender have any security documentation covering inventory?

Customer List, Business and Creditor Records, Mailing Lists
Make sure that these valuable assets are included in the sales agreement and that the seller is not entitled to use these lists in competition with you, or to give the records to any other party without your written consent.

Licences
Make sure that the completion of the purchase is conditional upon any licences that are necessary for the operation of the business (e.g., a liquor licence) being transferred. Have you checked all the licensing requirements and municipal bylaws (e.g., health, fire and safety regulations and zoning bylaws)?

Leases
A lease is an essential part of the purchase price of the business, unless of course you are buying the whole building. Ask questions such as: Is the lease transferable to the buyer with or without the consent of the landlord? Is the present lease negotiable with the landlord? Should you negotiate a whole new lease? Are there restrictions in the lease? Are there options for renewal? What rent-escalation clauses are built into the lease? There could also be leases for equipment, signs,

furniture, telephone systems etc. Some leases are assignable. Obtain the actual lease documents for your lawyer's review.

Non-Competition Clause
To avoid having the owner opening up a competing business across the street, include a clause in the sales agreement prohibiting the seller from establishing a business in competition with you. Build in a time limit and a specified geographic area.

Accounts Payable
Are all the accounts current or are some past due and how long past due? Do any of the creditors have liens or encumbrances against the assets of the business, or have they made claims for monies owing?

Prepaid Expenses
Make sure that any prepaid expenses (such as insurance, last month's rent or property taxes) can be assigned to you from the old owner without penalty.

Patents, Copyrights, Trademarks, Industrial Designs and Business Names
If you want these important, intangible rights as part of your agreement, they should be specifically included in the sales agreement.

Employees
Try to find out how many of the key employees who are experienced in the business would be prepared to remain with the business after you buy it.

Income/Earnings
The net income after expenses and before taxes is an important factor that has to be taken in context. For example, it relates to how the business operator keeps books, the efficiency of buying goods and services, how well labour costs are controlled, marketing, overhead and expenses, and the commitment to financial success. Some buyers or sellers put a high reliance on the gross sales figure because it reflects the volume of activity and cash flow.

Type of Business
Some businesses are more popular than others and therefore have greater buyer appeal. The higher the appeal, the higher the demand, and generally, a higher price.

Competition
Competition in the trading area affects profitability and gross volume of the business. Look for the following warning signs:
- Nearby major shopping centres which offer more attractive one-stop facilities for shoppers
- Heavy competition by discounters

- A large number of competing businesses
- Competitors who offer cheque cashing, delivery service, credit, delayed payments and other inducements to attract customers.

If these factors are present, you could be forced to try to offer the same features.

Customers
What is the existing customer base? Does the business cater to a few customers that make up the majority of the purchase volume?

Warranties
If the business offers products that are covered by warranty, find out what warranties have been extended and the lifetime of each warranty. They may be renewable contracts, which generate cash flow but to maintain customer goodwill, you might be obligated to honour them.

Accounting Practices
Make sure that a professional, qualified, credible accountant prepared the financial statements. Auditing can be expensive, but it might be necessary before you finalize the purchase. Also watch for:
- Unusually high depreciation which can artificially increase the profit figures
- Financial statements that are unrealistically overstated or understated
- Statements that reflect a lower than normal product cost or net profit percentage.

Management
If the current management has shown disinterest or incompetence, you should be able to purchase a business at a reduced rate and turn it around. However, if the business has a bad reputation, it may not be possible to substantially increase the customer base.

Financing
Determine if the seller will take a sizeable down payment and carry the balance of the purchase price over time with security. The security could be a debenture or a chattel mortgage on equipment and vehicles, or assignment of accounts receivable. The lower the down payment, the more potential buyers, and the seller can therefore ask a higher price. The converse holds true in cases where the seller demands all cash.

Geographic Area
A business situated in an area where the population has a higher disposable income may be more attractive than one situated in a low income or less travelled area.

Industry Ratio Comparison

Compare the business and the asking price with published industry standards, for example those published by Dun & Bradstreet. If the business is more efficiently and profitably run in comparison to key ratios, that could increase the purchase price. This is assuming of course that the backup documentation is accurate and not contrived.

Evaluating Goodwill

The area of greatest divergence of opinion in business evaluation is the value of goodwill. Some people define goodwill as simply the expectation of continued patronage. Others define it more precisely as the value of a business in excess of its suggested book value. Still others construe goodwill to be the difference between the tangible net worth of the company and its fair market value. The price you should pay for goodwill depends on the earning power and potential of the business. If the earning power is low, the buyer will probably resist paying any amount for goodwill.

Goodwill must result in profits or it cannot have value. Look at the business' ability to earn a fair return on investment, and at the present and future earning power as of prime importance. The seller contends that goodwill relates to the lease benefits, location, customer base, sales and inventory records, exclusive lines, connections with suppliers, licences, patents, trademarks and copyrights. The seller believes that these factors deserve compensation. Goodwill is intangible because it is an opinion and therefore difficult to evaluate.

When attempting to establish a value for goodwill, consider the following:
- Business and business owner's reputation
- Location
- Stability of company and industry trends
- Age of business
- Profitability
- Transition period in ownership changeover for training purposes
- Key personnel staying with the company under the new ownership
- Broad customer base
- Widely used trademark or trade name.

Be careful in apportioning the value to goodwill, because of the tax implications. The seller is able to use the amount paid for goodwill as a capital gain, and may want as high a factor as possible. You, as the buyer should try to have as low a value for goodwill as possible because you don't have the same tax advantages.

Methods of Evaluating a Business

The methods used by the seller for determining a value for the business do not necessarily reflect a realistic value of the business, but some value is needed for sale purposes.

The market value of a business refers to the highest estimated price that the buyer would be warranted in paying, and the seller would be justified in accepting, without any undue or outside influence involved. Undue or outside influences would include foreclosure, bankruptcy, receivership, competition, marital or partnership disputes, or health problems. Any of these factors should cause the price to drop. As a buyer, you should look for these factors in order to apply leverage in your negotiations.

Some of the methods used to evaluate a business include book value, liquidation value, replacement value and gross multiplier value. The capitalization of income value (CIV) is one of the more reliable methods, described below.

Capitalization of Income Value

This method is concerned with the present worth of future benefits from investment in the business. In other words, the business value is determined by capitalizing its earnings at a rate that reflects the risk associated with that firm. A high capitalization rate would be chosen if the buyer perceives a high degree of risk. The rate could vary from as little as 15% to as high as 100% or more. A capitalization rate of 20% is frequently the minimum amount for a small business that shows reasonable prospects for continued growth, and has relatively no risk. The higher the capitalization rate used, the lower the valuation for the business.

The capitalization of income value is used frequently because the business value is based on income or profit before depreciation, interest and income taxes, and by using an appropriate capitalization rate which is acceptable to the buyer. There are three steps to this process:

1. Estimate the level of future earnings of the company based on average net earnings over the past several years, together with an estimate of the increase in earnings. Average net earnings include owner's salary.
2. Select an appropriate capitalization rate based on the return on investment which buyers would be expected to demand. This is based on a fair return on investment, for example, 10% to 25%. The risk factor plays an important role at this stage.
3. Capitalize the income by dividing the income by the selected capitalization rate. The outcome would constitute the selling price.

For example, the buyer pays $60,000 cash or with borrowed money, and his projected net income from the business is $24,000; his return on investment (capitalization rate) would be 40%. The capitalization of income value also reflects the return on investment that the buyer wishes to recover from the business to meet specific needs. On a 40% return on investment, it would take 2½ years to recover the initial investment, in the example given.

Selling Price Formula

The formula given in Figure 3.1 is based on an evaluation of the business' existing earning power and profit potential. The selling price approach is given from the perspective of the buyer. Because each business and sales transaction is different, the formula should be used only as a guideline to indicate some of the major considerations in pricing.

FIGURE 3.1 ■ *Pricing Formula Worksheet*

1. Tangible net worth $ _____

   2.   Current earning power $ _____

   3.   Reasonable annual salary $ _____

   4.   Total earning capacity $ _____

   5.   Average annual net profit $ _____

   6.   Extra earning power (line 5 minus line 4) $ _____

   7.   Value of intangibles (line 6 × multiplier figure)$ _____

       Final price (a total of lines 1 and 7) $ _____

Methods of Buying a Business

There are two common methods of buying a business. One way is to buy the assets, which includes a goodwill component, and the other way is to buy the shares, assuming it is a corporation. If you have the alternative of buying either assets or shares, discuss the following considerations with your accountant and lawyer before committing yourself:

- Company financing
- Potential liability
- Company credit rating
- Leases and contracts held by the company
- Tax implications (i.e., depreciation of fixed assets, sales tax payable).

Purchase of Assets

If the business is a sole proprietorship or a partnership, the sale must be conducted as a transfer of assets, as there is no corporation in which shares can be purchased. The buyer typically sets up a new corporation and transfers all the assets and the lease into the new corporate name.

If a buyer is buying the assets of the company and therefore has a new corporation without a track record, the lack of a credit history could impair the credit that would be extended to the company in the initial stages.

If the assets of the company are secured by a creditor's lien, mortgage or other encumbrance, the transfer of assets cannot occur without the approval of the creditor. The creditor may not release the seller from the security, and may insist on having personal covenants of the buyer as well. Or, the creditor may consent to an asset transfer conditional on a re-negotiation of the terms of the security. Your lawyer should check the appropriate registries to see if there are any encumbrances or liens against the assets.

Purchase of Shares

The buyer may purchase the shares of the company from the shareholders. At the time of the sale, the shareholders resign as directors and officers. The buyer elects his or her own directors and officers. A modification to this approach is for the existing shareholders to sell their shares back to the corporation. The corporation then sells new shares to the buyer. A buyer may be able to purchase the shares of the business if the company has a high amount of debt by paying the owners the difference between the debt and the purchase price. For example, if the business assets were worth $200,000 and the debt was $175,000, the buyer could pay $25,000 to the owner and assume the shares of the business.

It may be difficult to have leases, contracts or licences assigned to a new company. If this is the case, then a purchase of shares in the corporation would permit the business to continue without others necessarily knowing that there has been a change in ownership. Another reason for buying the shares of a company is that a tax loss could be available that could benefit the buyer.

If you buy the shares of a business that enjoys a very good credit rating, you obtain the ongoing benefit of the excellent credit rating. If the credit rating is poor, that could have an adverse effect on future credit and overall goodwill.

If a buyer is making a share purchase, then any and all liabilities that the business might have from the past remain with the business. For example, there could be claims by Canada Customs and Revenue Agency (formerly Revenue Canada) for back taxes or reassessment of taxes, creditors may sue for past debts, customers may sue for an injury that was sustained on the business premises, or customers may make a claim on an express or implied warranty on products that have been purchased or product liability claims may commence.

Business Purchase Documentation

After you have decided on the structure of the purchase, make sure that you are properly protected with legal documentation. The legal documents include the offer to purchase and the formal purchase and sale agreement. The purchase and sale agreement would be for either an asset or share transfer.

Offer to Purchase

Whether you are making the offer directly yourself or through a realtor, business broker, or lawyer, the offer to purchase agreement must be in writing and specific. Never make an offer to purchase agreement without obtaining legal and accounting advice in advance. The terms of the offer to purchase normally include the apportioning of purchase price if you are buying the assets, employees, transition phase clause (owner staying on to assist in training), non-competition clause, financing considerations, and timing of completion and possession date. The offer to purchase agreement normally includes a provision that all the financial records of the company such as financial statements, balance sheets, income statements (profit-and-loss statement), sales records, contracts, leases and all other necessary documentation have been or will be supplied to the prospective buyer for review before any offer is firm.

Make sure that you can back out of the contract and avoid liability if for any reason you change your mind. For example, you may find hidden problems with the business and there could be other factors that you subsequently want to add. It is necessary in most situations to have a clause that states that a formal purchase and sale agreement will be negotiated and drawn up by the parties after all the subject conditions in the offer to purchase have been removed.

To minimize your risk when making an offer to purchase, remember the following:

Keep the Purchase Deposit to a Minimum
A deposit of 5% to 10% of the purchase price is generally requested as a gesture of good faith and sincerity. In fact, the broker or realtor usually wants the amount of their commission (approximately 10%) as the deposit. As it is negotiable, attempt to deposit as little as possible. An alternative is to pay a small deposit such as $100, $500, or $1,000 and then include a clause stating that the deposit will be increased to 10% of the purchase price, once all the conditional (escape) clauses have been removed.

Use Escape Clauses
Escape clauses are conditions that have to be met before the offer to purchase becomes a binding contract. Most benefit the buyer of a business and include: review and approval of offer to purchase by the buyer's lawyer and accountant; verification of all records by the buyer's accountant to the satisfaction of the accountant and buyer; appraisal of the business by an independent appraiser of the buyer's choosing; inspection of the business by a third party (potential partners or associates of the buyer); and approval by the buyer's bank for financing. These clauses are often referred to as unilateral conditions because it is totally up to the buyer in this example as to whether or not the escape clauses are removed.

Buy the Business Through a Corporation
You should probably incorporate a company to purchase the assets of the business, so that the offer to purchase is in a corporate name. This would also help you when the formal purchase and sale documentation is complete, because if you default on the final agreement, your company may be sued, but not you personally.

Do Not Sign Personal Guarantees

If you have incorporated a company and signed the offer to purchase in the corporate name, avoid signing a personal guarantee. Have all the risk assumed by your corporation.

Insert a Liquidated Damage Clause

The buyer should make sure that in the event that the contract is breached, the deposit shall be deemed to be liquidated damages.

Purchase and Sale Agreements

If the escape clauses in the offer to purchase have been removed, then a purchase and sale agreement is normally prepared on behalf of and at the expense of the buyer by the buyer's lawyer. The document is then reviewed and approved by the seller's lawyer. The contract is signed by all parties, followed by the transfer of payment and possession. These contracts are formal and can therefore be 25 to 100 pages, depending on the complexity of the business. Frequently there can be collateral agreements, in addition to the main agreement, that have to be signed by the parties, or one or the other of the parties. In addition, key documents are attached to the contract as exhibits. This includes financial statements, lists of assets, lists of inventory and supplies, copies of leases and other major contracts, lists of creditors, lists of customers and other documentation.

These key terms should be included in any contract involving a purchase of shares or assets:

- What is the amount of the purchase price?
- How will the purchase price be paid?
- How will the purchase price be apportioned?
- What assets are to be sold?
- What assets will be retained by the seller?
- How will inventory adjustments be made?
- How will accounts receivable be handled?
- How will other adjustments be determined?
- What about the seller's liabilities?
- What protection does the seller have if the buyer does not pay the assumed liabilities?
- What other warranties should the seller make to the buyer?
- What are the rights of the seller to compete?
- What restrictions should be imposed on the seller in operating the business prior to closing?
- What performance conditions has the seller included as part of the agreement?
- What happens to the records and books for the business at the time of closing?
- How are any disputes under the agreement resolved?

The contract to buy a business must be designed to meet the specific needs of the transaction. No two documents are or should be identical. Your agreement may contain most but not necessarily all the points here, as well as other provisions to fully protect yourself.

Professional Assistance in Purchasing a Business

Obtaining qualified legal and accounting assistance is particularly important when buying a business or a franchise.

Buying a business is serious business, involving serious money. It is false economy and very unwise to attempt to save on legal fees by doing all the work yourself. If problems occur in the purchase transaction, then you will certainly be retaining a lawyer at that time to initiate a lawsuit or protect you from one. Discuss your needs with your lawyer in the preliminary interest stage, before ever signing an offer to purchase.

Summary

While there are clear benefits of buying a business, there are many pitfalls that could catch the unwary purchaser. Before you sign any document or pay any money down, speak to a lawyer specializing in business. How to select such a lawyer is covered in Chapter 1, "Legal and Other Advisors."

To obtain helpful checklists and sample forms relating to buying a business, refer to the book, *The Complete Canadian Small Business Guide*, 3/e, by Douglas Gray and Diana Gray, published by McGraw-Hill Ryerson.

Four

Buying a Franchise

Introduction

Buying a franchise is different from buying an existing business because the franchisor provides support in getting the franchise started and for the life of the business. You may also be able to buy an operating franchise location. Studies show that approximately 90% of new franchisees continue in business more than three years. Less than 25% of non-franchise businesses survive over the same period.

Forms of Franchises

There are two forms of franchise—a product/trade name and a business format. A franchisor who owns an established product name, logo and/or trademark and sells the right to use its name, logo, trademark to another party is known as a product/trade name franchisor. The right is actually an exclusive or non-exclusive licence to market the product name to wholesalers and retailers. An example would be a company that has the rights to manufacture and use the name Coca-Cola.

With a business format franchise, the franchisor provides a product, name and logo, but also the management and marketing support to create a "turnkey" business operation. Examples of this type of franchise include McDonald's, Dairy Queen and Century 21. This chapter is primarily concerned with the turnkey franchise operation, and its advantages and disadvantages.

The business format franchisor may assist with site selection, owner and staff training, product supply, advertising and marketing, management and accounting, system controls and possibly financing. Besides the initial purchase price of the franchise, a percentage of sales is paid to the franchisor for ongoing support. The franchise agreement gives the right to sell the goods or services within a certain geographic area or territory and details the legal and commercial relationship between the two parties. The franchisee may sell goods or services supplied by the franchisor, or those that meet the franchisor's quality standards.

The guidelines and conditions can address sources of supplies, standards of cleanliness, pricing policy, hours of operation, staffing requirements and many other factors to maintain consistency of image, quality and service.

The Franchise Option

Is Franchising for You?

When considering the franchise option, you need to consider how a franchise will help you attain your goals compared with starting a business from scratch? Are you motivated by the challenge of doing it all yourself? Or does that concept cause you more than a little apprehension? If starting a business is overwhelming, then the franchise option may be well suited to your needs. Some entrepreneurs prefer the security and support provided by a large and experienced company. The franchisor obviously has a vested interest, as the more money the franchisee makes, the more money the franchisor makes. However, if your intention is to establish your business and then diversify or expand, you will be restricted from doing this with a franchise.

Advantages and Disadvantages

Advantages to the Franchisee

- Being associated with an established company
- A proven and successful business system
- Reduced risk of failure
- Increased chance of profitability within the first few years
- Easier to access financing (banks, suppliers, franchisor)
- Reduced costs of supplies and materials
- Access to extensive advertising (national, regional, local)
- Continuing managerial assistance
- Possibility of buying an existing operation.

Disadvantages to the Franchisee

- High degree of control
- Possible dispute over agreement terms
- Franchisor might not fulfil promises
- Services provided by franchisor could be more expensive
- Franchise fee comes off the gross revenue
- Franchisor in another jurisdiction could create contract enforcement problems
- Profits may be less than represented or anticipated
- Misleading statements by franchisor
- Franchisor could over-saturate market.

Advantages to the Franchisor
- Motivated franchisees
- Beating the competition to the marketplace
- Spread business risk
- Reduced management costs.

Disadvantages to the Franchisor
- Franchisee might not fulfil obligations
- Franchisee might damage reputation of franchise system
- Potential litigation by dissatisfied franchisee
- Growth by franchisor may be too rapid, causing operational problems.

Where to Find Franchise Information

To improve the quality of your comparisons and decision-making, review as many as possible of these sources outlined below.

- **Books.** Refer to *So You Want to Buy a Franchise* by Douglas Gray and Norman Friend, and *The Complete Canadian Small Business Guide*, 3/e, by Douglas and Diana Gray, both published by McGraw-Hill Ryerson.
- **Government agencies.** Contact Industry Canada and Consumer and Corporate Affairs.
- **Bank and accounting firm publications.** Most major banks and accounting firms have information on franchising.
- **Canadian Franchise Association (CFA).** CFA is a trade association representing firms in a wide variety of industries which employ franchising. CFA has several excellent publications including an information kit entitled *Investigate Before Investing* and *The Official CFA Directory*, an annual publication containing a list of the CFA members. For further information, contact CFA at 2585 Skymark Avenue, Suite 300, Mississauga, ON, L4W 4L5; 1-800-665-4232; *www.cfa.ca*.
- **International Franchise Association (IFA).** IFA has many products and services including its *Directory of Membership*, which details the operation of each of its franchise members. Contact IFA 2604 Elmwood Avenue, #347, Rochester, NY, 14618-2295 or at *www.ifausa.org*.
- **The Franchise Annual.** This directory describes the franchise concept as well as details of over 3,000 American, Canadian, and overseas franchise companies in various sectors.
- **The Info Franchise Newsletter.** This monthly publication from Info Press Inc., includes Canadian and American franchise information on legislation, litigation, trends and new franchisors.
- **Franchise Yearbook.** Published by *Entrepreneur Magazine*, this is a complete directory of all franchises in the United States and Canada.
- **Canadian Business Franchise.** This bi-monthly magazine includes articles on franchising as well as a selected list of Canadian franchise companies.

Obtain it from a bookstore or directly from the publisher, at 1-800-454-1662; *www.cgb.ca*. The publisher also produces the *Canadian Business Franchise Directory* annually.

- **Franchise shows and expositions.** CFA sponsors franchising shows in Toronto and Vancouver. National Event Management (Oakville, ON) produces the largest number of franchise and business opportunity shows throughout Canada. Valuable information on all aspects of franchising such as financing, buying, contracts, advantages, and obligations is available, as are on-site consultations with franchise specialists such as accountants, lawyers and bankers.
- **Franchise consultants/brokers.** A franchise consultant generally advises a franchisor on how to franchise and market a business effectively. A franchise consultant may also be a broker, so would have a vested interest.

Selecting a Franchise

When buying a franchise, make sure you thoroughly investigate your options and use a lawyer and accountant who specialize in commercial law and tax, as well as in franchise businesses. Before making a decision, answer the following questions: Did the franchise representative refuse to give you answers to any of your questions? Refuse to give you a list of franchisee references? Promise you high profits in exchange for minimum effort? Put high pressure on you to make a deposit or sign a franchise agreement immediately? Appear to be less interested in your ability to be successful and more interested in selling a franchise?

If the answer to any of these questions was yes, seriously reconsider pursuing that franchise company any further. The truly professional franchise will allow an objective and thorough investigation of each party by the other, without time constraints. If you are favourably impressed with the initial attitude, contact the owner of a franchise location close to you. Ask the franchisee if they are satisfied with the franchise owner and if not, why not?

What to Look for in a Franchise

The main areas to examine in evaluating a franchise include:

- **Background of franchise company.** This includes its financial condition, creditworthiness, relationship with suppliers, franchisees and customers and length of time in business.
- **Management.** Investigate experience, qualifications, reputation and commitment.
- **Viability of product or service.** Check on whether it is a new, trendy or well-established product, its suitability in your geographic area and proven market demand.
- **Potential profit.** Determine the potential net profit and check with other franchisees to determine if the projections are realistic. Are these comparisons based in communities that are similar to your own? Has there been an allowance for franchisee's salary separate from the profits? Will the projected net profit satisfy your economic and personal needs?

- **Location.** Satisfy yourself that the location is viable. The franchise owner may own the premises and lease them to the franchisee, or the franchisee could lease or purchase the premises from a third party. The franchisor will have to approve the site.
- **Premises.** How strict is the franchisor on appearance, design, layout, colours, fixtures and furnishings of the premises?
- **Operational controls.** Check for standardization of character, uniformity and quality of product, value of trademarks and strictness of operational controls manual.
- **Training and start-up systems.** Check on the duration, nature and extent of training, on-site or at franchisor's site, costs, supplemental training and start-up assistance.
- **Ongoing assistance.** Inquire as to the ongoing assistance provided: computer systems for inventory control, purchasing, invoicing and delivery, bookkeeping and accounting, financial management, selection of inventory, research and development, maintenance of equipment and hiring, training and firing of employees.
- **Advertising and promotion.** Franchisees are required to contribute to a fund for national or regional advertising, generally based on a percentage of the franchisee's gross sales. Does the system-wide advertising justify the costs involved? Are franchisees required to advertise at a local level at their own expense? Does the franchisor supply professional, prepared advertising and promotional material?
- **Franchisor financing.** Can this be done directly through the franchisor, or arranged in co-operation with a bank by the franchisor?

Key Areas of Consideration
There are three areas that are particularly important for you to consider, including territory, fees and costs, and renewal and termination.

1. Territory
Most franchisors provide some form of territorial protection to the franchisee. The area covered may be small, such as a few blocks, or as large as a province or number of provinces. In theory, the exclusive sales territory means that the franchisee has the right to sell the franchisor's service or product exclusively within that area. For example, "area franchising" implies that the franchisee would have exclusivity to a large sales region. The term "master franchise" implies that the franchisee would not only have a large sales area, but would also be able to sub-franchise to others within the allocated territory.

Problems can and do frequently arise, including the following:
- The franchisor may start up another franchise (either under the same franchise name or indirectly through a subsidiary company) or sell a location to a new franchisee within the territory, a breach of contract but expensive to challenge.

- The franchisor or other franchisees may sell or ship products into your territory from locations outside. Technically they do not have a location in your territory but they are encroaching into your market share.
- Frequently the term "exclusive sales territory" means that a franchisee merely has the right of first refusal to acquire any additional outlets within the territory before a second franchisee could accept. The size, cost and timing may not be at all attractive or financially feasible. Therefore, waiving your right of first refusal allows someone else to erode your market share and therefore profit potential.
- Some exclusive agreements are tied to population size within the sales territory. Over time, if the population exceeds the specified number, the company would be able to start up a franchise location in your territory.

2. Fees and Costs

Make sure that the contract specifically states the fees that are included in your initial franchise fee and royalty, and that the fees that are paid separately, periodically or optionally on the part of the franchisee. In some cases, the franchisor may be making unreasonable profits on the fees and costs, as compared to the normal expenses an independent business would incur. Your professional advisors can provide more insight on that important issue.

Know in advance the exact amount of all costs that you will have to pay, including initial and ongoing costs and what benefit you are receiving for your money. Here are the main fees and costs:

- **Initial franchise fee.** Usually paid at the time that the franchise agreement is signed, the amount varies depending on the type and size of the franchise. The fee normally includes the franchisor's costs incurred in selling the franchise and the franchisee's right to use the operating procedures and system, as well as trade name and trademark.
- **Training cost for franchisee or staff.** This cost could include room and board, transportation, meals and tuition.
- **Cost for ongoing training and management assistance.**
- **Start-up assistance and promotion charges.**
- **Periodic royalties or service fees.** Royalties are usually calculated as a percentage of the franchisee's gross sales, although they could be fixed fee. The royalties may be required to be paid on a quarterly, monthly or weekly basis and the percentage can vary considerably depending on the type of business. Retail operations generally have higher royalties than service operations. Royalties may not cover all ongoing services.
- **Product pricing fees.** In order to make a guaranteed profit, the franchisors require that the franchisee purchase all or most of the goods and supplies from the franchisor.
- **Average contribution to advertising.** This may be based on a specified percentage of the franchisee's gross sales, payable on a weekly or monthly

basis. This contribution is normally separate from local advertising that the franchisee pays for.

- **Local advertising.** Some franchisors require that the franchisee purchase a certain minimum of local advertising, with form to be determined either by the franchisor or the franchisee.
- **Buying or leasing equipment, supplies and opening inventory from the franchisor.**
- **Monthly lease or mortgage**.
- **Centralized bookkeeping, accounting and data processing services.**
- **Cost of site selection and development.**

3. Renewal and Termination

The term of a franchise agreement is normally between ten and 20 years, but it can vary considerably. The contract is automatically terminated at the end of that period unless there are provisions for renewal (the new contract may contain different requirements). If there are no renewal provisions, then you can't sell the franchise business to anyone else, an important resale and return on investment consideration.

Every franchise agreement has provisions for both parties to terminate the agreement. Termination rights of franchisors tend to be far more extensive than those of franchisees in order to protect the reputation of the franchise system. A franchisee who impairs the reputation of the franchise may receive a 30-day notice period in which the franchisee has the option to rectify the default. If the default is more serious, termination is normally given without notice.

Some franchise agreement termination clauses may invoke the claim that the franchisee:

- Made an assignment in (declared) bankruptcy
- Was petitioned into bankruptcy by creditors
- Ceased to do business on the premises
- Became insolvent and could not pay creditors
- Was placed in receivership
- Submitted financial reports that were inaccurate or misleading by understating gross sales on which royalties were based
- Sold unauthorized products or services
- Refused to cease activities that might damage the reputation of the franchisor's name and trademark
- Breached the terms of a lease or sublease relating to the franchise operation
- Failed or refused to pay amounts owing to the franchisor
- Constantly made late payments to the franchisor
- Failed to comply with established franchise operating procedures and standards.

The franchisee may have rights to terminate the franchise agreement including:

- Failure of the franchisor to acquire the location specified in the contract
- Inability of the franchisor to develop the site for operation

- Failure of the franchisor to meet contractual obligations to the franchisee
- Serious illness of the franchisee
- Full payment by the franchisee of all its outstanding debts and other financial obligations to the franchisor.

The Franchise Agreement

There is no standard franchise agreement, as they can vary widely depending on the type, size and sophistication of the franchise system, or whether a new or existing franchise is being purchased.

Some franchise agreements are very one-sided in favour of the franchisor, whereas others are more balanced. Be very careful with some clauses because they can be particularly restrictive to franchisees. A non-competition clause may state that if the agreement is terminated, the franchisee cannot compete in the same type of business in the same area for a specific time (e.g., two years). This provision may exist whether the agreement is terminated by the franchisor or franchisee. Another clause to be wary of is the limit on the amount of damages (financial losses) that the franchisee could claim from the franchisor for breach of contract If the amount is unrealistically low, it would be unfair to the franchisee.

Sources of Conflict

Franchisees are normally happy to pay royalties, assuming that business is good at the beginning. However, as revenues increase and the monthly royalty cheques get bigger, their perceived value of the franchisor's support often drops.

Many of the problems relate to different and often unrealistic expectations. The franchisor may have considered the franchisee to be more capable and aggressive. The franchisee may expect more support, quicker, higher or unrealistic revenues and greater advertising exposure than actually received. The franchisor may have erred in site selection or exaggerated revenue projections.

Lack of perceived value in a franchise system can often be attributed to ineffective communication between the franchisor and its franchisees. The old adage goes "no news is good news," but in franchising no news is considered to be bad news. Franchisors must maintain consistent communication and stay proactive in order to build perceived value in the franchise system. As soon as franchisors become reactive, most of their time is spent "putting out fires" instead of working constructively to improve the franchise.

Everyone who buys a franchise expects leadership and consistency. They may not always agree with the direction of the franchisor, but they must know in which direction he or she is headed. Inconsistency is common among new franchisors who manage by crisis rather than objectives, because they have not developed an effective system with which to operate the franchise. Some of the areas of potential concern in a franchisee-franchisor relationship follow.

Lack of Support

Some franchisees need more ongoing assistance than others, and some believe that they need more than they are getting. Often it's not the quality of service that the franchisor gives, but the quality of service that the franchisee *perceives to be getting* that is the critical element.

If the franchisee's revenues are lower than projected, the perceived level of service is low and the franchisee inevitably looks for someone else to blame. Reduced cash flow usually means that not everyone can get paid, but payroll, rent, suppliers, advertising and utilities, if left unpaid, will have an immediate impact on the day-to-day operation of the business. So, an easy target is the franchisor and, in particular, the ongoing royalty payments. In order to justify withholding the royalty payments, the franchisee must have a reason. He or she generally becomes convinced that the franchisor has not provided the proper level of service, a subjective assessment.

If the franchisee does withhold payment, the franchisor can commence an action if the delinquent franchisee does not comply with a letter demanding that the royalty is paid. The franchisor can then attempt a court application for a mandatory injunction, requiring the franchisee to pay the royalties. If the franchisee is unhappy with the level of service and has exhausted all dispute resolution methods, he or she can initiate a legal action claiming non-performance of the franchisor's obligations under the agreement, but royalties must be paid in the meantime. Franchisors worry that lack of compliance may spread to other franchisees, interrupting cash flow and jeopardizing the entire franchise system.

Unrealistic Estimates of Income and Expense

Lower-than-projected revenues may result from exaggerated or inappropriate initial projections provided by the franchisor. Low sales may also be due to insufficient grand opening promotion or failure to allow for seasonal fluctuations. Projected expenses for items such as the cost of labour or freight may have been too low.

Sales Quotas

A few franchise agreements (usually those from supply-motivated franchise systems) call for the franchisee to make certain sales quotas as a condition of the franchise. This is common in automotive franchises. Changes in the appeal of the product, the economy or demographics of the trading area can reduce demand. Any quotas that are set should be reasonable and capable of being adjusted to changing market conditions.

Diversification of Products and Services

The franchisee expects the franchisor to carry out ongoing research and development to identify products and services that may replace or supplement existing offerings. Problems can arise if the franchisee considers these new products and services incompatible with the franchise image, or the diversification requires an expenditure by the franchisee which appears unjustified or unreasonable.

Franchisees may demand unreasonable or unnecessary changes to the product range or wish to offer products or services that are totally incompatible with the franchise profile. Franchisees are often responsible for much of the positive innovation within a franchise system, as they deal directly with the consumer and their changing demands. One of the key elements in franchising is consistency, and any change must be for the overall good of the franchise system, not the benefit of just one franchisee.

Promotions and Discounts

Franchisors who are more concerned about increasing their royalties than in the profitability of the franchisee will be in a conflict-of-interest with the franchisee. An increase in overall sales will benefit the franchisor who receives a percentage of gross as royalties, whereas the franchisee's profits can diminish if the increased sales are achieved by discounting product lines. The franchisee should have the right to opt out of any promotion that may have a negative financial impact, especially if the products being discounted are those that he can normally sell at full mark-up.

Rebates and Discounts

The franchisor who receives unreasonable or undisclosed rebates or discounts from manufacturers or suppliers is almost certain to create conflict. There is nothing fundamentally wrong with a franchisor receiving rebates and discounts as long as they are reasonable and disclosed. The franchisee must have the ability to purchase supplies or products at lower prices than if the company was operating independently.

Some franchisors have the potential to earn greater revenues from rebates and discounts than from ongoing royalties. Some franchisors use all or some of the rebates and discounts to supplement the advertising fund. This win-win strategy can result in higher sales to the franchisees, which creates goodwill within the system and increases the royalty stream to the franchisor.

Contention Over Advertising Funds

The use of advertising funds by the franchisor is a prime source of conflict. Concerns regarding the franchisor diverting funds to cover other expenses can usually be prevented by the franchisor segregating the funds from the general account and providing regular accounting to the franchisees.

Contention over the disproportionate use of funds in one area when the intent of the fund is to equally benefit all franchisees can be alleviated by giving the franchisees some input as to the use of the funds. Having franchisee representation on all committees of the franchise system can eliminate many problems.

Territories

Territories that are not clearly defined, of insufficient trading area or that encroach on another franchise, are all potential problems. Such problems can be prevented by both parties having a clear understanding of the rules before the game starts. Negotiate any exclusive territory and provide for any options or rights of first refusal at the outset, and include these issues in the franchise contract.

Competition with Company-owned Stores

A franchisee should not be placed at a disadvantage or be faced with unfair competition because the franchisor operates company-owned stores. The provisions concerning exclusivity in the franchise agreement should provide the franchisee with adequate protection against the franchisor opening company-owned stores in direct competition with the franchisee.

Ruth Learns the Hard Way About Her "Exclusive" Territory

Ruth attended a business opportunities show and was very impressed with a particular restaurant franchise. The financial projections looked impressive. She bought a franchise location, arranged for financing of $250,000 and started up her business. Within a year, she realized that she had a problem. She was always arguing with the franchise company over their refusal to let her try innovative ideas to increase revenue. They wanted her to comply with the rigid franchise manual and not deviate from it.

Despite these frustrations, the business was doing very well as the location was excellent, and Ruth worked hard. One day, Ruth heard rumours that the franchise company was going to open a "corporate" owned restaurant a block away. Ruth checked her franchise agreement. It said that no other franchises could open up within 20 blocks— it had no restrictions for a corporate owned restaurant. Ruth was fed up and wanted to sell. However, she encountered difficulties finding a purchaser, as no one wanted to have a competitive restaurant so close.

A franchise lawyer could have helped avoid many of the problems that Ruth encountered, by reviewing the franchise agreement and advising her of the downside scenarios. Also, Ruth should have asked to speak to between five and ten other franchise owners to get their opinions and concerns with the franchise company.

Payment Schedules

If a franchisee is late in the payment of royalties, supplies or rent, it is bound to negatively impact the relationship with the franchisor. Late payments are normally a symptom and not the underlying problem, and the franchisor must look beyond the franchisee's tardiness and address the source of the problem.

Accounting Procedures and Requirements

Franchisees who submit incomplete, inaccurate or tardy reports can take up an inordinate amount of a franchisor's time. Expect franchisors to be stringent about reporting and deadlines, as they depend on timely, relevant accurate information to monitor performance. Reporting also forms the basis for management information systems that enable the franchisor to provide the franchisees with valuable data that will help improve their individual performance.

If you as a franchisee are unable to meet a deadline, ask the franchisor for an extension, or if the reporting requirements are unreasonable, the matter should be discussed to search for a compromise.

Quality Control Issues

Franchise systems with weak or no quality controls should be avoided. Quality controls should apply product specifications, customer service, store appearance, uniforms, employee performance, warranties and guarantees, and the promotion of the franchise. The requirement for the franchisee to purchase equipment, products and supplies only from the franchisor or its designated suppliers may cause prospective franchisees to be concerned with competitive pricing. The franchisee must be able to source and have the franchisor approve alternative sources of supply, if products supplied by the franchisor become too expensive. However, the enforcement of high quality control standards is essential in order to protect the business image of the franchise system, and control over the source of supply is critical in achieving acceptable standards.

The franchisee also relies on the franchisor to maintain consistently high standards across the franchise system. A failure to do so can negatively affect his or her particular location. Visiting other franchised locations prior to investing will provide a good indication of the franchisor's enforcement of high standards.

Buy-back Agreements

Most agreements provide for the franchisor to repurchase the franchised business or some of the equipment, leasehold improvements and supplies, if the franchise agreement is terminated for whatever reason. A problem can arise where the agreement stipulates that the repurchase price will be based on "book value," as shown in the franchisee's financial statements. Depending on the amount of time the franchisee has been in business, or how long he or she has owned certain assets, the assets could be completely depreciated on the books. A more equitable method of evaluation should be agreed upon before an appraisal is necessary.

Resolution of Conflict

Refer to Chapter 16 on "Litigation and the ADR Process." In addition, many franchise companies have their own ADR (alternate dispute resolution) procedure built into the contract.

Summary

As you can see, the franchise option is not for everyone. Many people have made money in franchises. Others have lost their shirts. Go into the franchise option with a clear and realistic perspective of the downside risk, as well as the upside potential. Carefully examine your personality, style and needs to decide whether the accountability and control involved with following someone else's program is a good fit for you or not. Do your due diligence research thoroughly, comparison shop, look at other alternatives and speak with a franchise lawyer before you sign any documents.

Five

Buying Real Estate

Introduction
When operating a business, you could be faced with buying a house or condo that would contain a home office, buying an office condo or buying a building. You may buy real estate with others for investment purposes. All these actions involve legal and financial implications.

Types of Ownership of Property

Types of Interest in Land
There are several types of legal interests in land, the most common being freehold and leasehold.

Freehold
Freehold ownership in land entitles the owner to use the land for an indefinite time and to deal with the land in any way desired, subject to legislation (e.g., municipal bylaws, hydro utility easements or rights-of-way, provincial mineral rights), contractual obligations (e.g., subdivision restrictive covenants) and any charges that encumber the property title and that are filed in the provincial land titles office (e.g., mortgages, liens). Another term for freehold is *fee simple.*

Leasehold Interest
In this type of interest, the holder has the right to use the land for a fixed period of time, e.g., 50 or 99 years. The owner of the property (landlord or lessor) signs an agreement with the owner of the leasehold interest (tenant or lessee) setting out terms and conditions. The leasehold interest can be bought and sold, but the leaseholder can only sell the right to use the land for the time remaining in the lease, subject to any conditions contained in the original lease.

Both freehold interest and leasehold interest can be designated as an asset of your estate or specifically bequeathed in your will.

Types of Joint Ownership

There are two main types of legal joint ownership—joint tenancy and tenancy in common.

Joint Tenancy

In joint tenancy, an owner has an undivided but equal share with the other owners. No one person has a part of the property that is specifically his or hers, because all the property belongs to all the owners. At the time of purchase, all the joint tenants will show up on the title of the property equally and each of the joint tenants has the right in law to possession of the whole property. If any of these essential conditions are not met, then the ownership is deemed to be a tenancy in common and not joint tenancy. The title of the property will generally state that all parties are joint tenants.

One of the main features of a joint tenancy is the right of survivorship. If one of the joint tenants dies, the others automatically and immediately receive the deceased person's share, equally divided. The deceased person's share is not passed on as an asset of his or her estate to beneficiaries, whether or not a will exists. It is fairly common for a married or co-habiting couple to hold the legal interest in the property by means of joint tenancy.

Tenancy-in-Common

In this form of ownership, the tenants can hold equal or unequal shares in the property. Each party owns an undivided share in the property and therefore is entitled to possession of the whole property. For example, there could be five people who are tenants-in-common, but four of them could own $\frac{1}{10}$ of the property each, and the fifth person could own $\frac{6}{10}$ of the property.

The holder of a tenancy-in-common property can sell or mortgage the interest in the property. When a buyer cannot be found, the tenant-in-common can go to court and, under a legal procedure called partition, request that the court order the property to be sold and the net proceeds to be distributed proportionately.

Tenancy-in-common does not carry an automatic right of survivorship, as in joint tenancy. If one of the tenants-in-common dies, the interest does not go to the other tenants, but goes to the estate of the deceased. If there is a will, it is distributed under the terms of the will. If the deceased person does not have a will, provincial legislation would dictate how the person's assets are to be distributed to relatives.

If you purchase property for investment purposes with people who are not relatives, you would not want them to automatically have your interest in the property in the event of your death, so you would prefer tenancy-in-common over joint tenancy. If you have been previously married, have children from a previous relationship and have since remarried, you may want to specify in your will that a portion of the estate goes to those children individually or collectively. The only way to do this is with a tenancy-in-common situation, because the interest would be deemed to be an asset of one's estate. If the partners invest unequal amounts of money in the property, a tenancy-in-common structure would reflect those different contributions in terms of the percentage interest in the property.

Written agreements setting out the procedures if one tenant-in-common wants out of the situation are prudent. Giving the others the first right of refusal on a proportional basis to buy out the interest; or a clause requiring the consent of the other tenant-in-common in approving a potential purchaser; or a provision requiring notice to the other tenants before the property is sold are all possible clauses. A tenancy-in-common arrangement might be preferable when one of the owners wants the independence to raise money for outside interests. In many cases, the tenancy-in-common portion could be mortgaged without the consent of the other parties.

Understanding the Purchase and Sale Agreement

The agreement of purchase and sale sets out the terms and conditions between the parties and is legally binding if no conditions exist in the contract that have to be met before it becomes binding. All contracts dealing with land must be in writing to be enforceable, including a lease.

Elements of a Contract

Five main elements have to be present in order for a contract to be valid, including the following.

1. Mutual Agreement

There must be an offer and an acceptance. The terms and conditions of the contract must be specific, complete, clear and unambiguous. The parties to the contract must be sufficiently identifiable.

An offer may be withdrawn (revoked) any time before acceptance by the other party, as long as that revocation is transmitted to the other party ideally in writing. If the offer has already been accepted without condition and signed before receipt of the revocation, a binding contract has occurred.

2. Legal Capacity

The parties to a contract must have the capacity to enter into a legally binding contract, otherwise the contract cannot be enforced. Each party to a contract:

- Must be over the "age of majority," which varies from province to province but is usually 19 years or older
- Must not have impaired judgment, i.e., the party must understand what is involved in signing the contract; if a person is impaired by drugs, alcohol, stroke or mental infirmity (diminished capacity), that would invalidate the contract if it could be proven
- Must not be medically or legally insane
- Must be able to act with free will, i.e., not under duress or threat or intimidation.

3. Exchange of Consideration

The parties must exchange something of value in order to bind the contract. Usually money changes hands, but "consideration" could mean another property, a service or product or other benefit, or a promise to do something.

4. Intention to be Bound

The parties must have the intention of being bound by the agreement, and they must expect that it could be enforced by the courts.

5. Compliance with the Law

A contract, to be enforceable, must be legal in its purpose and intent. The courts will not enforce a contract that is intended to, or has the effect of, breaching federal, provincial or municipal legislation.

Getting Out of a Signed Contract

There are instances where either the vendor or the purchaser may wish to back out of the agreement. Be careful because litigation is expensive, time consuming, stressful, protracted and uncertain in outcome. Get legal advice before you act. Some conditions of backing out of a contract are discussed below.

Recision

In several jurisdictions in Canada, there is a "cooling-off" or recision period, whereby the purchaser of a property has a period of time (usually from three to 30 days) to back out of the contract by giving notice to the vendor in writing before the deadline. The vendor is obliged to pay back without penalty all the money that the purchaser has placed on deposit. In cases where legislation does not give an automatic right to recision, the documents that are a part of the property package may have a recision period built in. If you do not have a statutory (bylaw) right to recision and it is not part of the documents relating to the purchase of a *new* property, then you may want it as a condition of your offer.

Specific Performance

If the vendor or purchaser refuses to go through with a purchase and sale agreement when there are no unfulfilled conditions attached to the agreement, the other party is entitled to go to court and request the court to order the breaching party to perform the terms of the agreement, i.e., complete the transaction. The party who succeeds in obtaining the court order would be entitled to ask for the costs of the application from the court. Generally, court costs awarded represent about 25% to 40% of the actual legal costs incurred; therefore those who "win" at court ultimately "lose" financially.

Damages

If one party refuses to complete the agreement, instead of suing for specific performance of the terms, the other party can sue for damages. Damages include the financial losses that have been incurred because the other party failed to complete the bargain. To get financial damages (compensation), you have to prove you have suffered financial damages. For example, if a vendor refused to complete the deal because he thought he could make $50,000 more on a property sale if the price had gone up considerably and if it could be shown that he did sell it for $50,000 more after refusing to go through with your signed commitment, then you could claim $50,000 damages plus court costs. Your loss could be quantified, assuming that there were no other reasons that could explain the differential in price. Alternatively, if the purchaser fails to complete and the vendor can show that he or she was relying on those funds for another purchase, and so on down the line with other sales all relying on the first, there could be considerable damages for which the purchaser may be liable. These are called "consequential" and "foreseeable" damages. This is a complex area of law and skilled legal advice is critical.

Conditional Contract

If the vendor or purchaser has preliminary conditions built into the purchase and sale agreement ("subject to" clauses), and those conditions cannot be met, no valid binding contract exists and neither party is liable to the other.

Void Contracts

A contract is void and unenforceable if the required elements that make up a contract are not present, or if the contract is prohibited by statute (e.g., municipal, provincial, or federal law).

Voidable Contracts

If one of the parties has been induced into entering the contract on the basis of misrepresentation, whether innocent, negligent or fraudulent, that party may be entitled to void the contract. If the misrepresentation was innocent, generally the contract can be cancelled and any money returned, but no damages can be recovered in court. If there is negligent or fraudulent misrepresentation, however, not only can the contract be cancelled, but damages can also be recovered in court. For example, if the vendor was going to provide vendor-back financing and relied on the purchaser's representations of his or her creditworthiness, and prior to completion of the transaction (through a credit check or other investigation) the vendor learns that the purchaser is a terrible credit risk, then that could be deemed negligent or fraudulent misrepresentation. The contract could be cancelled.

Key Sections of the Purchase and Sale Agreement

Most purchase and sale agreements come in standard formats, with standard clauses, and are drafted by the builder, the local real estate board or commercial stationers. Additional, customized clauses can be added. A contract prepared by a builder has distinctly different clauses from those of a standard form for resales, or from those created by real estate boards.

Standard or additional clauses may not be comprehensive enough for your needs; some people may not even understand the implications and yet sign the agreement anyway. That is why it is so important to have a lawyer review your offer to purchase before you sign. Regrettably, only a small percentage of people do this, perhaps thinking it is an unnecessary expense, or they are too trusting. It is false economy to save on a legal consultation, as the costs are very reasonable relative to the risk involved in signing a bad contract. Alternatively, some people insert a condition that states the offer is "subject to approval as to form and contents by the purchaser's solicitor, such approval to be communicated to vendor within 'x' days of acceptance, or to be deemed to be withheld."

Some of the common clauses and features contained in the purchase and sale agreement follow.

Amount of Deposit

A deposit serves as a partial payment on the purchase price, a good-faith indication of seriousness, and an assurance of performance if all the conditions in the offer have been fulfilled. The deposit is generally 5% to 10% of the purchase price. If there were conditions in the offer that were not met, then the purchaser is entitled to receive the full deposit back. Such conditions or "subject to" clauses in the offer protect one's interests. Most agreements for purchase and sale have a provision that gives the vendor the option of keeping the deposit as "liquidated damages," in the event that the purchaser fails to complete the terms of the agreement and pay the balance of money on the closing date.

When making a deposit, be very careful about to whom you pay the funds. If you are purchasing on a private sale and no realtor is involved, never pay the funds directly to the vendor; pay them to your own lawyer in trust. If a realtor is involved, the funds can be paid to the realtor's trust account or your own lawyer's trust account. If you are purchasing a new property from the builder, do not pay a deposit directly to the builder. The money should go to your lawyer's trust account, or some other system should be set up which ensures that your funds cannot be used except under certain conditions set out in the agreement. If you give a deposit to a builder, if the builder does not complete the project and goes into bankruptcy, you could lose all your money and could have great difficulty getting it back. Although several provincial governments have brought in legislation dealing with new property projects and public deposits, legislation provides only partial protection.

If you are paying a deposit, ensure that interest is given at the appropriate rate or formula to be paid to your credit. In many cases, deposit monies can be tied up for many months, representing considerable interest.

Conditions and Warranties

Understand the distinction between *conditions* and *warranties*, as it is critical to the agreement wording.

A condition is a requirement that is fundamental to the very existence of the offer. A breach of condition allows the buyer to get out of the contract and obtain the full amount of the deposit back. An inability to meet the condition set by a vendor permits the vendor to get out of the contract.

A warranty is a minor promise that does not go to the heart of the contract. If there is a breach of warranty, the purchaser cannot cancel but must complete the contract and sue for damages. Therefore, if a particular requirement on your part is pivotal in your decision to purchase, *frame your requirement as a condition rather than as a warranty*. Both vendors and purchasers frequently insert conditions into the agreement, also referred to as *subject clauses*. Clauses should:

- Be precise and clearly detailed
- Have specific time allocated for conditions that have to be removed, e.g., within two days, 30 days, etc. It is preferable to name the precise date, rather than merely refer to the number of days involved.
- Specifically state that the conditions are for the sole benefit of the vendor or purchaser, as the case may be, and that the party requiring the condition can waive them at any time. You may wish to remove a condition even though it has not been fulfilled, in order for the contract to be completed.

Here is just a sampling of some of the common subject clauses. There are many others that you or your lawyer may feel it appropriate to insert.

For Benefit of Purchaser

- Title being conveyed free and clear of any and all encumbrances or charges registered against the property on or before the closing date at the expense of the vendor, either from the proceeds of the sale or by solicitor's undertaking
- Inspection being satisfactory to purchaser by relative, spouse, partner, etc. (specify name)
- Inspection being satisfactory to purchaser by house inspector/contractor selected by purchaser
- Sale of purchaser's other property being made
- Confirmation of mortgage financing
- Deposit funds to be placed in an interest-bearing trust account with the interest to accrue to the benefit of the purchaser
- Approval of assumption of existing mortgage
- Granting of vendor take-back mortgage or builder's mortgage
- Removal of existing tenancies (vacant possession) by completion date
- Existing tenancies conforming to prevailing municipal bylaws
- Interim occupancy payments being credited to purchase price

- Review and satisfactory approval by purchaser's lawyer of the contents of the agreement of purchase and sale
- Warranties, representations, promises, guarantees and agreements shall survive the completion date
- No urea formaldehyde foam insulation (UFFI) having ever been in the building
- Vendor's supplying a certificate of estoppel at the expense of the vendor within days of acceptance of the offer
- Vendor's warranty that no work orders or deficiency notices are outstanding against the property, or if there are, that they will be complied with at the vendor's expense before closing.

Additional Clauses if Purchasing a Condominium
- Receipt and satisfactory review by purchaser (and/or purchaser's lawyer) of project documents, such as disclosure, declaration, articles, rules and regulations, financial statements, project budget, minutes of condominium corporation for past year, management contract, estoppel certificate, etc.
- Confirmation by condominium corporation that the condominium unit being purchased can be rented.

Additional Clauses if Purchasing a Revenue Property
- Review and satisfactory approval of financial statements, balance sheet, income and expense statement, list of chattels and inventory, names of tenants, amount of deposits and monthly rents, dates of occupancy, list of receivables and payables, list and dates of equipment safety inspections, list and dates of repairs, service contracts, leases, warranties, property plans and surveys.

For Benefit of Vendor
- Removal of all subject clauses by purchaser within 72 hours upon written notice by vendor of a backup *bona fide* (legitimate) offer
- Confirmation of purchase of vendor-back mortgage through vendor's mortgage broker
- Satisfactory confirmation of creditworthiness of purchaser by vendor or vendor's mortgage broker
- Issuance of building permit
- Builder receiving confirmation of construction financing
- Registration of a subdivision plan
- Deposit funds non-refundable and to be released directly to the vendor once all conditions of the purchaser have been met
- Review and satisfactory approval by vendor's lawyer of the contents of the agreement of purchase and sale.

Risk and Insurance

It is important that the parties agree to an exact date when risk is going to pass from the vendor to the purchaser. In some cases, the agreement will state that risk will pass at the time that there is a firm, binding, unconditional purchase and sale agreement. In other cases, risk will pass on the completion or possession date. In any event, make sure that you have adequate insurance coverage taking effect as of the date that you assume the risk. The vendor should wait until after the risk date before terminating insurance.

Fixtures and Chattels

This is an area of potential dispute unless it is sufficiently clarified. A *fixture* is technically something permanently affixed to the property; therefore, when the property is conveyed the fixtures are conveyed with it. A *chattel* is an object that is moveable or not permanently affixed. Common chattels include the carpets and drapes.

It is unclear sometimes whether an item is a fixture or a chattel. For example, an expensive chandelier hanging from the dining room ceiling, gold-plated bathroom fixtures, drape racks or television satellite dish on the roof might be questionable items. One of the key tests is asking whether the item was intended to be attached on a permanent basis to the property and should be transferred, or whether the vendor intended to remove or replace these items before closing the real estate transaction.

In general legal terms, if it is a fixture and it is not mentioned in the agreement, it is deemed to be included in the purchase price. On the other hand, if it is not a fixture and no reference is made to it in the agreement, then it would not be included in the purchase price. Most agreements for purchase and sale have standard clauses stating that all existing fixtures are included in the purchase price except those specifically listed. In addition, a clause should list and describe the chattels specifically included in the purchase price.

Adjustment Date

This date is used for calculating and adjusting taxes, maintenance fees, rentals, and other such matters. As of the adjustment date, all expenses and benefits go to the purchaser. For example, if the maintenance fee has been paid for the month of March by the vendor and the purchaser takes over with an adjustment date as of the 15th of March, there will be an adjustment on the closing documents showing that the purchaser owes half of the amount of the prepaid maintenance fee to the vendor for March.

Completion Date

This is the date when all documentation is filed in the appropriate registry and all monies are paid out. It is customary for the closing funds to be paid to the purchaser's solicitor a few days prior to closing. As soon as confirmation has been obtained from the registry office that everything is in order, the purchaser's solicitor releases the funds to the vendor's solicitor. More discussion of closing is presented later in this chapter. Note: The adjustment date and the completion date are frequently the same.

Possession Date

This is the date on which you are legally entitled to move into the premises, usually the same as the adjustment and completion date. Sometimes the possession date is a day later in order for the vendor to move out; in practical terms, though, many purchasers prefer that all three dates be the same. The risks of the purchaser take effect as of the completion date, and there is always a risk that the vendor could cause damage in the premises if he or she remains there beyond that date. As soon as your lawyer has advised you that all the documents have been filed and money has changed hands, the realtor or lawyer arranges for you to receive the keys to the premises.

Merger

Merger is a legal principle that if the agreement for purchase and sale is to be "merged" into a deed or other document, the real contract between the parties is the document filed with the land registry. To protect yourself, include that the "warranties, representations, promises, guarantees and agreements shall survive the completion date." There are exceptions to the document of merger in cases of mistake or fraud.

Commissions

At the end of most purchase and sale agreements there is a section setting out the commission charged, which the vendor confirms when accepting an offer.

Buying with Others

Most people prefer to invest in real estate on their own, if possible. On the one hand, some people prefer to start out investing with a group as it may provide mutual support, shared and therefore reduced risk, pooled skills and expertise, greater investment opportunities, shared responsibility and time, and collective energy, synergy and momentum. On the other hand, if you do not select your group investment wisely, it could be a financial and emotional nightmare. Know the benefits and limitations of the various group investment options and never go into a real estate purchase without obtaining prior advice from your lawyer and accountant. Always have a written agreement in advance.

Factors to Consider

Approximately 80% of business partnership "marriages" don't work out. The odds therefore are very high that any real estate group relationship in which you are involved may not survive. By cautiously assessing the individuals that will make up a potential group, you can minimize the risk immensely. Following are some of the key factors to consider.

Goals and Objectives

Ensure that your goals and objectives are consistent with those of the rest of the group. For example, some members may want a long-term investment (e.g., five years) with positive cash flow from rents; others may want a medium-term investment (e.g., three years) and are prepared to subsidize the negative cash flow because of hopes of property appreciation; still others may want to quick flip within a few months of purchase, in a hot market.

Expertise

You probably know the skills that you can contribute to the investment. If you are going in with friends or relatives, you may have a clear idea of the skills that they offer. But if you are going into an investment group with strangers or acquaintances, clarify exactly what, if any, skills that they will bring to the group. If they are just silent investors, it may not matter. If they are active investors in a small group, you need to determine their contributions. If the group is going to be totally managed by one group member, query the person's credentials and track record, and get it in writing. If you are going to rely on the person to protect your investment, be careful and cautious.

Liquidity

Liquidity refers to how easily and quickly you can get your money out of the investment. Your financial resources and needs will determine your liquidity needs. For example, if you need to get your investment capital back quickly, then you probably won't want a long-term investment. Reconsider the investment if you would suffer if your money were tied up or at risk. Don't invest money you could not afford to lose. Be cautious about investing retirement or contingency reserve funds, if you need immediate liquidity.

Most investments are tied up for the duration of the deal, related to the investment group's goals and objectives. If you are buying shares in a real estate investment on the public stock exchange, you may have liquidity but not necessarily at an attractive price. Also, consider a buy-out clause in the investment group agreement. This means the group would buy you out within a fixed period of time, although normally at a discount price, to act as a disincentive for people to get out early.

Liability

Make sure, if at all possible, that your risk is limited to the amount of your investment. Avoid personal exposure for any financial problems that occur, either to mortgage companies, other investors, or the investment group as such. For example, if you invest in a corporation that is holding property for the group and the corporation has taken out a mortgage with a lender, the lender may require personal guarantees of the shareholders of the corporation If you went into a general partnership with two others and financial problems occurred created by the others, you would still be liable for the full amount of the debt if the other two couldn't pay. A third risk example would be if you signed an investment group agreement that stated that any shortfall of funds would have to be paid by the investors on a proportional interest basis. Finally in a limited partnership, if you stopped being an inactive partner and started to actively involve yourself with the management of the investment, you could have exposure. Some limited partners are asked to sign personal guarantees up to a certain limit; avoid this scenario. Your lawyer should look at the agreement and advise you of the ways of limiting or eliminating personal liability risk.

Legal Structure

Group investments fall into variations of a general partnership, limited partnership, corporation or joint venture agreement. Some legal structures allow more flexibility and varying degrees of personal liability exposure, depending on the structure and the group investment agreement, discussed previously.

Control

Control relates to the influence that you have on the management of the investment and related decision-making. Obviously smaller groups tend to allow more individual control than others do. For example, in some cases, unanimous consent is required for major decisions; in other cases, 75% consent is required; and in still other cases, a simple 51% majority vote of investors is required. In some instances you do not have any vote. You put your money in and hope for the best. If you are buying into a limited partnership, thoroughly check out the promoter's previous history, experience and reputation.

Tax Considerations

One of the main reasons that you would be investing in real estate would be for the tax benefits. Be very cautious about salespeople or financial advisors who attempt to induce you into buying a tax shelter. That area is ripe with pitfalls and risk. Get objective and impartial advice from your lawyer and tax accountant before making your investment decision. You want to buy from an investment viewpoint first, with tax benefits then taken into account.

Compatibility

Are the other people in your investment group similar in personality, age, financial position and investment objectives? How do group members look on issues such as control, management and liability? What contributions, if any, are they making? If the people in the group have diversified skills, this could save the group money and make the investment more secure. Ego, power, greed, arrogance and unrealistic expectations are common group stressors.

Risk Assessment

Objectively look at the overall potential risks of the nature of the investment, the potential for profit, the degree of potential personal liability, the type of legal structure, the nature and degree of control, the quality of management and your compatibility with other members.

Contribution

Determine what contribution is expected of you in terms of money, time, expertise, management, personal guarantee and contingency back-up capital. Do you feel comfortable with the expectations?

Percentage of Investment

Do you feel comfortable with the percentage of investment that you are getting, relative to the contribution you're making? For example, in one holding company, one inactive partner finds and manages the property, and the other three are silent investors. The active partner has 55% of the property interest, did not put any money in, and did not sign any personal guarantees. The three silent partners put up all the money equally, signed personal guarantees for the mortgage, and have 15% of the investment each. Would you feel comfortable with that investment percentage if you were a silent partner? What if you were the active partner?

Getting Out or Buying Others Out

What if you want out for any number of reasons? Is there a formula for getting out? What penalty do you pay, how is it calculated, and how long will it take to get your money? Conversely, what if you want to buy the other investor(s) out, due to a personality conflict or for other reasons? Can you do it? If there is nothing outlined in the agreement to get out before the property is eventually sold, you could have a problem.

Don't Get Trapped in a Bad Investment Deal!

Chester, Peter and Dan decided to invest in an office condo, as a business investment. They decided to hold their respective interests in the condo in joint tenancy as equal owners, as they each put in $100,000. As time went on, the business started having problems. Conflict occurred between the partners. They decided they would leave the premises, work out of their homes, and rent out the office condo to cover the mortgage. However, they could not come to an agreement on how much rent to charge.

Good legal advice at the outset would have set out an agreement between the investors, setting out the recipe for resolving problems if they arose. This would include a buy/sell provision for getting out or getting others out. This structure would have saved stress, hassle and legal fees. Also, the ownership should have been in tenancy-in-common. Otherwise, joint tenancy meant that when one partner died, the others would automatically get his interest, in terms of property value.

Management

Is the group investment going to be managed by a professional management company, a resident manager, a group of investors, one of the investors, or the original promoter? How confident are you with management? What fees are being charged? Are the fees reasonable in the circumstances?

Profits and Losses

Determine how the group will deal with excess revenue from an income property? Is that to be kept as a contingency fund, or is a portion of it paid out to the investors? What about selling the shares of a corporation holding the property or the property itself? How are those decisions made? These decisions have tax implications for you. What about losses? Is the shortfall to be covered by a bank loan, or remortgaging of property, or by the group of investors? In practical terms, how is that to be done?

Types of Group Investments

The most common options available in group investing consist of co-tenancy, general partnership, limited partnership, joint venture, syndication and equity sharing.

Co-tenancy

Each co-tenant has a proportional interest reflected in the title to the property filed in the land title office. For example, if three people decide to invest together on an equal basis, it would show up on the land title as each party having "an undivided one-third interest each, tenants-in-common." In law, co-tenants or tenants-in-common can generally deal with the property without the consent of the other co-tenant. In addition, if a co-tenant dies, his interest in the title to the property goes to his estate, it does not go to the surviving owners, as in a joint tenancy type of legal ownership. When people buy for investment purposes or to buy a property together to live in, but the parties are not living together in a common-law or legal marriage, tenancy-in-common is the common way to hold it.

The ownership of the land through tenancy-in-common reflects percentage ownership on title; it does not involve partnership type obligations to third parties. To prevent misunderstandings have your own lawyer either prepare a co-tenancy agreement or review it if someone else prepares it. Consider including the following points:

- That the co-tenants are not partners of each other, as set out in the provincial partnership act
- That the co-tenants do not have the power to act for each other, except as outlined in the co-tenant agreement
- That the co-tenants are not agents of each other
- That the co-tenants can compete with each other in other real estate investments

- That the co-tenant is individually responsible for any tax or other financial liability relating to his or her percentage interest in the property
- That there are no fiduciary duties; a co-tenant can make money from the co-tenancy, without it being considered a conflict of interest.

In addition, the co-tenant agreement should set out the living accommodation rights, duties and responsibilities, if the parties are living in the same dwelling. A sketch map of the living area should be attached.

It is common for friends, relatives or people who cannot afford to buy a principal residence on their own to invest in real estate through a co-tenant arrangement. A co-tenancy is a reasonably simple structure and relatively easy to get out of.

General Partnership

There are many potential liability risks involved in a general partnership, as well as investment limitations. Never go into one without competent legal and tax advice. A general partnership is governed by the partnership act of each province. The risks involve individual liability for all the debts or liability of the partnership, regardless of how many other partners there are. For example, if there is $50,000 owing by the partnership and the two other investors do not have any money or assets and you do, creditors will go after you for the full amount. A lot of people assume that if there are three partners, the liability is split three ways.

In addition, the provincial partnership act outlines automatic rights that each partner has in law; as well as tax, control and ownership implications; non-competitive provisions; fiduciary duties, dissolution rights; automatic break-up of the partnership on death of a partner; and inability to pledge the partnership interest as security to a lender. Lack of control and limited management and investor options make the general partnership option an inflexible one, and the implications onerous for most investors. Although a partnership agreement can lessen some of the limitations, it does not eliminate them. General partnerships normally only involve a few people.

Limited Partnership

A variation of a general partnership and a corporation, a limited partnership has less of the legal disadvantages of a general partnership but maintains the tax advantages. For example, the rights and liabilities of the partners are set out in the limited partnership agreement. The liability of each partner is limited to the amount of the investment. That is why the partner is referred to as a limited partner, due to the limited liability. The limited partner is an inactive partner, and has no control over management of the limited partnership other than voting on who should be the manager. The general partner is normally a corporation and is responsible for the active management of the limited partnership investment. The general partner can be sued, but usually is operated by a corporation without assets.

It is important that a limited partner is not involved in any fashion with the management and decision-making of the limited partnership. To do so could expose the limited partner to unlimited liability in the same manner as a general partner is exposed.

The operation of a limited partnership is governed by the limited partnership agreement, provincial limited partnership legislation and possibly the provincial securities legislation. Limited partners hold their interest in the form of "units" issued by the limited partnership. These units are similar to shares in a corporation and represent the proportionate share in the limited partnership held by the investor. Units can be sold to other group investors or outsiders, subject to the restrictions set out in the limited partnership document. Many limited partnerships have a large number of investors, as the financial cost can be considerable.

Keep in mind that the promoter of a limited partnership is out to make a personal profit. This may or may not be consistent with making money for you from the investment. Minimize the risk of false or misleading representations by requesting cash flow guarantees from the promoter, secured against assets of the promoter. Attempt to get a written commitment from the promoter to purchase your unit if you so wish, after a period of time. Make sure that long-term financing is in place, so that you don't have to come up with more money in a short time. Finally, make sure that your lawyer and tax accountant review the project and documentation, and advise you as to the legitimate tax benefits, degree of risk, and realistic nature of the projections.

Corporation

You may wish to hold real estate by owning shares with others in a corporation. A corporation is normally governed by the provincial company legislation for most real estate investments. A corporation is a separate legal entity and can sue and be sued, but its liability is limited to the assets of the corporation. Individual shareholders are not personally liable for corporate liability, unless personal guarantees of the corporation were signed by the shareholder.

A corporation can be a convenient vehicle for real estate group investments. It is structured to make it easy to sell or transfer shares, subject to the articles of incorporation and shareholders' agreement. If a shareholder dies, the corporation and its investment continue. The shares would go to the estate of the deceased or be purchased by the corporation, depending on the shareholders' agreement. Generally there is a limit on the number of shareholders in a corporation, beyond which the corporation could be governed by provincial securities legislation. This would involve stringent public reporting requirements and accountability, as well as limitations in the management of the corporation. Obtain legal advice to ensure that you are not covered by securities legislation. Many holding corporation investments are generally comprised of not more than ten people.

Corporations are a popular means of holding revenue property such as apartment buildings. Income from the corporation is tabulated and taxed in the corporation. Investors pay taxes on income only if they receive money by means of dividends or salaries from the corporation. Otherwise, investors have to wait until the property is sold. If the shares are sold to a new owner, the investor could have a taxable gain on those shares.

Joint Venture

A joint venture could involve individuals or corporations who want to pool money, resources, skills, expertise, land or other assets to make a profit by means of development or investment. Generally it is a specific, one-time project. Joint ventures can be formed as a co-tenancy, general partnership, limited partnership or holding corporation, in which the shareholders are the joint venturers. It is also possible that a corporation could be formed to hold the property in trust for the joint venturers. The nature of joint venture structure depends on legal, tax, and financial issues, as well as the purpose of the joint venture. Most joint venture groups are small in number. It is essential to have a joint venture agreement drawn up and signed. Make sure that the agreement makes it clear that the relationship is not one of a general partnership, due to the tax and legal implications. Have your lawyer and tax accountant give you advice.

Syndication

This is usually in the form of a limited partnership and is designed to provide passive investors with limited liability, capital appreciation and tax deferral. All the management is done by the promoter of the syndicate or company contracted by the syndicate. The syndicate makes money from the investors as well as the investment itself. Generally, the cost to the investor is directly related to the degree of risk and financial and performance guarantees by the syndicate promoter. Have your lawyer and tax accountant assess the risk, before signing any documentation. Many syndicates have a larger number of investors and are therefore governed by provincial security legislation.

Equity Sharing

In a way, equity sharing is a combination of a partnership and co-tenancy. For example, one approach is for an investor to look for a tenant who wants to buy a house but doesn't have the down payment. The investor buys the house and the tenant moves in and pays slightly more than fair market rent. The rent is sufficient to cover all mortgage costs, property taxes, utilities, insurance and maintenance. Therefore, there is no negative cash flow. The tenants have a place to live and a house to maintain and upkeep with pride.

The above parties sign an agreement setting out the arrangement. Generally, the investor has title to the property with a stipulation that if the tenant remains, say three years, the tenant has the option to purchase the house for the appraised value minus the normal real estate commission and an agreed upon percentage for the equity increase over the three-year period (e.g., 10% to 25%). This could bring the house price down sufficiently that the tenant would be able to get financing to buy it. If the tenant can't or doesn't want to purchase at the end of the term, the tenant loses the option and all equity sharing and purchase rights.

The secret to making the equity sharing plan work is the right selection of the property at the right price and terms, the right match of investor/tenant, and a well-written agreement that is fair to both parties. The agreement should be drawn up by a lawyer and cover what happens if the tenant stops paying, breaches other terms of the agreement or dies; or the investor declares personal bankruptcy; or a disagreement occurs over the appraised value of the property; or the investor does not want to sell after three years because the market is depressed.

Equity sharing can also include putting the tenant on title for an agreed percentage interest at the outset. This approach is not recommended, as it would be difficult for the investor to get the full title back without considerable legal fees if a falling-out occurs.

From an investor's viewpoint, the advantages of an equity sharing concept include the benefits of ideally assured positive cash flow, a committed tenant with pride and no management problems. From the tenant's viewpoint, the arrangement allows the tenant to select a house and provides a financial backer to get into the market, as well as a sharing of the equity build-up with an option to buy at a discounted price. One of the main disadvantages to an investor, though, is the sharing of the equity build-up. You can do equity sharing arrangements yourself with advice from your lawyer or invest in companies that offer the service. The problem is that you lose control with these companies as groups of eight to ten investors are put together. In addition, you have to pay the equity sharing management company an administrative fee.

Generally, the smaller the investment group, the more control and involvement; the larger the group, the less control or no control, and lack of individual identity or involvement with the investment. In some of the very large groups, you are totally detached from any involvement or input. Consult your legal and tax advisor before venturing into any arrangement.

Putting the Arrangement in Writing

After you have considered the options and decided which group investment you want, the next step is to ensure that you have a written agreement, with the help of your lawyer. Each type of group discussed earlier has a different format of agreement. The agreement you sign should be customized for the specific investment, and take into account the factors discussed earlier.

The main points and procedures consist of the following:
- Type of legal structure
- Name and location of investment group
- Goals and objectives of group

- Duration of agreement
- Names and categories of investors (e.g., general, limited, active, silent)
- Financial contribution by investors
- Procedure for obtaining additional capital
- Role of individual investors in the investment management
- Authority of any investor in conduct of investment group
- Nature and degree of each investor's contribution to the investment group
- How operating expenses will be handled
- How operating income will be handled
- Debts of investment group separate from individual investor
- Separate bank account
- Signing of cheques
- Division of profits and losses
- Books, records and method of accounting
- Draws or salaries
- Absence and disability of investor
- Death of an investor
- Bringing in other investors
- Rights of the investors
- Withdrawal of an investor
- Buying out other investors
- Management of employees
- Sale of investor interest
- Restrictions on the transfer, assignment, or pledging of the investor's interest
- Release of debts
- Settlement of investor disputes and arbitration procedures
- Additions, alterations or modifications to investment group agreement
- Non-competition with the investment group in the event of departure by the investor.

Why People Lose Money when Purchasing Real Estate
There are many reasons why people have problems when buying or investing in real estate including:
- Not understanding how the real estate market works
- Not having a clear understanding of personal and financial needs
- Not having a clear focus and lacking a realistic real estate investment plan, with strategies and priorities
- Not doing thorough market research and comparison shopping before making the purchase
- Not selecting the right property, considering the potential risks, money involved, and specific personal needs
- Not verifying representations or assumptions beforehand
- Not doing financial calculations beforehand

- Not buying at a fair market price
- Not buying real estate at the right time in the market
- Not buying within financial debt servicing capacity, comfort zone and skills
- Not understanding the financing game thoroughly, and therefore not comparison shopping to get the best rates, terms and type of mortgage
- Not making a decision based on an objective assessment but on an emotional one
- Not determining the real reason why the vendor is selling
- Not having the property inspected by a building inspector before a purchase decision is made
- Not selecting an experienced real estate lawyer and obtaining advice beforehand
- Not selecting an experienced tax accountant and obtaining advice beforehand
- Not selecting an experienced realtor with expertise in the type of real estate and geographic location you are considering
- Not negotiating effectively
- Not putting in the appropriate conditions or "subject clauses" in the offer
- Not buying for the right reasons, i.e. buying for tax shelter reasons rather than the inherent value, potential and viability of the investment property
- Not independently verifying financial information beforehand
- Not obtaining and reviewing all the necessary documentation appropriate for a given property
- Not selecting real estate investment partners carefully
- Not having a written agreement with real estate investment partners, prepared by a lawyer
- Not detailing with exactitude precisely what chattels are included in the purchase price
- Not seeing the property before buying it, but relying on pictures and/or the representations of others
- Not managing the property well, or not selecting the right property management company
- Not selling the property at the right time in the market or for the right reasons.

Selling Your Property

Selling is an integral part of the real estate process, whether it is your own home, business or an investment property. Many people take the selling process casually, without a full appreciation of the skills and techniques that should be used. They rely on luck or their realtor to get the top price. If you don't know how to maximize the selling price, you could lose your potential profit.

Ask yourself before deciding to sell why you are selling, the timing, the price, the terms and the benefits. Also consider how you are going to sell, including selecting and negotiating with a realtor, a lawyer and the buyer.

Determining When to Sell
Of course, you want to make sure the sale is not perceived as a distress sale. The following factors could justify a decision to sell:

- Market is reaching its peak in terms of upward momentum of sales
- Appreciation of the property has plateaued or is starting to decline
- Income has plateaued
- Return on investment is decreasing
- Capital expenditures are going to increase
- Declining tax shelter or tax benefits
- Financial needs have been met
- Interested in other priorities or opportunities
- Area is not economically healthy, either stagnating or declining
- Reached appropriate stage in original strategic holding period
- Reduction in net operating income
- Getting frustrated with property management problems.

In short, monitor the market and your investment regularly. Anticipate problems and act accordingly.

Preparing to Sell Your Property
Once you have made the decision to sell, you have to consider the following:

- **Timing.** Sell when everyone else is buying, although this is not always possible. The best times for selling homes would generally be in the spring, summer or early fall, rather than the winter.
- **Pricing.** The property has to be priced right for the market, based on objective assessment or value. Determine the ideal price and then add another 5% or more for negotiating margin.
- **Documentation preparation.** Prepare all necessary documents to provide to the realtor or purchaser. For example, if a mortgage is assumable without qualification and has an attractive interest rate, get a copy of the mortgage. If you have a revenue property or small apartment building, get all the financial records for a purchaser to review.
- **Financing.** If you have an assumable mortgage or you are prepared to take a first or second mortgage back in terms of vendor financing, clarify the terms.
- **Professional advice.** Obtain advice from your tax accountant and lawyer with regard to pricing, apportioning value and timing.
- **Select a realtor.** Most experienced real estate purchasers utilize a realtor. Make certain your realtor is experienced in selling the type of real estate you have.
- **Competition.** Check out similar properties for sale and compare the positive or negative features of your own property.
- **Promotion.** Have your realtor expose the property as extensively as possible, normally through a Multiple Listing Service (MLS), open houses for the public and realtors, newspaper advertising and lawn signage.

- **Make property attractive.** First impressions are lasting, so give your property special "curb appeal."
- **Set terms.** Determine your best deal and bottom line position and why. The purchaser will be attempting to negotiate the best deal, so be prepared.
- **Calculate closing costs.** Determine what you are going to net after all costs and before taxes. For example, you might have a three or six-month penalty clause in your fixed term mortgage for prepayment. There would be an exception, of course, if the mortgage were assumed by the purchaser.

Disadvantages of Selling the Property Yourself

There is primarily one reason for attempting to sell the property yourself, and that is saving on a real estate commission. You may indeed save money, but the saving could be an illusion. Depending on the nature of the property, the market at the time, the specific realtor and real estate company, you can negotiate a reduced real estate commission. The problem with a reduced commission structure, though, is that if you want it listed on MLS, other realtors will see the reduced commission and may not be inspired to spend time attempting to sell it, when they can make a higher commission on other properties.

The following remarks are not intended to dissuade you from attempting to sell your own property, but to place the process in realistic perspective. In general, the disadvantages of selling your property yourself are as follows:

- **Inexperience.** If you don't know all the steps involved, from the pre-sale operation to completing the deal, you could make costly mistakes. If you use a realtor who knows the market well, you can capitalize on the correct decisions being made.
- **Emotional roller coaster.** Many people get emotionally involved in the sale process because of the direct interaction with the prospective purchasers. For example, you may be frustrated by negative comments or fault-finding, people whose personality you don't like, or people who negotiate toughly on the price. These one-on-one dynamics can sometimes be taken personally, and therefore be a cause of stress.

  If you use a realtor, you rarely (if ever) meet the prospective purchaser directly, either before the agreement of purchase and sale is signed, or before or after closing. This degree of anonymity reduces stress.
- **Time commitment.** Showing your property may not necessarily be convenient. In addition, you'll have to spend time preparing the ad copy and responding to telephone calls or people knocking on the door.

  A realtor will save you time. The realtor shows the property and answers phone calls.
- **Expense, nature and content of advertising.** Costs include the daily or weekly newspaper classified and/or box ads, internet listing, as well as a lawn sign. In addition, you may not know what specific types of advertising would be appropriate for your type of property; how to write ad copy that

would grab the attention of a prospective purchaser; nor how to identify and emphasize the key selling features of your property.

A realtor coordinates all open houses and pays all the advertising costs, the nature of which is negotiated at the time the listing agreement is signed. Not only could you get listed in the weekly MLS book, circulated to all member realtors, you could also be in the MLS computer database, accessible to all realtors. Ads could be placed in daily and/or community newspapers plus in special weekly real estate newspaper publications, available in most major cities. In addition, your realtor can promote your property on the Internet. An experienced realtor should also know how to write good ad copy and accentuate the key selling features of your property.

- **Limited market exposure.** There is obviously a direct correlation between the nature and degree of market exposure and the end price. Clearly, self-advertising leads to limited exposure.

- **Potential legal problems.** The prospective purchaser may supply you with an agreement of purchase and sale. This contract could be legally risky, unenforceable, unfair, or otherwise not beneficial to you. You may not recognize these potential problems or risks. In addition, you could end up agreeing to take back a mortgage when it would not be necessary or wise, or to accept a long-term option or other legal arrangement that could be risky.

  A realtor should know and recognize what aspects of the agreement are unfair, unenforceable, or unclear, and advise you accordingly, as would your real estate lawyer. Professional assistance is a cheap price for peace of mind.

- **Lack of familiarity with market.** You may not know exactly what a similar property in your market is selling for, or the state of the real estate market at that point in time. This can place you at a distinct disadvantage. For example, if you are unrealistic in your pricing, along with limited advertising exposure, you could literally price yourself out of the market. Prospective purchasers may not even look, let alone make an offer. You may eventually sell your property, but only after several price reductions and a long period of time. Naturally, this depends on the market and the nature of your property.

  A realtor should be familiar with the market in your area, especially if you select someone who is experienced with your type of property and geographic area. The pricing and overall marketing strategies would be customized for market conditions and general saleability.

- **No pre-screening of prospective purchasers.** You could waste your time talking to people over the phone or showing them through the office, who are not and never will be serious prospects. You could also end up accepting an offer from someone who does not realistically have a chance of financing the business purchase, or who asks for unrealistic time periods for removing purchaser conditions, which would tie up your property during that time.

If you use a realtor, when the pre-screened offers are finally presented, you will have more serious prospects.

- **Offer price not necessarily the best.** Any offers you receive may not be the best price you could get. You may have started out too low or too high, based on emotion or needs (not reality); you may have received a "low-ball" offer from the purchaser that was only intended to reduce your expectations; you may be inexperienced in real estate negotiating skills; or you may be subjected to effective closing skills on the part of the prospective purchaser.

   The realtor would normally do the initial research and set the original asking price realistically and objectively, depending on the market conditions and condition of the property; recognize a "low-ball" offer as a tactical ploy, and attempt to determine if the prospect is serious; help you deal with offers and counteroffers; and be skilled in negotiating and closing.

- **Purchaser wanting discount in price equal to commission saved.** It is not uncommon for the prospective purchaser to determine the fair market value and then ask to have a discount equal to the real estate commission you are saving. The reason purchasers are attracted to a "For Sale by Owner" deal is the prospect of a better deal than a property listed with a realtor, due to the built-in commission. A compromise may be possible whereby the price is further reduced by 50% or 75% of the commission saved. It is normally an illusion to think that you will save the full amount of the commission. The other related issue is if you save (say $5,000) on a commission, after the purchaser saves an additional $5,000 on the purchase price (e.g., splitting the commission saving), would you not have a lingering doubt that you could have netted more if it was listed?

- **Tough to sell in a buyer's market.** Buyers in this type of market are very price sensitive, negotiate toughly because they want the best deal, and have the time to be selective. You are at a disadvantage if you don't get all the exposure possible and use all the negotiating and selling skills available. You could wait a long time before finally selling, and the market could go down further by that time in a declining sale market (i.e., substantial supply of property but limited demand).

   If you use a realtor, whether the market is a buyer's or seller's market, for the reasons outlined in this section, the statistical odds are that you would benefit, in general terms, in terms of your net sale proceeds.

There are distinct benefits to consider selling through a realtor, who is experienced and carefully selected. Of course, there are exceptions in certain situations, but you have to be very aware of the pitfalls. Most real estate investors realize the benefits of using a realtor and do so as a business decision, whether for buying or selling.

Key Factors to Consider when Selecting a Mortgage

Before finalizing your mortgage decision, you have to decide on amortization, term of the mortgage, open or closed mortgage, interest rate, payment schedules, prepayment privilege and assumability. A brief explanation of each of these concepts follows.

Amortization

Amortization is the length of time over which the regular (usually monthly) payments have been calculated on the assumption that the mortgage will be fully paid over that period. The usual amortization period is 25 years, although there is a wide range of options available in five-, ten-, 15- or 20-year periods as well. The shorter the amortization period, the more money you save on interest.

Term of the Mortgage

The term of the mortgage is the length of time the mortgagee will lend you the money. Terms may vary from six months to ten years. If the amortization period was 25 years, that would mean that you have several different mortgages, in effect, possibly ten to 20 separate mortgage terms before you have completely paid off the loan. In reality, many people sell their investment property after five to ten years of ownership, depending on circumstances.

At the end of each term, the principal and unpaid interest of the mortgage become due and payable. Unless you are able to repay the entire mortgage at this time, you would normally either renew the mortgage with the same lender on the same terms, renegotiate the mortgage depending on the options available, or refinance the mortgage through a different lending institution. If you renew with a different mortgage lender, there could be extra administrative charges involved. As there is considerable competition among lenders, frequently there is no administrative fee if you are transferring a mortgage to another institution. Some institutions will absorb the legal costs as well, as an inducement.

Some people take out short-term mortgages (e.g., six months), anticipating that interest rates will go down. The problem is that if rates have gone up instead of down at the end of the six months, your monthly mortgage payment will increase and you may not be able to afford, the increased rates. If you negotiate a long-term mortgage (e.g., five years), you can budget over a five-year period with certainty. The lender is not obliged to renew the mortgage at the end of the term, but will generally do so as long as you have met your payment terms. Upon renewal, an administration fee of $100 to $250 is often charged. In a competitive market though, this could be waived.

Interest Rate

There are various ways to calculate the interest: the fixed rate, which means the interest rate remains fixed for the term of the mortgage (e.g., one year); and the variable rate, which means that the interest rate varies every month according to the premium interest rate set by the lender. In this latter case, although the actual monthly payments that you make usually stay the same, the interest charge proportion of that monthly payment of principal and interest will vary with that month's rate.

How often interest is compounded will determine the total amount of interest that you actually pay on your mortgage. The more frequent the compounding of interest, the more interest you will pay. The lender can charge any rate of interest, within the law, and compound that at any frequency desired—that is why it is important for you to check.

By law, mortgages have to contain a statement showing the basis on which the interest is calculated. Mortgage interest has traditionally been compounded on a half-yearly basis. If a mortgage is calculated on the basis of straight interest that means there is no compounding, but just the running total of the interest outstanding. Some mortgages, such as variable rate mortgages, may be compounded monthly. The initial rate quoted for a mortgage is called a *nominal* rate, whereas the real interest rate for a mortgage compounded semi-annually, for instance, is called the *effective* rate. As an example, a mortgage that quotes a nominal rate of 8% has an effective rate of interest of 8% when compounded yearly, 8.25% when compounded half-yearly and 8.47% when compounded monthly.

Be careful when comparing interest rates in the newspaper or elsewhere. Make sure that the "best rate" is not artificially low because it is based on monthly calculations, rather than semi-annual interest calculations.

Interest Averaging

If you are considering assuming an existing first mortgage because the rate and term is attractive, but you are concerned about the current interest rate of second mortgage financing, do an interest averaging calculation. You might find the average interest rate to be less than the prevailing first mortgage rate. Here is an example of how you calculate it:

1st Mortgage	$60,000 × 8%	= $ 4,800
2nd Mortgage	$30,000 × 10%	= $ 3,000
	$90,000 × "x"%	= $7,800 Total Interest Paid

Average interest rate "x"% = $7,800/$90,000 = 8.6%

Open or Closed Mortgage

An *open* mortgage allows you to increase the payment of the amount of the principal at any time. You could pay off the mortgage in full at any time before the term is over without any penalty or extra charges. Because of this flexibility, open mortgages cost more than standard closed mortgages.

A *closed* mortgage locks you in for the term of the mortgage. There is a penalty fee for any advance payment. A straight closed mortgage will normally have a provision that if it is prepaid due to the property being sold, a three-month interest penalty will be applied, or waived entirely if the new purchaser of the property takes out a new mortgage with the lending institution. Most closed mortgages have a prepayment feature, discussed shortly.

Payment Schedules
There are many payment options available including weekly (52 payments a year), biweekly (26 payments a year), semi-monthly (24 payments a year), monthly (12 payments a year) and other variations. The more frequently you make payments, the lower the amount of interest that you will be paying and the sooner you will pay off the mortgage. Some lenders give you the option of increasing the amount of your monthly payments, once a year, for example 10-20% more. Other lenders permit you to make double payments. Do your research.

Depending on your negotiations, you may make payments on interest only, or have a graduated payment schedule, which means that at the beginning of the term of the mortgage your payments are lower and increase over time. The ability of the borrower to make the payment may increase over time, and the payment schedules are graduated to accommodate that. This could be an advantage with revenue real estate purchases or a business. There are some limitations to a graduated payment mortgage.

Prepayment Privilege
This is a very important feature to have in your mortgage if it is a closed mortgage. If it is an open mortgage, you can pay in part or in full the balance outstanding on the mortgage at any time without penalty. If you have a closed mortgage without prepayment privileges, you are locked in for the term of the mortgage (e.g., three years) without the privilege of prepaying without penalty.

Another option, though called a closed mortgage, is in fact partly open and partly closed, permitting prepayment at certain stages and ways. For example, you may be permitted to make a prepayment of between 10% and 20% annually on the principal or original amount outstanding, depending on your mortgage terms. This could be made on the anniversary date of the mortgage, or at any time in that year, depending on your mortgage. Another variation would also give you the option of increasing the amount of your monthly payment by 10% to 20% once a year or at any time in the year. This would make an incredible difference in interest saved and reducing the amortization period. Every time a prepayment is made, or every time you increase your monthly payments, the balance owing and thus the monthly cost of interest is reduced. The net effect is that a larger portion of each payment will be applied toward the principal, since monthly (or other agreed-upon regular) payments usually remain the same. Make sure that you completely understand and negotiate your prepayment options, as there is a considerable variance between lenders.

For example, you may want to pay up to 20% any time in that year, rather than waiting for the anniversary date; to have the pre-payment amount based on the original amount, not the outstanding principal at the time; and to be able to increase your monthly payments by up to 20% at any time in the year, not just the anniversary date. In other words, you want to have it all!

A lender may be prepared to give you a "side letter" which confirms a modified term arrangement. For example, the lender may have pre-printed mortgage documents and a standard policy that is not as attractive, say 10% prepayment annually. The "side letter" could permit payments of up to 15% or 20%. If you negotiate effectively, you may be able to get them to modify the terms, however their policy may not permit this.

If you are buying real estate strictly for investment purposes, you may have a policy of not paying down the principal outside of the normal payments. This would preserve your cash and make it available for other purposes, for example, other real estate investments. In this scenario, you would presumably be counting on equity appreciation over time.

Assumability

Assumability refers to the buyer taking over the obligation and payments under the vendor's mortgage. Most mortgage contracts deal with the issue of assumability very clearly. The lender can agree to full assumability without qualifications, assumability with qualifications, or no assumability. For example, if a vendor reluctantly gave a vendor-back second mortgage for $50,000 for two years, the vendor (the lender) may not want to have that mortgage assumed by anyone else, as the vendor would prefer to be paid out in full if the property is sold, rather than carry the mortgage any longer.

You could have a wider range of potential purchasers if purchasers who may not otherwise qualify for your mortgage could assume it without qualifications. Most mortgages allow the mortgage to be assumable with qualification by the lender.

If someone assumes your mortgage, make sure you obtain a release of any claim from the lender first. If you have already sold a home with the purchaser assuming the mortgage, and did not obtain the release, you should be automatically released as soon as the lender extends the term or varies the mortgage in any way. Without a release, if the purchaser assumes your mortgage and then defaults, you could be personally liable for the mortgage arrears.

Portability

Portability allows that if you sell one property and buy another during the term of your mortgage, you can transfer the mortgage from one property to the other. Check carefully, though. Some lenders require that you purchase the new property within a short period of time after you sold your original house, for example a few months. You could save money if interest rates have gone up before buying the new home. Otherwise, you would be taking out a new mortgage for your new home at current, higher mortgage rates. Remember, the higher the interest rate, the lower the mortgage amount that you qualify for. Conversely, if mortgage rates have gone down since you bought the first house, you would probably not be interested in transferring your existing mortgage, unless you had a fixed rate mortgage, with a mortgage differential penalty that was larger than the savings.

General Contents of a Mortgage

Most mortgage documents are fairly detailed. Have a competent and experienced real estate lawyer review it and interpret the key areas for you. In addition, the laws are constantly changing. In any mortgage, the basic provisions are: the date of the mortgage, the names of the parties who are signing, a legal description of the property, the amount of the loan, the payment terms including interest and frequency, the respective obligations of the lender and the borrower and the signatures of all the parties. The common clauses are discussed following.

Personal Liability

Under a mortgage, the borrower is personally liable for the debt to the lender, assuming the mortgage is in an individual's name rather than a corporate name. In the event of default, the lender can sue the borrower for the full amount of the mortgage; the lender is not obliged to commence foreclosure or power of sale proceedings and take over or sell the property. In practical terms, however, the lender normally commences a form of foreclosure or power of sale action to protect its interest as well as suing the borrower personally. If the property is sold, then the borrower would be responsible for the shortfall plus all the associated costs that the lender has incurred.

If you have a co-covenantor or guarantor on the mortgage, in other words, someone else that promises that he or she will meet all the obligations of the mortgage, the lender can sue both the borrower and the co-covenantor for the debt under the mortgage. The lender may refuse to give funds covered by a mortgage without extra security protection by means of a guarantor or co-covenantor. If you are married and are purchasing the property under your personal name, the lender will almost always insist on your spouse signing as a guarantor or co-covenantor, regardless of your creditworthiness.

If you have an incorporated company to purchase real estate and take out a mortgage in that name, in most cases the lender will ask you for a personal guarantee of the corporate mortgage. Refer to Chapter 12 on "Creditor Proofing Your Business."

Insurance

This clause requires that the mortgagor insure the building against fire. The insurance policy must show that the mortgagee is entitled to be paid first (if a first mortgage) from the mortgage proceeds in the event of a claim.

There is also a provision in the mortgage that sets out the amount of the insurance (replacement). It states that if you fail to pay the premium, the mortgagee can do so, or if you fail to get sufficient insurance, the mortgagee can do so, and all the additional premium costs can be added onto the principal amount of debt.

Requirement to Pay Taxes

This clause states that you are obliged to pay all property taxes when they become due, and that if you do not do so, the lender is entitled to pay the taxes and add the amount paid in taxes to the principal amount of the mortgage. Some lenders set up a separate tax account set up at the time you take out the mortgage. You pay an extra amount every month on your payment for the tax portion, and once a year the lender pays the property taxes directly. Attempt to look after the taxes yourself, if you can. The reason is that you receive a low interest rate on the advance payment of taxes, from the bank. Alternatively, attempt to be released from this provision at the end of a year. Some lenders require proof that taxes have been paid every year.

Maintain Property

This clause in the mortgage states that you are required to keep the property in good repair. The lender obviously does not want the property to deteriorate through neglect, thereby reducing its property value and compromising the security.

Home Must be Occupied

This clause is to protect the lender from a rental house being vacant, or the borrower being absent from the house for an extended period of time, for example, three months. The potential risk is that the house is subject to vandalism, arson or deterioration if no one is around. Insurance coverage could be void in this situation as well, leaving the lender at risk.

Requirement to Keep any Subsequent Mortgages in Good Standing

This provision states that you must maintain all your financial obligations on the second and third mortgages so that they do not go into default. If they do go into default, foreclosure proceedings could occur. If the property was sold, the first mortgage would be paid off first, followed by the second and the third, etc.

No Urea Formaldehyde Foam Insulation (UFFI)

Many mortgages state that no UFFI is permitted in the premises at the time the mortgage is granted or subsequently.

Assignment of Rents

If you are purchasing a revenue house or building, the lender may request that you sign a document entitled "Assignment of Rents." If you fail to make your monthly payments to the lender, the lender can formally notify the tenants that you have assigned the rent payments to the lender directly.

Must Comply with All Laws

This provision would advise that all federal, provincial and municipal laws concerning the use and occupancy of the property must be fully complied with. This is important if you intend to rent out the property. Although there may not be a strict prohibition against rental, there could be relevant municipal zoning bylaws.

Quiet Possession

This provision states that unless the mortgagor defaults, the mortgagee cannot enter or will not interfere in any way with the peaceful enjoyment of the property by the mortgagor.

Prepayment Privileges

Make sure that the prepayment privileges, previously discussed, are set out clearly in the agreement.

Assumption of Mortgage Privileges

Assumption of mortgage privileges, also discussed earlier, should be clearly set out in the mortgage document.

Special Clauses Relating to a Condominium Purchase

See the section on types of mortgages.

Acceleration Clause

This clause states that if the mortgagor defaults on any of the mortgage terms, then at the option of the mortgagee, the full outstanding amount of principal plus interest is immediately due and payable. In some provinces, legislation restricts the mortgagee from exercising the right of acceleration, even though it may be in the mortgage document.

Default

This section of the mortgage deals with the circumstances that could place the mortgage in default and sets out the rights of the mortgagee in the event of default.

Summary

In this chapter, we have covered a wide range of issues you need to consider when buying or investing in real estate, on your own or with others. It is so important to select a lawyer who specializes in real estate, in order to protect your interests before you sign any agreements.

For further information on buying real estate, refer to the book, *Canadian Home Buying Made Easy*, by Douglas Gray, published by McGraw-Hill Ryerson.

Six

Leases

_____

Introduction

When starting or operating a business, your options include operating out of your own home, renting a turnkey office space on a month to month basis, or leasing space. The best choice depends on the nature of your business, your financial resources and your risk comfort zone.

Advantages and Disadvantages of Leasing

Few small business owners have the financial resources to consider buying a building and property. Even if they do, the decision to buy rather than lease space should be made only after considerable discussion with their accountant and lawyer. Leasing provides flexible options that minimize the risk. The following outline discusses some of the main advantages and disadvantages of leasing from the perspective of both the tenant (lessee) and landlord (lessor). From a negotiating viewpoint, it helps to understand both parties' points of view.

Advantages to the Tenant

- Capital is not required to purchase the property, thereby freeing up capital for other business purposes.
- The lease payments are generally 100% tax deductible as an expense.
- It is generally easier to sell the business if no land is involved.
- It may be possible to negotiate an option to purchase the building and land at the end of the lease. The advantage is the chance to acquire the land and building when the tenant can afford it. In an option-to-buy situation, it is common to have a predetermined fixed price with a time limit within which to exercise the option. There may be an adjustment formula for inflation (cost-of-living index).
- It may be possible to negotiate a lease with a variable monthly lease payment based on seasonal cash flow income of the tenant. The total annual rent would be fixed.

- Protections can be built in to minimize personal and business financial risk, as discussed in the last section of this chapter.

Disadvantages to the Tenant

- In some situations, the tenant cannot depreciate improvements made on the lease property in terms of tax deductions.
- When the lease expires, the potential value of the business (goodwill) will not be of financial benefit to the tenant unless the landlord agrees to renew the lease. This can be offset by having a renewal option in the lease.
- The tenant does not reap the extra benefit of appreciation of the value of the property, even though the increased value may be directly related to the presence of the tenant. Any capital gain in the property value accrues to the benefit of the landlord.
- It may be more difficult for the tenant to borrow money with leased premises, if there are no assets to pledge as collateral other than the lease agreement.
- The total cash expended by the tenant in rental payments may be greater, over the term of the lease, than if payments were made for principal and interest on the purchase of the property.
- Improvements made to the property by the tenant at his or her own expense are totally lost to the tenant upon termination of the lease. The landlord automatically assumes legal title to all improvements done to the property, unless there was an agreement in the lease allowing the tenant to remove certain improvements upon termination of the lease. Improvement costs can be substantial, especially if the tenant is the first tenant in a new building.

Advantages to the Landlord

- During the course of the lease, the tenant may pay more rent than would be paid if the property was purchased, and the landlord still owns the property at the end of the lease.
- The tenant improvements made to the premises become the landlord's property at the end of the lease, unless there is a written agreement to the contrary.
- The landlord can deduct depreciation on the building from taxes.
- The landlord is taxed on a capital gains basis if the appreciated property is ever sold.
- The tenant may be responsible for all maintenance and repairs on the space being rented, as well as all or part of the taxes, thereby minimizing the financial outlay and risk of the landlord.

Disadvantages to the Landlord

- It is sometimes difficult to find financially responsible tenants willing to lease at the rental rate desired to service the debt and provide a return.

- Some tenants will break the lease at the earliest opportunity if it appears that the business is not going to be viable. Statistically, the high failure rate of small business means the odds are that a percentage of tenants will go out of business before the end of the term.
- There is a risk of loss of continuity of cash flow if the tenant leaves, thereby creating debt servicing problems. The empty space could also deter other tenants from coming into the building.
- Even a very creditworthy tenant may get into financial difficulties. This would leave the landlord with rent collection or eviction problems, as well as possible litigation to recover the balance outstanding.
- The landlord may incur sizeable expenses or difficulty in leasing the space again at the termination of the lease. The tenant may have made specialized improvements to the rented space for the business' specific needs, which are unsuitable to anyone else. The landlord may therefore undertake extensive reconstruction on the premises to attract a new tenant.

Types of Leases

To obtain a leasing arrangement suitable to your business needs, compare the following types of leases. The name used to describe each lease may vary in your region, but the concept is the same.

Ground Lease

A buyer may purchase a building or business property without actually purchasing the land under it. The land may be leased separately on a long-term lease basis (e.g., 99 years). By purchasing a building and leasing the underlying land, the financial outlay of capital for the land is eliminated and yet the benefit of its use can be obtained. The cost of leasing the land can also be written off as a tax-deductible expense.

Net Lease

In a net lease situation, the tenant pays a flat rate which is all-inclusive of heat, light, water, taxes, common area use, ground maintenance, building repairs, etc.

Net Lease Plus Taxes

This is similar to the net lease, except that there is an agreed-upon extra expense for taxes, normally to be passed on once a year. Any taxes over and above the base tax rate are passed on to the tenant totally or partially, depending on what is negotiated.

Triple Net Lease

In this lease situation, the base rent is a certain price (for example, $10 per square foot of area rented), but the tenant is responsible for paying his or her proportionate share of all the extra charges incurred by the landlord, normally outlined in the lease agreement. These extra operating expenses could add up to another $6 or $7 per square foot, for example. The operating costs may fluctuate each year based on taxes, maintenance, insurance, administrative and management costs.

Index Lease

In this lease, the rent varies based on a formula of costs incurred by the landlord. For instance, the lease may vary every year based on the cost-of-living index to account for inflation.

Variable Lease

A variable lease is one in which the annual rent may vary depending on the seasonal nature of the cash flow of the business. For example, there could be a very low or no-rent period of three or four months because business activity is slow. The rent for the remaining months of the year would be high to compensate.

Graduated Lease

This type of lease requires an increase in rental payment every month for a specified period of time. This is usually done to assist a business during start-up, so that the monthly payments relate to the increase in cash flow of the business. At the end of the graduated period, the rental payments by the tenant would then be at a fixed rate, usually as in a net or triple net lease.

Percentage Lease

In one type of percentage lease, the landlord obtains no minimum rent but simply a percentage of the total monthly business sales. The landlord attempts to determine the tenant's potential revenue and bases the percentage on that amount. The percentage could be set at a higher percentage for a lower volume of sales, and a lower percentage for a higher volume. The tenant would have to calculate whether or not the base percentage could be too difficult for the business to pay, assuming that the gross revenues are obtained.

The other variation is that the landlord calculates a minimum rent based on the tenant's potential revenues, but the rent paid is based upon actual revenues. In other words, it is a percentage of the gross monthly revenue of the business. In this example, the landlord is able to budget on a minimum guaranteed rent until such time as the tenant pays a higher rent because revenues justify it. In this type of lease, the landlord requires very tight accounting and reporting controls.

Another arrangement is for the percentage to be based on net profit. This type of arrangement has to be defined very carefully in the lease. The most common way is for the profit to be calculated before depreciation and/or interest and income taxes. There is usually a limit on the owner's salary; otherwise the owner could inflate the salary paid as a management fee or to relatives in order to increase expenses so that there is no net profit. The landlord also frequently requires that a minimum amount be spent on advertising by the tenant so that sales and net profit are generated. Frequently, the landlord requires a minimum amount spent for maintenance, so that the premises are kept in good condition.

The percentage lease is commonly used in the renting of retail stores in shopping centres. The landlord therefore obtains the benefit that the tenant obtains in terms of the large traffic volume.

Be extremely careful that you obtain competent professional advice from your lawyer and accountant before committing yourself. The relationship with the landlord in a percentage lease is almost that of a partner, because the landlord has very tight controls on reporting and expenditure of monies. As the success of the tenant's business may only be partially due to the location, try to negotiate a fixed maximum dollar amount that the landlord would be entitled to receive.

Legal Aspects of a Lease

The terms of the lease contract and all the rights that you and the landlord have under that contract will affect your business profit, your business survival and the ability to sell your business in the future. Thoroughly research the ideal location for your business, carefully review the terms of the lease, and then discuss it with your lawyer and accountant before signing any documents. Once you have committed yourself, it could be very difficult or impossible to get out of the lease without severe financial consequences and litigation.

As leases are prepared by landlords for landlords, they tend to be one-sided. In other words, the lease requires obligations and restrictions of the tenant, but does not have the equivalent balance on the part of the landlord. Your lawyer may be able to renegotiate the terms of the lease to be more equitable and balanced, and in accord with your budget and acceptable risk.

Oral or Written

If you intend to rent premises on a month-to-month basis, you may not be required to sign a lease. If you are operating a business with that degree of uncertainty, you are probably not too concerned about your long-term rights or options. On a month-to-month lease, normally either party can give the other party one month's notice to vacate. The goodwill component may be minimal if you were to sell your business, unless you had an attractive long-term lease in place.

The landlord may prefer to sign a month-to-month lease because the property is due to be torn down or construction work is scheduled which limits the appropriateness of a long-term lease. To protect yourself fully, insist upon a written lease. To be enforceable, a lease has to be in writing in most jurisdictions in Canada.

The landlord usually insists that a lease be in writing to be sure of the duration of cash flow income. The landlord's bank may require proof of lease documentation in order to finance the landlord. Any potential purchaser of the landlord's building and land will want to take a look at the leases and tenants in determining the purchase price.

Offer to Lease

When you are considering a space to lease, present an offer to lease. Most landlords have property management agents, real estate agents, or other sales personnel employed to solicit offers to lease. In other cases you may be dealing directly with the landlord. When an agent is involved, there is generally a commission paid to the agent by the landlord, which can vary considerably. For example, the agent may receive 10% of the gross base rent in the first year of a three-year lease or 15% in the first year of a five-year lease or 10% on the first two years of a five-year lease—the longer the term, the higher the commission. Keep in mind that the landlord's agent is acting on behalf of the landlord, and has an incentive to have you sign the offer.

Offer to lease forms vary considerably. Make sure that your offer to lease has escape clauses, conditions that have to be met before you have a binding offer.

Be certain that you have a copy of the formal lease to review before you submit your offer to lease. The formal lease document should be attached to your offer to lease as a schedule. Be wary of an offer to lease that states that a "standard lease document" will be required to be signed without that document being given to you in advance. Very rarely are any two leases the same.

The offer to lease sets out the basic terms between the parties that are to be incorporated in the formal lease document: the length of the lease term, rental terms, use of the premises, names of the parties, description of the property, frequency of rental payments, renewal options if any, and any other unique terms. The offer to lease would include a reference to the formal lease and the modifications, including additions and deletions that have been noted on the lease document. After it has been submitted, it may be difficult or impossible to negotiate further changes. If you find an alternative location that you prefer, or the terms of the other location are more favourable to you, your lawyer must notify the agent immediately in writing that the offer has been withdrawn, assuming it has not yet been accepted.

The offer to lease ideally should be in the name of a corporate entity rather than your personal name. If you have paid a low deposit at the time of the offer, that minimizes your financial risk if you need to get out of the contract. If you have included various subject conditions that have to be met by the landlord or yourself, and the conditions are not met, then you get your deposit back. You may put a provision in the offer to lease that if the offer is accepted, you will increase the deposit to the amount of the first and last month's rent. Ask for the deposit to be held in an interest-bearing account. The landlord may accept the offer as presented, or suggest a compromise. You may prefer your lawyer or accountant to act for you in negotiating the terms. It is hard to remain objective when caught up in the enthusiasm and stress of such a major business decision.

Be particularly cautious if you are making an offer on a building currently under construction. It is common for delays in construction, and even though the lease may give a specific date for occupancy, there is always a provision in the lease that gives the landlord an "out" in terms of legal liability if delays occur. A description of clauses to consider, negotiation hints and pitfalls to avoid follow this section.

Formal Lease

Once your offer to lease has been accepted, you now have to sign a formal lease. The landlord may have purchased from a stationery supplier a commercial lease document that has approximately four to six pages. On the other hand, the landlord may have a lawyer prepare a document which could be anywhere from ten to 100 pages in length. Leases prepared by major Canadian real estate companies, national property management companies and shopping centre leases tend to be over 40 pages. Attached to the formal lease document would be various schedules, including a sketch or map of the exact location or construction plans. Key terms that might be found in a lease will be discussed later in this chapter.

Impact of Government Legislation

Government legislation also affects a landlord-tenant relationship, including the following types of legislation.

Municipal Legislation

Municipal legislation in the form of bylaws affect zoning requirements. These bylaws regulate the types of businesses that can be operated in areas throughout the city. Health and safety regulations could also have a bearing on your business.

Provincial Legislation

The provinces may have different titles and content in the following legislation, but the underlying purpose is the same:

- **Commercial Tenancy Act.** This legislation governs the relationship between the landlord and tenant, whether a lease is signed or not. Certain provisions of this Act can be waived in the lease, but the Act provides rights and remedies to both the landlord and tenant.
- **Short Form of Leases Act.** Some leases that are very short (a few pages in length) refer to the fact that the lease is to be governed by the Short Form of Leases Act. This saves the landlord from drawing up a lengthy lease because the essential terms of the landlord-tenant relationship would be governed by that Act.
- **Rent Distress Act.** If a tenant fails to pay the rent when it is due, the landlord is entitled to restrain (in other words lock up the premises) until the rent is paid. There are other protections for both the landlord and tenant which are set out in the Act.
- **Real Estate Act.** The Real Estate Act covers the registering of a lease by the tenant or landlord in the Land Titles Office or the equivalent, depending on the province.

Federal Legislation

The federal *Bankruptcy and Insolvency Act* sets out provisions when a landlord or tenant is petitioned into bankruptcy or voluntarily declares bankruptcy.

Key Terms of a Lease

There are many key terms or clauses in a lease that you should be aware of to avoid pitfalls in your negotiating. The inclusion and sequence may vary but shopping centre leases or leases prepared by major property management companies tend to have many more terms than outlined below.

Rent Clause

It has to be clear for your protection exactly how the rent is calculated and when it is due and payable.

In addition to the different rent possibilities discussed in the previous section, there could also be extra charges that the landlord would have the right to change arbitrarily every year. A shopping centre complex could include a provision for a fee for administering and promoting the mall. A clause in the lease might entitle the landlord to increase its administrative fees from time to time. This open-ended clause could limit your ability to budget carefully.

Commencement Date Clause

This is the date that you are responsible for commencing your rent payments, not necessarily the same date as taking possession of the premises. The landlord may have allowed you a rent-free period.

The occupancy date of premises which are being constructed may not be specific or accurate because of unanticipated delays. You could expend a lot of money ordering inventory and equipment, to find that you have to wait for three or six months longer before you can move in. You may not have any legal recourse against the landlord depending on the terms of the lease. Be particularly cautious about relying on good faith that the landlord's proposed date of completion of the building and occupancy is accurate.

Use Clause

This provision sets out exactly what your business intends to use the premises for. It is to your advantage to have the use description as broad as possible, in case you may want to expand the range of products or services that you offer. If the use clause is too restrictive, that could limit your profit and possibly impair your business survival. Once the use clause has been agreed upon, the landlord may not be prepared to modify that provision later. If you ignore that clause and offer a service or product that is not included, then you could be deemed to be in breach of the lease.

Non-competition Clause

This clause would protect you from a competitor coming into the premises and causing your business to suffer. For example, if you were a dentist you might want to have a clause in the lease stating that no other dentist could rent office space in the building during the term of your lease. On the other hand, a gift store could argue that there is no restriction in their lease in the type of jewellery product that they sold if a jewellery store in the same building complains.

Demolition/Construction Clause

A clause could allow the landlord to give short-term notice (for example, six months) to the tenant to leave the premises, even if you have a ten-year lease. The landlord could arbitrarily give this notice if there is a clause allowing it, to demolish the building or make substantial construction changes. Be extremely cautious in signing any lease that has such a clause; in effect, you just have a short-term lease. You would have great difficulty selling your business because of the high risk.

Acceleration Clause

The landlord may have a provision that in the event of your default on the terms of the lease, the full face amount of the lease could be accelerated and you could be sued. If you had a five-year lease at $1,000 per month, the face amount of the lease would be $60,000 over the term. If you are one year into the lease and breach the lease, with an acceleration clause the landlord could attempt to sue you for $48,000. In reality, though, the landlord would have an obligation in law to mitigate (minimize) its damages (financial losses) by immediately attempting to re-rent the premises.

Default Clause

Many provisions throughout the lease set out the basis on which the landlord can deem you to be in default. One obvious ground for default would be failure on your part to pay rent. There could be others including using the premises outside the terms of the lease, going into bankruptcy, failing to have the required insurance, failure to keep your business open during the hours required by the shopping mall, failing to maintain your premises, subletting without permission, and many others.

If a default occurs, generally there is a time period within which you have to remedy the default after you have been given notice (for example, three days or one week or month). If you fail to remedy the default within the time required, other legal and financial actions could occur including your eviction from the premises.

Penalty Clause

The penalty clause provision generally sets out that if you are in default of any of the lease terms, a three-month penalty is imposed on you in addition to the other rights and remedies that the landlord may have. If you pay $1,000 per month, then you would have to pay the three-month penalty of $3,000. A penalty clause can be broad in terms of what constitutes a penalty, or limited to the terms specified.

Entry Clause
The entry clause provision sets out the basis on which the landlord can enter your premises. Obvious situations such as leaking water pipes causing water damage, fire and other reasons relating to safety and limiting damage would permit the landlord to enter. There could also be other reasons as specified. The subject of entry is key in terms of the legal rights of the tenant. For example, if the tenant had paid rent until the end of January but moved out on January 20, and the landlord entered the premises to show the premises to a prospective tenant on January 25, the tenant could claim that the landlord had terminated the lease. If there were four years left, this could be a substantial loss to the landlord if he or she was unable to re-rent the space for the next four years.

Assignment Clause
The assignment clause is normally combined with the subletting clause. It may state that the tenant is unable to assign the lease under any circumstances, or that an assignment may be acceptable with the prior written consent of the landlord, such consent not to be unreasonably withheld. The landlord has the right to investigate the creditworthiness of any prospective assignee. If the landlord believes that the assignee is not a good risk, the landlord can refuse to approve the assignment. The tenant would have to either find a new purchaser of the business, continue operating, or breach the contract and leave the premises.

Another type of assignment clause to be wary of is one that states that if the tenant requests the landlord to assign (or sublet) the premises, the landlord has the right to immediately, or 30 days thereafter, deem the lease to be terminated. The landlord may want to insert this provision to give him or her the option, if rental rates have increased, to renegotiate the terms of the lease. If a tenant is two years into a five-year lease and paying $10 per square foot and the prevailing rate is now $20 per square foot in the premises, the tenant could sell the business at a very attractive profit because of the immense savings to the prospective buyer in terms of rental. On the other hand, the landlord may not accept the assignment and could immediately declare the lease to be at an end unless the prevailing rate of $20 per square foot was renegotiated into the lease. Naturally, this would have a serious effect on the ability of the tenant to sell the business.

Subletting Clause
This clause relates to the tenant subletting a portion of the space to a third party. The normal provision in the lease is that the landlord would permit subletting but only with the prior written consent of the landlord. This enables the landlord to do a check of the prospective subtenant. It is possible the subtenant might be

contravening various non-competition clauses in the master lease between the landlord and other tenants. The sublease clause may be important to consider for potential sale of the business, or for the survival of the business if downsizing is required.

Improvement/Fixture Clause

This clause sets out the provision that all improvements and fixtures on the premises shall be deemed to belong to the landlord. Upon installation, they immediately become part of the building, and cannot be removed without the consent in writing of the landlord. Depending on the type of business that you have, you could be putting in expensive fixtures that you would like to take away with you at the end of the lease term. If this is the situation, negotiate very toughly at the outset on this point and specify the exact improvements that you want in writing.

The landlord may be concerned about damages that could occur to the premises if a tenant tried to remove improvements and fixtures. The landlord may therefore require a provision in the lease, that any structural or other cosmetic damage that may occur to the premises as a consequence of your removal of the specified improvements, shall be repaired at your cost. On balance, you may feel that this is a fair stipulation.

Utilities

The utility provision sets out the expenses that the tenant is responsible for such as electricity, water, telephone, sewage, garbage removal, or any other matters under these categories. The tenant may be responsible to pay a portion or all of the cost, depending on the circumstances. Find out from the landlord what the average rates will be, and then modify those rates based on your anticipated usage of utilities.

Insurance

Most leases have a clause stating that the tenant is responsible for maintaining various types of insurance of a specified minimum amount. For example, there could be a requirement for a minimum $1,000,000 general liability coverage. It is a normal stipulation that the landlord obtain proof of coverage and proof that the premium has been paid.

Maintenance/Repairs

In some leases, the landlord is responsible for all maintenance and repairs to do with the building and surrounding area such as parking and landscaping. In other leases the landlord wants to pass on to the tenants virtually all the maintenance and repair costs. This is usually done on a percentage basis, proportional to the amount of square footage that the tenant occupies.

If you are responsible for these extra costs, have an estimate of the past costs and projected costs over the next number of years. For example, possibly the landlord needs to completely re-roof all the premises or repair the parking lot because of numerous potholes, or completely repaint the premises inside and outside. You might feel that these costs should be borne by the landlord. The time to negotiate the maintenance/repair costs is at the very outset before anything is signed.

Security Deposit
Depending on the length of the lease, the landlord may ask for the last one, two, or three months' rent as a security deposit for any damage caused by the tenant. It is also common to have the landlord request the first month's rent, although technically that is not a security deposit.

Make sure that you try to negotiate a provision in the contract giving you interest on the security deposit monies. If your rent was $2,500 per month and you paid two months' rent as security deposit, that is $5,000. If the lease is a five-year term and you negotiated a flat rate of 70% per year on the security deposit, you would have an additional $1,750 to your credit by the end of the term. If you negotiated that the security deposit monies bear interest at the bank prime rate, which is variable, then you could take advantage of the changing rate of interest. You could also attempt to negotiate that the security deposit monies bear interest that is compounded, which would earn you even more money by the end of the lease.

Guarantees
If the lease is in the name of a proprietorship or a partnership, the owners are automatically liable personally for the full amount of debts or liabilities of that partnership, including any liabilities due to a breach of the lease. For this reason, many people incorporate a company before signing a lease. The landlord may request a personal guarantee or a guarantee from another company of a corporate lease. However, you should always try to negotiate out of the guarantee provision. Some suggestions for doing this are covered in the next section.

Promotion and Administrative Cost Clause
In shopping malls it is common to have a provision, that the tenant pays a portion of the landlord's administrative and promotional costs, as detailed in the section on rent clauses

Renewal Clause
You may want to negotiate an option to renew the lease for a further term(s) upon the expiry of the present lease. Some option to renew provisions include limiting the rent increase if the option were renewed, having the rent increase based on a cost-of-living index, having the rent increase negotiated between the parties and if an agreement cannot be reached, then an arbitrator under a provincial Arbitration Act could assist in the decision.

Holdover Clause

There should be a clause that states the terms if the tenant stays on the premises beyond the termination date. Normally the tenant remains on a month-to-month basis after the lease has terminated and on the same rental terms. On a month-to-month lease, either the landlord or tenant can give each other one month notice.

Option to Purchase

If the tenant wants the option of purchasing the premises, then this provision should be negotiated and clearly stated in the lease. Do not rely on the landlord's oral promise. The purchase price should be specified, or a formula for calculating the purchase price, and a stipulated period of time during which the option will be held open. This clause also protects the tenant from someone else buying the property for the duration of the option period. The landlord may require an additional payment for this option, which could be a flat sum or a nominal amount paid every month over the term of the lease. The extra charge may or may not be applied against the eventual property purchase. The tenant may also negotiate a provision which allows him or her to apply a percentage of the monthly rent payments toward the down payment or purchase price.

Minimizing Personal and Business Risk

There is always a potentially high degree of personal and business risk in signing a lease. The location may turn out to be a poor one, competition may start to affect the business, or health, marital, or partnership problems may impair the business operation. For these reasons, it is vital to build precautions into the lease to minimize risk, including the following.

Incorporate

It is wise to incorporate in any business situation which involves high risk such as a long-term lease. Statistically, approximately 75% of small businesses fail within three years of start-up.

Penalty Clause

You may wish to negotiate a three-month penalty as the total damages that the landlord would expect from the tenant in the event that the lease is breached. The landlord may require the penalty to be paid in advance and represent the last three months of the term or the penalty, whichever comes first. Again, make sure that the funds go into an interest-bearing account.

If the tenant gave three months penalty under the lease, no other security would be given and the landlord would have no further recourse if the tenant left before the term of the lease.

Alternatively, it may be negotiated that if the tenant breaches the lease, a penalty of three months' rent would be paid by the tenant representing the full amount that the tenant would be responsible for. No penalty deposit would be paid in advance.

Another option is that the amount of the penalty be decreased based on the length of time that the tenant remained in the premises. For example, in a five-year lease, the clause might state that if the lease is terminated with four or more years left, there would be a five-month penalty; with three to four years left, it would be a four-month penalty; with two to three years, a three-month penalty; and so on.

Short-term Lease with Options to Renew

To minimize the risk of a long-term lease, you may decide to keep the initial lease period relatively short. After that, you can decide whether it is viable to remain in the leased premises for a longer period of time. For example, rather than signing a five-year lease you might negotiate a one-year lease with two renewable two-year options.

This type of structure would give you the option of the full period, but with limited time interval commitments. A clause would then set out the amount of the increase, or a formula under which it would be calculated, if any rent increase was to occur.

No Personal Guarantee

For a corporate lease, it is not uncommon for a landlord to request a personal guarantee or guarantees by the directors. The majority of landlords could be persuaded to waive this request through effective negotiating techniques, perhaps by suggesting that other premises will be leased unless the personal guarantee provision is removed.

You may also negotiate a provision that the personal guarantee automatically expires at the end of the first year of the lease. This clause could state that if the lease is terminated by the tenant before the end of the year, the personal guarantor shall be responsible for the balance of the first year's rent. From the perspective of the landlord, the first year is probably the highest risk with a new tenant. A personal guarantee could be limited to a fixed amount, such as a maximum of three months' rent. Whenever a lease is terminated, the landlord is required by law to exert his or her best efforts to locate another tenant. If unable to re-rent the premises immediately, the personal guarantor would only have to pay up to three months' rent.

If your attempts to avoid giving a personal guarantee have been unsuccessful, your next step would be to minimize the overall exposure. Wherever possible, do not agree to more than one guarantor. Refer to Chapter on Creditor Proofing Your Business.

Free or Reduced Rent

Often a landlord is willing to offer a free rent period or reduced rental payments as an incentive to rent the premises, usually when the space has been vacant for some time. Try to limit the financial outlay as much as possible. Following are some suggestions:

- Request graduated or reduced rental payments. Have the payments start low and graduate upwards to the higher amount every month over the first year or possibly longer. The aggregate amount may be less than the normal annual aggregate rent for the subsequent years of the lease.
- Negotiate from one to six months, or more, rent free. The amount of free rent will depend on the length of the lease, the improvements you are paying for, the type of business (if it enhances the image of the building) and other factors. Alternatively, possibly the first, fourth, eighth and twelfth months would be free. This would provide the landlord with some cash flow but would also provide the tenant with a quarterly rent saving in the first year.
- Try to have the landlord pay for the costs of renovations up to an agreed maximum. The landlord might be desperate to have a good tenant in the building to draw in other prospective tenants, as well as customers. The tenant might agree to a ten-year lease on the basis that the landlord pay $50,000 for improvements. Everything depends on the circumstances and your negotiating leverage.
- Request that the first year of maintenance be waived. In the case of a triple net lease, the operating expenses over and above the base rent could be considerable. In this example, request that the first year is a net lease with a flat rate, with the triple net lease feature commencing in the second year. There would be no carrying forward of the triple net extras from the first year to subsequent years.

Construction Allowances

If you are renting premises that are being newly constructed, provisions may be negotiated with the landlord to save you renovation expenses. The provision may state that the landlord would pay to have all the leasehold improvements done that the tenant requires, as a condition of signing the lease. It is less expensive for the landlord to do such work if it is being done at the same time as the overall construction of the building.

Lease Assignment

Remove your personal liability and risk from the lease before selling your business and assigning the lease to a buyer. Otherwise, if the buyer defaults on the terms, the landlord has the right to sue not only the buyer as the assignee, but also you as the assignor. Ask the landlord to remove your personal guarantee (assuming you gave one) at the time that the lease is assigned. Be certain this agreement is in writing and signed by the landlord. The landlord can obtain personal guarantees from the new buyer of the business if necessary.

If the landlord will not release your company from the lease, then incorporate a new company and transfer any assets to the new company. If the landlord refuses to release the personal guarantee on your original lease, then arrange with the buyer to negotiate a completely new lease with the landlord. This may involve the buyer having to pay more rent and you may have to reduce the purchase price accordingly. The key point is to have your personal name released from any future liability exposure.

Negotiating a Lease

In most situations, the tenant does not negotiate directly with the landlord. Normally a sales agent in the form of a realtor or property management company advertises and negotiates the rental of the business premises for the landlord. Sales agents tend to be sophisticated in negotiating as well as in effective sales techniques. Therefore, the small business owner is often at a disadvantage in this type of business experience.

With any negotiation, it is important to understand the needs of the other side. The sales agent's motivations include earning a commission and satisfying the landlord so that ongoing business can be obtained. As the sales agent is acting on behalf of the landlord, don't disclose to the sales agent any information that could impair your negotiating position. Being overly enthusiastic about the location may reduce your negotiating stance. Try to keep the sales agent guessing as to whether or not you are planning to select that location.

Keep in mind the benefits you provide to the landlord when you become a tenant:

- The more tenants in the building, the easier it will be for the landlord to attract other tenants. Occupancy implies stability and traffic flow, important factors for tenants as well as the landlord. If a location is newly opened or soon to be open, this fact should provide you with better negotiating leverage in being one of the first tenants to sign up for the building.
- Landlord needs cash flow to debt service the bank loan. A landlord has to account to the bank in generating the cash flow. The more unrented space in the premises, the less cash flow and therefore the more pressure the landlord is under from the bank. The landlord may be motivated to rent the space and may be more flexible in negotiating the lease. It may take the immediate cash flow pressure off the landlord, even though the tenant may not be around a year later.
- Full occupancy enhances the selling price of the building. A prospective buyer would find it far more attractive and the selling price would be accordingly higher if the tenancy is at full occupancy. If the landlord wishes to borrow money on the building to invest in other buildings or for other business reasons, the bank will lend money to the landlord based on the amount of cash flow being generated by the tenants in the building. Therefore, this may provide incentive for flexibility on the landlord's part.
- In order to maintain maximum occupancy and remain competitive in lease costs, a landlord has to be flexible in negotiating leases.

It is helpful therefore when negotiating to understand the context. In many situations you are doing the landlord a favour by becoming a tenant, not the other way around. This philosophical and negotiating viewpoint will help to balance an otherwise one-sided lease arrangement.

Sue Doesn't Negotiate to Protect Her Interests

Sue decided to lease space in an office building for her expanding technology business. She initially wanted only 3,000 sq. ft., but the landlord's sales agent convinced her to commit to 5,000 to allow room for growth. Sue did not speak to a lawyer or negotiate the lease package. She signed the five-year lease in her personal name. Within two years of moving into the space, Sue had to downsize due to a cyclic drop and related demand for her technology products. She now only needed about 1,000 sq. ft. The landlord refused to negotiate a lower lease rate, or let Sue out of her lease.

Unfortunately, Sue should not have signed any lease without speaking to a business lawyer, who could assist her in the negotiating process. Also, she should have incorporated the company first, and negotiated out of a personal guarantee. Sue should also have considered committing only to a one-year lease for 3,000 ft., with two renewable two-year options. That way, she could monitor her company needs, but have a reasonably short lease commitment. She should also have attempted to negotiate an attractive lease package, such as one month free rent and the commitment by the landlord to pay for some leasehold improvements.

Steps in Negotiating a Lease

1. Thoroughly understand leasing terms and concepts. Speak to your accountant and lawyer for clarification.
2. Determine your overall criteria regarding the ideal location, the amount of money you are prepared to spend and other factors.
3. Thoroughly research potential locations and short-list them to three locations, if at all possible. Any one of these locations should be acceptable to you. Prepare a list of your questions and concerns, to be answered by the landlord or his or her representative.
4. Obtain all documents required to assess the three locations, including a copy of the lease, building plans if the building is being constructed, and other information that your lawyer or accountant may request.
5. Review the documentation and prioritise your preferred locations.
6. Set up a meeting with your lawyer and accountant and discuss the prospective premises.
7. Decide on your negotiating position regarding terms after consultation with your professional advisors.
8. Decide whether you or your lawyer will be doing the negotiating. If it appears tactically advantageous for you to do it, then make sure your game plan is well thought out in advance. If you involve your lawyer, it is

common for the other side to involve its lawyer, especially in the case of negotiating legal terms in the agreement.

9. Submit your offer to lease in detail with the formal lease attached, with any suggested modifications.

10. Advise the agent that you are seriously considering other premises and if they are not serious about agreeing with your terms, then you will have no alternative but to take your business elsewhere. If you say this, make sure that you mean it, and be prepared if necessary to walk away from the deal.

11. Put pressure on the agent and the landlord by placing a deadline, perhaps two or three days, on acceptance of the offer to lease. A major Canadian property management company may require the documents to be approved at head office and this could take a longer period of time. The offer should not be open for any longer than a week, the shorter the better. Placing a deadline implies that you are serious about going elsewhere if they are not in agreement.

12. If the landlord does not accept the offer, or if a counteroffer is made to you and you are not in agreement, then try the next location on your priority list. This approach will eventually get you the location and lease terms that you want. Use your accountant and lawyer to assist with lease negotiations. This will give you the peace of mind of knowing that your decision is based on expert advice that will limit your personal exposure and risk.

Alternatives To Leasing

To minimize the potential risk of leasing, consider other options that may be appropriate for your business needs.

Packaged Offices

You can rent an office area that is already set up to provide "turnkey" operational services to businesses. Companies that provide this service are referred to as "packaged offices," "executive suites" or "business centres." Look in the phone book under "offices for rent." These types of businesses are available in office spaces or industrial buildings.

"Packaged offices" typically include fully furnished offices of various sizes, and amenities such as a furnished waiting room, receptionist, telephone answering service, voice mail, support services such as word processing and equipment such as photocopiers, faxes, etc. Also available is a boardroom in most cases. You can utilize as much or as little of the services provided.

The benefit of the packaged office concept is that your costs are variable, depending on your needs. Also, you can rent on a monthly basis or sign a six- or 12-month contract depending on your requirements. This type of flexibility reduces long-term risk as well as capital, equipment and staff outlay, during your start-up or ongoing business operation.

Subletting from Someone Else

With some research, you could find a business that has downsized, does not need the full use of their space, but has a long term lease in place. They could use additional cash flow to compensate for their extra leasing costs. You could rent part of their space on a monthly or longer term basis. At the same time, you could use their reception or other staff services as you require. This concept is a variation of the packaged office option, but is not set up as such. If this arrangement was made with a company that had complementary business activities, there could be some natural synergies.

Working Out of Your Home

There are many tax write-off benefits to a home office. You could renovate your home to build an appropriate home office if need be. You can also meet clients at your home office, depending on your type of business. Refer to Chapter 7 on "Regulations, Zoning and Licencing" for more information on operating a home business.

If you are going into a business with other partners, or using independent contractors or hiring employees, they could possibly work out of their respective homes also. For example, in a computer-related type of service or consulting business, this option is common.

Summary

It is so important to understand the leasing options for your business. There are many complex issues, protections to build in and tactical considerations. An experienced business lawyer will assist you in negotiating the lease. The risks of not using a lawyer are high.

Seven

Regulations, Zoning and Licensing

Introduction

Across Canada, there are local, regional, provincial and federal laws that regulate the operation of a business. In some cases there are private regulations that impact on home business operation. It is important to know the rationale behind these regulations and how they operate, whether you are permitted to operate out of your home, and if not, what your options are.

Municipal, Provincial and Federal Regulations

Municipal government regulations relate to business permits, noise and parking bylaws, health, land use and building codes. Provincial government regulations that impact on business include matters dealing with sales tax, building codes, employees, safety, health, consumer protection, etc.

Federal regulations which may affect your business include those related to building codes, health, safety, product safety, customs duties, tax, trade practices and payroll deductions. Here are the most common regulations to consider.

Municipal

- City business permit
- Zoning bylaws (opening hours and location, noise, fumes, home-based business, parking)
- Health regulations (preparation of food, removal of waste products, training of staff, etc.)
- Land use regulations
- Business taxes
- Property taxes
- School taxes
- Water taxes

- Building permits (applicable to alteration also)
- Building codes (plumbing, electrical, fire and health hazards).

Provincial

- Business registration (proprietorship, partnership, and/or trade style name)
- Bulk sales
- Directors' liability to statutory creditors (that is, to provincial government departments with legislation and claim rights, such as employment standards, Workers' Compensation Board, sales tax, environmental protection, human rights, etc.)
- Incorporation (provincial)
- Land use regulations (certain provinces)
- Environmental protection regulations
- Provincial business licence (certain provinces)
- Provincial income tax (corporate or personal)
- Quebec place of business tax (Quebec only)
- Provincial Sales Tax
- Provincial building codes (electrical apparatus and equipment, fire, safety and health hazards)
- Minimum age, wage, termination and hours of employment
- Trade practices
- Consumer protection, including sale of goods
- Annual vacations and public holidays
- Human rights
- Pay equity
- Workers' Compensation
- Quebec Pension Plan (Quebec only)
- Safety and health
- Liquor licence
- Provincial health insurance
- Maternity leave.

Federal

- Incorporation (federal)
- Federal income tax (corporate or personal)
- Federal sales tax
- Goods and Services tax (GST)(some provinces combine their provincial tax with the federal GST, a harmonized sales tax (HST))
- Export/import permit
- Customs duties
- Building codes
- Directors' liability to statutory creditors (that is, to federal government departments with such legislation and claim rights, such as employment standards, GST, income tax, environmental protection, human rights, etc.)

- Health and safety standards
- Employment insurance
- Human rights
- Pay equity
- Canada Pension Plan (except Quebec)
- Payroll tax deductions (monthly remittances to government)
- Environmental protection legislation
- Trademarks, copyrights, industrial designs, patents
- Product safety
- *Competition Act* (includes false or misleading advertising).

Operating a Home Business

Municipal Regulations

Municipal government has the authority to make its own regulations relating to home business operation. These regulations are intended to protect the general public and prevent or minimize public nuisances and misleading business practices. There can be a considerable range of differences between one community's bylaws and another's with regard to home-based businesses. Some of these regulations may be based upon clearly stated rationale, but others may be antiquated statements designed in and for a different era. Unless challenged, these regulations may go unnoticed. Such situations may be found in smaller communities or areas where major corporations are the primary employers. With the trend in home businesses, entrepreneurs and city officials are updating the bylaws to be more representative of present-day communitities.

There are basically two types of regulations which attempt to meet the above objectives—zoning and building regulations.

Zoning Regulations

Zoning regulations divide a community into four basic classifications—residential, commercial, industrial and agricultural. Each of these areas include further sub-categories such as residential single-family or residential multiple-family. The types of activities that can be carried out in each classification vary by locality. Home-based businesses are usually referred to as "home industries" or "home occupations."

Since municipal government is run by elected officials, the government concerns reflect the concerns of the residents. Each community may have its own personality which could encourage either a liberal or a conservative attitude. Factors that may impact on city council's decision on the regulations include the rural, urban, or metropolitan nature of the community; the vocalness of a powerful community lobby group; or the prevalence of, and economic spirit generated by, local entrepreneurs.

Some of the considerations of local government officials include:

- Preserving the economic well-being including preventing unfair competition of commercial areas

- Preserving neighbourhood amenities
- Preserving the appearance and character of residential neighbourhoods
- Preserving residential property values
- Controlling traffic and property use in residential neighbourhoods
- Protecting residential neighbourhoods from nuisances such as noise and odour
- Maintaining the tax base revenue in commercial and residential areas
- Fulfilling the perceived needs and expectations of the community
- Avoiding criticism or complaints from the community.

In general terms, local governments are becoming more receptive to the growth in home businesses. Although business owners in commercially zoned areas sometimes perceive that the home business entrepreneur is not paying the same taxes, not meeting the same regulations, and competing unfairly, in most cases this is untrue. The home-based owner may be targeting a different market completely. Almost 50% of home businesses eventually move out of the house, which favourably increases the revenue tax base and economic well-being of the community. Fostering the home business concept is therefore enlightened self-interest for local governments. It provides employment in the community, either self-employment or through hiring of other employees. It provides an incubator for people who by choice or necessity would not be able to start a business except from home.

Many local governments recognize the reality of home-based business and are classifying and licensing them.

Ultimately, the elected officials attempt to keep the interests of the community foremost in mind. Some, all, or none of the following local regulations relating to home-based business may be applicable in your community:

- Control of nuisances, such as noise, smoke and odour
- Control of unsightly garbage or junk
- Control over use of employees at home (perhaps only family members can work at home)
- Control of traffic to avoid congestion, noise or parking problems; restriction on trucks being used in the business
- Control of signage or advertising on the premises (restriction on number and size, restriction on location, or total restriction)
- Control over types of businesses allowed (there could be regulations allowing certain businesses and prohibiting others; some communities distinguish between a business and a profession, and generally allow more flexibility under the "professional" category)
- Control over the maximum number of customers served at home at any one time, or possibly restriction against any business-related foot traffic
- Control over the amount of space that can be used for the business (e.g., not more than 25% of the total residential square-footage)
- Control over retail sales (total or limited restrictions)

- Control over storage of inventory (permitted, restricted, or prohibited)
- Control over manufacturing (permitted, restricted, or prohibited)
- Control over entrance (separate business entrance either required or prohibited).

Many governments require that business take out a licence to operate. Some smaller communities do not require this. Before issuing a licence, the city may first investigate whether you have complied with the appropriate zoning, health, building, sanitation and other business bylaws. Some of these regulations are local, but others could also be governed by provincial or federal regulations.

Building Regulations

If you are going to make any modifications or additions to your house for your small business, enquire as to whether a building permit is required. There is generally some flexibility. Depending on the nature and purpose of the work, provincial or federal regulations may apply. Local building regulations may also involve electrical, fire, health, plumbing and other types of inspection.

Does the Zoning Permit Home Business Operations

With the wide range of potential zoning restrictions on home business, you may find that there are no, some, or a total restriction. Or, you may be able to get temporary permission while the regulations are under review. There are three steps in ascertaining the zoning issues, and your rights and options.

1. Determine if your local community has zoning regulations by contacting your local government office. Contact the planning department, zoning department, licensing department, or the building inspector. You do not have to give your name and address at this stage, as you are asking for public information.
2. Determine how your property is zoned by locating your property on the official map at your local city hall zoning department. If your home business is in an area zoned agricultural, you can be almost certain that you can operate a business, since farmers were the pioneers of "home businesses." Many commercially zoned areas permit usage for both businesses and residential—the family living in the back or upstairs of a "mom and pop" business is common—however, some industry zoning restricts any residential use. This can present problems for those who want to rent and live in a warehouse or other industrial building and operate a home-based business such as an artist's studio. Residential zoning is more restrictive of home business operation, limiting the scope of home business activities.
3. Since there is a wide range of possible restrictions, enquire specifically what is and what is not permitted in your zone and for your intended business. Refer back to the discussion on zoning regulations and restrictions, so that you are conversant with them. Remember, you are entitled

to this public information. If you are still unclear as to your rights and options after doing your initial research, speak to a lawyer who is conversant with municipal law.

If Your Home is Not Zoned for Home Business

Adjust to Meet Regulations

After you know your restrictions, you may modify your projected operation to comply with regulations. For example, if you can't have non-family employees working at your home, you may ask your employees to work from their own homes. If you can't make retail sales from your home, consider mail-order merchandising or distribute your product through sales representatives, or directly through distributors or retail stores.

Establish and Maintain Good Relations with Neighbours

Find out how your neighbours look upon the idea of you working from home. They could be very supportive of your intentions. Your business could be providing a local service which is desired, or you could be creating employment for neighbourhood youths. Also, you could be providing a form of security in the neighbourhood if you are home during the day. Your neighbours could provide important local support when making special requests to the zoning department.

Apply for a Use Permit

After you have discussed your business plans and intended facilities with the zoning officials, you could be permitted to use the premises for the purpose stated, without the need for public hearing. Technically speaking, your business can operate, although it is not lawfully permitted. In some cases, if you have such a *non-conforming use status* under the existing bylaw, that right could be cancelled automatically if you cease doing business for a certain continuous period of time (e.g., six months), or sell the house. Generally, a non-conforming use status can be revoked at any time if your local government policy changes.

Apply for a Variance

You can request the local zoning board, planning board, or appeals board to waive the zoning restrictions in your particular case. A variance normally requires a public hearing. There are several arguments that you may be able to present in order to accomplish your objectives:

■ Show that there would be no harm done to the neighbourhood. Attempt to get the written support of your neighbours beforehand, and have them attend the hearing. If there are no objections at the hearing, you could succeed.

■ Show that what you intend to do is comparable to a home business which is permitted.

■ Show that you would suffer hardship and be deprived of a livelihood if the zoning bylaw was enforced in your circumstance.

Attend several zoning board meetings to see how they are conducted, and note which board members seem to be the most influential. Speak to a lawyer familiar with municipal law, if possible, who can assist in evaluating your situation and planning your appeal.

Lobby to have Local Zoning Regulations Amended
Due to the greater acceptance of the important role of home-based businesses, you may wish to lobby for changes. You could locate other home business owners through professional, trade, chamber of commerce (in many communities, 50% or more of the members operate a business from home), civic organizations, the yellow pages or local newspaper advertising. You could form a group and educate the community and elected officials about the benefits to the community of home-based businesses in order to elicit their support. It would be helpful to retain a lawyer to assist in your efforts.

Rent a Private Mailing Address or Use a Packaged Office
To get around the problem of having your home address as your business address, for business image or zoning compliance purposes you could rent a mailbox or mail forwarding service. They can receive and send mail and parcels, or accept or send courier parcels for you, as well as other services. Their primary clients are home-based business owners. "Packaged offices" offer "corporate identity package" services to those who wish to create the impression that they are operating out of a business address. Mail is delivered to that address and held for you to pick up. Normally the "package" includes a telephone answering service, but this could be an option. Renting an "office" address in this manner effectively keeps mail, parcels and visitors from coming to your home or apartment, which may satisfy your neighbours. You may also wish to rent a "packaged" or fully furnished office on a month to month basis, including all the trappings of an office, such as waiting room, reception, answering service, voice mail, word processing services, etc. Most "packaged" offices tend to be in larger cities. Look in the phone book under "offices for rent."

Jack Solves his Problem and Keeps his Neighbours Happy
Jack had always wanted to operate a mail order craft business out of his home. However, his city had restrictive bylaws about offering a service business from home. Also, Jack felt that his miserable neighbour would complain to city hall, if delivery trucks were seen coming and going. Jack did not want the stress and expense of signing a long term lease with a landlord, or having to hire staff.

After doing his research, Jack found a perfect solution. He signed up for a "business ID" package through a local "packaged office" that he found in the phone book, under "offices for rent." This entitled him to use a boardroom or fully furnished office, up to ten hours a week to see his business associates. This created a very professional image. His business cards showed the business address. In addition, the package included a personalized telephone answering service during the weekdays, and voice mail after that. If there were any urgent calls, the service would contact him at home. Also, the service would send or receive any parcels for him. This enabled Jack to have the freedom to operate his business in a cost efficient manner, and avoid any problems with city hall regulations or his neighbour.

What if you Violate Zoning Regulations?

In practical terms, possibly nothing. Many people ignore the local zoning regulations, either because they don't realize that they apply or because they think that no one will find out about it because local officials don't have the time or resources to look for violators. This is not meant as an encouragement to ignore zoning laws, but a simple statement of reality.

There are many ways that officials could find out about zoning violations:
- Unhappy neighbours could complain about traffic congestion, cars parked in front of their homes, or too much noise.
- Spiteful, envious, or feuding neighbours could complain as revenge.
- An application from provincial sales tax licence, a business licence, or a business telephone hook-up could alert authorities.
- Advertising in the local newspaper could alert authorities.
- Competitors could complain, anonymously or otherwise.
- Potential customers could make innocent enquiries at city hall to see if you have a business licence, or, if they are dissatisfied with your service or product, complain to city hall.

If a complaint was made, you would receive a notice requesting you to stop the violation, and setting out the reasons for the request. You would have the right to appeal the notice and give reasons why an exception should be made. Some reasons for appeal were discussed earlier in the section on variances.

Private Regulations

In addition to government regulations, there could also be private regulations to consider. Some of the common ones are:

Residential Tenancy Agreement
The terms of the written agreement between you and your landlord could forbid operating any business out of the house, apartment or condominium. If you were in breach of this clause, it could permit the landlord to evict you.

Condominium Bylaws
The bylaws of a condominium development, as well as the rules and regulations, could restrict any business activity by owners or renters of the unit. If you were

a tenant and were in violation, you could be evicted. If you were the owner, you could be fined by the condominium corporation. If the violation continued, the condominium corporation could obtain an injunction restraining you from continuing the violation. You would have to pay court costs, possible damages (financial losses claimed by the party initiating the action) and your own legal expenses. Before buying a condominium, have your lawyer check the "fine print" in this regard.

Restrictive Covenants

If you bought a house in a subdivision, it is common for restrictive covenants to be registered against the title to the residential property by the developer. There could be a restriction prohibiting any business from being operated from the home; and though local government would permit the operation of a business, private regulations take precedence. Therefore, other property owners would have the right to enforce the restrictive covenant, which restricts the use of property to strictly residential purposes. If the restrictive covenant was enforced in civil court, you would be out court costs, possible damages and your own legal expenses.

Before starting out, research the zoning regulations to see how they affect you. Get advice from your professional advisors, as well as your local business development office and chamber of commerce. By taking a positive approach and having a responsible attitude toward your neighbours, potential problems may be avoided.

Insurance Policies

Your insurance policies could restrict certain types of business activities; for example, your standard policy terms could state that your home is to be used for personal use only and not for business. Therefore, if you did not add on extra coverage for home business use of your home, any claims could be denied, for example, if there was a fire or theft of your business equipment, or if a customer was injured on your property. Refer to Chapter 9 on Insurance.

Summary

There are many municipal, provincial and federal government regulations to consider when running a business from your home. This is in addition to any private regulations, such as landlord or condominium regulations that could be applicable in your situation. Be aware of what regulations apply to your specific type of business operation and make sure that you comply with them. If you don't comply with certain government regulations, e.g. provincial and federal sales tax, income tax, paying employees, taking off and remitting employee deductions, etc., then you could be personally liable as a director of an incorporated business, or if you are operating a proprietorship or partnership. Refer to Chapter 2 on Business Structures as well as Chapter 12 on Creditor Proofing Your Business.

Eight

Raising Money

Introduction

One of the basic needs of any small business is money. Where to get it, how much to get, and how to repay it are fundamental concerns when starting out, and at other stages in your business. One of the main reasons for business failure is being undercapitalised. This chapter will cover how to avoid the pitfalls and the different sources of money available.

Methods of Debt Financing a Business

Financing your business by borrowing money is called debt financing. There are numerous methods of debt financing your business, including the following.

Demand Loan

Demand loans are generally short term and have no fixed repayment schedule. The interest rate is a floating rate and changes with the chartered bank prime rate. If your company is creditworthy, you may be able to negotiate a rate which is at the prime rate, or ½ to 1% above the prime. Depending on the degree of risk, the bank may require up to 4%, 5% or 6% over the prime rate. A demand loan means that the loans are payable on demand at any time.

Operating Loan (Line of Credit)

A line of credit provides day-to-day working capital needs of the business and is normally secured by receivables, inventory or assets. The bank agrees to lend up to a maximum amount, as required, providing certain conditions are met. Normally of a revolving nature, the amount borrowed goes up and down depending on deposits and payables. Interest is paid on the amount outstanding on a daily basis. Avoid continuous operation at the upper end of a credit line, as the effect is the conversion of a line of credit to a term loan.

Bridge/Interim Loan

This temporary financing is used to bridge the commencement of a project until government subsidies, long term loans, grants, or financing are received.

Conditional Sales Purchases

The manufacturer of new equipment will frequently assist in financing the purchase by requiring only a down payment of one-quarter to one-third of the purchase price, and carrying the balance by means of a conditional sales contract. The purchaser has possession of the asset, and the vendor maintains ownership until the bill is paid in full. A conditional sales purchase is normally secured with a Specific Security Agreement.

Floor Financing

With floor financing, the lender maintains legal ownership of the items "on the floor" while the retailer displays them for sale. This conditional sales contract arrangement allows title of the goods to transfer once the borrower has sold them, enabling the business to have a high volume of product for sale. Floor financing is used commonly by large appliance, furniture and car dealers.

Leasing

Leasing involves the use of vehicles, machinery, equipment, or space on a rental fee basis. Ownership rests with the bank, leasing company, or landlord, while the business has the possession and use of the benefit. Each lease or purchase consideration must be looked at independently with your accountant. Leasing is used in the following situations:

- When there are high capital requirements for equipment, and little or no cash available
- When your cash is needed as working capital
- When the equipment will depreciate or need replacement within a three- to five-year period.

Refer to Chapter 6 on Leasing.

Letters of Credit

A letter of credit is a guarantee issued by a bank, on behalf of the client, to a supplier. It is a guarantee of payment, upon delivery of merchandise to the client in accordance with the specified conditions. Primarily used when importing or exporting goods, a letter of credit is usually irrevocable.

Accounts Receivable Financing

In accounts receivable financing, lenders pay cash advances to borrowers using accounts receivable as security, allowing a continuous source of operating cash. The borrower can generally obtain up to 75% of the outstanding receivables under

60 days old. In exchange, the lender normally requires an assignment of book debts (accounts receivable) as well as a regular monthly listing of all the outstanding receivables. If the borrower does not pay, the lender can advise the customers directly that all funds are to be remitted from that point on directly to the lender. This type of financing is available from banks, commercial finance companies and factoring companies.

Another method is to assign the receivable to the lender, who obtains the money directly from the customer. Car dealers frequently use this approach, as well as mobile home dealers. The borrower collects the accounts receivable from customers and remits the funds to the lender.

Factoring

A factor is a business that purchases outright the accounts receivable of another business. If the factor purchases the receivables on a non-recourse basis, it means that it cannot go after the business for any bad debt losses. Unlike accounts receivable financing, factoring is not a loan. The factor purchases accounts receivable for their value, usually advancing from 70% to 85% of approved receivables pending collection of those receivables. When the customer pays, the factor pays out the remainder due, less the factor fees and interest charges. Traditionally used in the garment industry, factoring can be used for other businesses as well. A factoring arrangement could have a "with recourse" provision, whereby you would be responsible for any bad debts. Naturally, interest and fee charges without recourse are higher than with recourse due to the greater risk.

Factors can help a business expand, finance an acquisition, fill seasonal inventory, or generate cash to buy out partners. Many banks provide factoring through association with factor companies. Factors do not require extensive loan documentation. Their primary interests are:

- Credit reliability of their client's customers
- The basic integrity of the business owner
- The track record of the business owner and the company
- The willingness of the client to service merchandise, honour warranties and handle customer complaints
- Diversified receivables without a heavy concentration of debt in one or two accounts.

Inventory Financing

Inventory financing is used to either support a loan or obtain additional credit to increase inventory. The financing may be secured by a General Security Agreement, or *Bank Act* security on the raw materials, work in progress, or finished inventory. Banks advance a lower percentage of the inventory's value than they would for receivables. Financing by banks or commercial finance companies can range from 50% to 75% of the value of the goods. Inventory financing may be combined with receivables financing to build inventory for peak selling seasons.

Trade Credit

Trade credit is a common form of business financing. Suppliers allow terms of credit (e.g., 30, 60, 90 days or longer), thus avoiding payment in advance for the merchandise. In effect, the supplier is giving a loan at no interest, as long as it complies with the payment terms. A discount may be offered for payment made within ten days. Interest would run on any overdue charges.

Credit Card Financing

A business credit card can be used to pay its various expenses. Payment terms are either 5% of the declining balance monthly (Visa, MasterCard) or payment in full monthly (American Express).

Personal or Shareholder's Loan

The owner may borrow money personally and pledge personal assets as collateral for the loan. The money is then used either to buy shares in the business (equity), or a shareholder's loan (for a corporation) or a personal loan if it is a proprietorship or a partnership. Banks and consumer finance companies may provide personal loans.

The advantages of a shareholder's loan follow:

- Interest is a tax deductible expense for the company.
- Lenders can consider the loans as equity as long as they are left in the company. Normally a bank will require a postponement of claim form to be signed by you stating that you will not withdraw the shareholder's loan until the bank loan is paid in full. Obtain tax advice on the implications of a postponement of claim before signing. Consider negotiating out of it, or proposing less onerous alternatives.
- You can take money out of the company without tax by paying back your shareholder's loan in part or in full, assuming you have not signed a postponement of claim.
- It is easier to repay a loan than to sell shares back to the company or to other investors.

Government Assistance

The amount of financial assistance available to small and medium-sized businesses through government amounts to billions of dollars a year. Federal, provincial as well as a few municipal governments and crown corporations offer assistance programs. Because all levels of government are aware of the vital importance of small business to the economic well being of the country, new programs are always being added and existing ones discontinued or modified.

Government financing and assistance programs are available for all stages of a business, including developing your business management skills, financing, researching, developing, manufacturing and marketing the product and developing your employees' skills. Generally, government programs do not give you financing for existing debts, unless approval is given to consolidate debts and advance additional funds in a unique situation. Government funding for working capital (ongoing monthly expenses) is uncommon.

Generally, government financing assistance has fewer requirements for collateral security compared to the private sector, and the amount of equity you are required to have is less. This means less financial risk and, therefore, a reduced need to obtain funds from friends, family or other investors. Government loans are usually less expensive, and some grant programs do not have to be repaid. After you have obtained government financing, you are more credible and attractive to other lenders or investors.

Financial Assistance Programs

Financial assistance programs take various forms, as follows:

- **Loans at reduced interest rates.** These loans are at rates of interest lower than conventional sources of financing. Loans from the Business Development Bank of Canada (BDC), a federal government crown corporation, are an example.
- **Loan guarantees.** The government will guarantee a loan made to you by an approved conventional lender. An example would be a business improvement loan (BIL) regulated under the *Small Business Loans Act*. Loan limits could vary over time, but presently it is $250,000. This federal government program is designed to assist small businesses in the purchase, installation, renovation, or improvement of equipment, usually fixed equipment. It also includes renovation, leasehold improvements, purchase of land, construction, and purchase of premises. Funds are advanced by chartered banks, some trust companies and credit unions. If you go out of business, the government guarantees the lender that they will be reimbursed for the debt outstanding, up to a certain amount, for example 90%. Part of this program currently requires the lender not to ask for a personal guarantee from you of more than 25% of the loan amount. Another example, the Export Development Corporation, issues guarantees to banks making export loans or issuing performance and bid guarantees.
- **Forgivable loans.** These loans may be repayable in part or full, unless certain conditions exist, in which event the loan is forgiven. The Program for Export Market Development (PEMD), offered through Foreign Affairs and International Trade Canada, assists Canadian companies to export by paying for the company representative to attend trade shows outside Canada. If the company receives export orders within two years of the trip, for example, the money is repaid. If it doesn't, the loan is forgiven.
- **Loans with favourable repayment schedules.** The repayment schedule of the loan is structured to be comfortable with the cash flow history of the company. This is common in businesses that are seasonal in nature, or at various phases in the project. A Business Development Bank of Canada loan is an example.

- **Grants.** This is money paid by the government directly to the company or organization without any requirement that it need be repaid. Many federal and provincial governments use such programs to stimulate job creation or research and development.
- **Cost sharing.** This form of assistance involves the government sharing the cost of the project.
- **Subsidies for wages**. Many of these programs sponsored by Human Resources Development Canada may partially or completely pay for an employee's wages in order to create new employment.
- **Subsidies for training and education.** Human Resources Development Canada has programs which fund up to 75% of the cost of employee skill upgrading (e.g., computer training) or management training for business owners. The NEBS (New Exporters to Border States) program, conducted through the Business Development Bank of Canada (BDC) and/or provincial governments, can provide financial assistance up to 75% of the program cost.
- **Subsidies for consulting services.** The CASE (Counselling Assistance to Small Enterprise) program administered by the BDC is one government department offering reduced cost consulting programs. Experts can provide a wide range of consulting advice. Various provincial and federal government departments also provide researching, negotiating and marketing assistance free or reasonably priced.
- **Insurance coverage.** The federal government and some provincial governments have insurance protection if a supplier does not pay you when exporting. This minimizes the inherent risk.
- **Tax or other concessions.** The federal or provincial government may provide tax incentives for people to invest in your business or project, such as the provision of provincial tax credits up to a certain percentage (e.g., 30%) to people who invest in a provincially approved venture capital program (VCP) or employee share ownership program (ESOP). Another example would be the federal government immigrant investor program. In this case the federal government will sometimes grant landed immigrant status to people from other countries who invest money in an approved investment.
- **Equity financing.** The government, in this situation, would become a minority equity partner in your business by investing money. The BDC is an example of a federal crown corporation with this program.
- **Government contracts.** Federal and provincial governments and their crown corporations buy billions of dollars of goods and services each year, and have a mandate to purchase from Canadian suppliers first. For information on selling to the government, contact Public Works and Government Services Canada, (blue pages of your phone book under "federal government") and the provincial government purchasing department (blue pages of your phone book, under "provincial government").

Methods of Equity Financing

Equity is the money that is put into the business in exchange for shares. A balanced debt to equity ratio is an integral part of a successful business operation. The greater the debt, the greater risk. Equity financing for your business could work when:

- You have borrowed to your lending limit, or have used all available assets as collateral
- Buying out a retiring or deceased partner's share of the business
- A company is expanding and its working capital needs have exceeded retained earnings
- A major equipment purchase, plant expansion, or introduction of a new product line
- Research and development needs
- Turnaround purposes when purchasing an insolvent company
- Temporary refinancing purposes before going public on the stock exchange.

The primary source of equity financing is usually the owners of the company, coming from personal savings and the sale of assets. If your personal resources are insufficient, other sources include:

- Family and friends
- Employees, clients of professional advisors, suppliers or customers
- Major companies seeking vertical or horizontal integration of their operations
- Foreign investors immigrating to Canada, or foreign-controlled banks with branches in Canada
- Federal or provincial government equity plans, either directly (e.g., through the BDC or provincial government development corporations), or indirectly (through incentive programs for the private sector)
- Venture capital firms—usually interested in high risk businesses where there is potential for a higher return on investment; with large investments, may require majority control position on board of directors (not usually interested in daily business operations unless the business' survival is at stake)
- Pools of funds from individuals, pension plans, trust companies, insurance companies, private investment syndicates, corporate holding companies (usually arranged by a stockbroker or investment dealer).

Love Money or Family and Friends Financing

"Love money," also referred to as "F&F" financing, refers to the risk capital contributed to a start-up or early-stage company by those who are closest to the entrepreneur—family and friends. These are the people whose most natural inclination is to want to help the entrepreneur be happy and successful.

Consider all of the implications for you and your family and friends before approaching them for investment monies. No one ever looks at you the same way again if you have lost money for those who financed your business. Relationships are almost always damaged when money is lost. Even when the prospective investor has confirmed in advance that he or she can afford to lose the money, and is willing to take the risk of doing so, when it actually happens it is quite another thing. At the worst, it will destroy your relationship with that person; at the least you will definitely lose credibility.

With all of the "slings and arrows of outrageous fortune" that life throws at each of us, our family and friends are the safe refuge with whom we can seek comfort, solace and sanity. Their value to us goes infinitely beyond calculation in dollars and cents. Thus, go slowly and thoughtfully before bringing your family and closest friends into a business deal with you. How will you feel if you let them down? How will you feel if they never look at you with quite the same degree of trust and respect again? While people can forgive, few will ever forget. Parents are generally the most forgiving of financial loss, while friends tend to be the least. Here are some candid recommendations.

Tess and David Explore Creative Financing

Tess and David decided to go into business together, but they needed about $200,000. They owned a home with about $225,000 equity. However, as both Tess and David had been "downsized" by their former employers, they did not have any income sources, which made it difficult to get any bank loans. They went to David's parents to raise capital, but were concerned about the effect on the relationship if the business ran into problems.

Tess and David could structure the money from David's parents as repayable loans, rather than payment for shares. If the business did well, the parents could have the option of converting debt to equity. Also, a collateral mortgage could be placed on Tess and David's home to secure the debts to the parents. That way, they would have first claim before any other creditors. Any assets purchased for the business could be pledged to the parents under a General Security Agreement to provide additional security. Tess and David could also consider renting part of their basement to nearby college students as a revenue source.

Use your Business Plan

Before they invest, show each of the F&F prospects your business plan. Have them review all elements, particularly risk factors. If, after reviewing your business plan, they don't think the business is viable, then you may learn something. If these people won't fund the project, it may well not be worth financing. Show the business plan to an outside consultant. If he or she approves of the project, that will help preserve your relationship in the event of failure. Then you can both say, "Hey, even the expert consultant liked the deal!" On the other hand, if the professional recommends against it, listen to the reasoning.

Use a Shareholders' Agreement

In the case where there will only be a small number of investors, make use of a shareholders' agreement. "Small" will vary according to circumstances, but is likely under ten people. A carefully written agreement that sets out the possible upside and downside, the risks and benefits, the rights and remedies, is essential to attempting to preserve good relationships with your investors when things go bad, or at least are off target as they frequently are. A properly written shareholders' agreement will deal with all the critical issues. Refer to Chapter 2 on Business Structures.

Report to your Investors Regularly

Since these investors are your family and friends, you do not want or need to have, lurking silently behind every conversation with these people, their unspoken question "What's happening to my money?" Tell them, and often. A brief reporting letter once a month to your F&F investors is recommended. No less than once every two months. Summarize the functional areas of the company, its progress and problems.

Investors are much happier if they are advised of problems as they develop, rather than getting very bad news at the last minute. This is against the inclination of many, if not most, entrepreneurs who optimistically believe, or at least hope, that the solution is just around the corner. Most investors can accept your failure and their financial loss if they know that you have kept them fully informed throughout, and that you have done your very best to make the project work. In addition, each investor likely has a wide sphere of influence and acquaintances, so he or she may be able to find assistance for you.

Angels

The term "angel" is generally applied to an investor who is not a family member or friend of the entrepreneur, so as to distinguish him from providers of love money. Angels have been described as investors who are willing to take an unusual risk for an unusual rate of return. These people are willing to sacrifice security, liquidity and interest in order to achieve a very significant potential upside return. Angels go in where chartered banks will never tread.

Who Are the Angels?

Angels are any affluent members of your community and across the country, who are ready, willing and able to invest some of their own money into other people's ventures. They are financially comfortable individuals, such as successful businesspeople and executives; doctors, dentists, lawyers, accountants and other professional people; self-employed tradespeople such as plumbers and electricians; successful commission salespeople; government administrators and others. They are frequently not the wealthiest people in your province, or owners of very successful businesses, as these people often have significant investments of their own with professional investment advisors.

Angels are generally successful middle-class and upper-middle-class people. Many have a sense that they are missing out on profitable private business and investment opportunities because they are not directly engaged in business.

What kind of Investments do Angels Want?

Most angels do not have a well-formulated private investment strategy. This will generally work in your favour. As private individuals who earn their living in some way other than the financial business, angels simply respond to individuals who approach them on a case-by-case basis. It is thus your responsibility to enrol the angel in becoming part of your dream.

In every instance, you must satisfy the four elements of the SLIP test: Security, Liquidity, Income and Potential upside. The potential upside is the key element in the SLIP test. This needs to be enticing or at minimum, very attractive. However, financial return is not the only, or sometimes even the most important, reason for an angel to invest. That is certainly the case with family and friends. Many people will invest with you for reasons that are not strictly monetary in the conventional sense, including:

- **Participation in something exciting.** Many hobbyists or afficionados of a sport or pastime will invest in a young venture because it excites them; they feel emotionally stimulated by participating in the deal. As a real example, almost all of the largest Canadian helicopter skiing operations, which have become the pre-eminent heliskiing operators in the world, were funded initially by the private subscription of avid powder skiers. Millions of dollars were raised privately from business and professional people who were absolutely wild about powder skiing. By being in a small way an "owner" of the heliskiing business, these "powder hounds" fulfilled some of their longing for excitement in a sport that they adore.

- **Opportunity to help.** Many people will invest in order to help the struggling entrepreneur when they are either interested in the entrepreneur, or more likely, the field of endeavour itself. For example, medicine and the environment are two areas where many professional people would obtain a sense of satisfaction in helping a young company become successful when the company is developing a product that could contribute to a better world.

- **Get a job or perform a service.** Sometimes people with substantial savings will invest in a business on condition that they be retained to perform consulting services for the company or even be hired as an employee by the company. Or, on a variation of this, sometimes lawyers, accountants and consultants in other areas will perform their professional services in exchange for stock in the company. This is as good as cash for the company when these services would have to be paid for in any case.

- **Opportunity to learn.** Someone may invest in a company to become acquainted with a new technology, or to learn something about an area that is of interest to him. This may be a rancher who invests in someone's dairy technology, or a doctor who invests in a private clinic.

Strategic Alliances or Corporate Partnering

You can accomplish your goals without further diluting equity, or accumulating debt, in your company. The method is in making a commercial agreement with an existing company, probably significantly larger than your own, either domestic or international, currently involved in some aspect of its business which interacts with your needs and interests. This type of contractual arrangement goes by many names, such as strategic alliance, strategic partnering, corporate partnering, business collaboration or joint venture. No matter what the name, each company has decided that the other has something that it wants, and it chooses to combine resources rather than each pursuing these particular aims independently.

Three broad goals that can be achieved through forming strategic alliances include:

1. Developing alternative ways of financing product development, production and marketing
2. Facilitating more rapid expansion of new technology applications and penetrate distant markets
3. Building a stronger competitive position through establishing relationships with other companies.

Strategic alliances are not only being pursued by small companies with few resources, but by major trans-national corporations with sales in the billions.

Types of Business Collaborations

There are a number of ways that you can create a relationship with another company. For example, if a small firm has a concept, prototype or product of interest to larger companies, the larger companies are often willing to enter into research, development, licensing, manufacturing, marketing or distribution agreements with the smaller companies. Another approach is to divide the world into territories for a product, and sell rights to individual countries or areas.

The number of possible business arrangements is only limited by your imagination, and that of the other party and your professional advisors.

Advantages and Benefits of a Strategic Alliance

Some of the potentially positive aspects of a strategic partnering arrangement include:

- Increased financing
- Increased probability of business success
- Larger projects are made possible
- Achieve success to new markets and improved market intelligence
- Avoid expensive duplication and save money
- Boost credibility of a small firm.

While these are some of the more obvious advantages of forging an alliance with a corporate partner, there are many disadvantages as well. Each situation will have to be evaluated on its own merits. Do not assume that in every case the advantages will outweigh the drawbacks.

Disadvantages and Drawbacks of a Strategic Alliance
Some of the potentially negative aspects of a corporate partnership arrangement include:

- Expensive to set up and administer
- Excessive use of senior management's time
- Friction and misunderstanding between corporate cultures
- Loss of proprietary technology and trade secrets.

Going Public
"To go public" or "to take a company public," generally refers to the process whereby a formerly privately-owned company arranges to have its shares listed for trading on a recognized stock exchange so that members of the public can buy and sell the shares. The phrase usually implies that money has been raised as part of the process of "going public" through the sale of shares. In other words, part of the ownership of the company is now held by the public.

Advantages of Going Public
The decision to go public is a major one, perhaps the biggest one that you will ever make for your company, and it has far-reaching implications. Some implications are necessary to ensure the very survival of your company, while others may be sufficient to cause its demise and failure. The benefits to going public include the following:

- Better access to capital
- Better access to borrowing
- Less dilution of founders' position
- Stock liquidity and valuation
- Employee incentives
- Facilitation of mergers and acquisitions
- Prestige and recognition
- Personal wealth for the founders.

Disadvantages of Going Public
The drawbacks of going public include the following:

- Expenses—upfront and ongoing
- Continuous disclosure of material information
- Loss of control
- Public accountability for decision-making and loss of privacy
- Shareholder expectations
- Increased taxation
- Directors' liability
- Collapse of stock price and inability to raise further capital.

Methods of Internal Financing

Many business owners who are unable to access money may be forced to reassess their needs, resources and business management. For example, quick handling of accounts receivable, effective inventory control, customer prepayments, and cutting down on unnecessary expenses can free up funds. It forces your business to operate in a more efficient fashion, lessening your need to look outside the business for financing. Some of the methods of internal financing are as follows.

Customer Prepayments

A business can encourage customers to make a deposit, prepayment or payment on delivery. This is a very common technique in the mail-order business and in service-type businesses.

Employees

Employees with access to capital may be willing to invest in the company because they understand its products and services and trust the management. A financial stake in the company's future could have a positive influence on the employee's work habits and commitment to the business. Conversely, it could prove difficult to remove or retire the employee if the employee becomes unproductive or unco-operative. Any such investment should be written up in a contractual form through the assistance of your lawyer. Make sure that you have buyback or payback provisions built into the agreement as a precaution and to protect the business.

Inventory Control

Effective inventory control will ensure that there is the right amount of stock to satisfy customer demand. Determine guidelines and adjust your purchases to meet the peaks and valleys of your annual business sales. Too much money tied up in slow-moving inventory, debt servicing payments on inventory loans and lost customer loyalty due to insufficient stock, is costly to your business.

Collecting Receivables

Receivables can be reduced by tighter credit-granting policies, better monitoring of accounts, and more effective collection policies. You may wish to consider credit cards or cash only for sales.

Delayed Payables

Establishing a good working relationship with your suppliers can result in extended payment terms or a discount on volume or regular purchases. Make certain they are aware of your loyalty to that firm and your repeat business.

Restructuring Payment Arrangements

There are times when a small business is not able to maintain monthly payments plus interest on loans. By using creative negotiating techniques you can get around short term problems through alternative repayment plans including:

- A period of grace for principal loan payments during the start-up period
- Blended payments that feature a long amortization period resulting in low payments of principal in the early years
- Graduated payments; that is, low payments on principal in the early years and higher ones later on
- Payments of principal during the high season only, so that the business does not have a cash-tight period during the low sales volume season.

Selective Product Lines
Only handle product lines on which you get the most favourable terms from suppliers and which have the highest sales turnover and profit margin.

Fixed Assets
You may wish to sell your assets to a leasing company and lease them back, thereby freeing up cash for working capital purposes. On reviewing your assets, some assets may be less necessary to the business and may be sold to free up additional cash. By purchasing second-hand equipment and machinery, you can reduce financial outlay.

Renting or Subletting
You may decide to rent space for a store or factory rather than buying, to improve your leverage and your cash flow. By subleasing space you can offset your monthly rent payments, thereby increasing your working capital. Refer to Chapter 6 at Leases.

Operating as a Subcontractor
Operating as a subcontractor, saves on employees' expenses and overhead. You may decide to operate from your home.

Stringent Management
By determining how to conserve on capital and save on expenses, financial resources can be freed up and the business risk minimized. The business owner should analyze the financial condition of the business on an ongoing basis, by asking the following questions:
- Are salaries too high?
- Is the owner taking out too much for personal earnings rather than keeping it in the company for working capital?
- How do the company's costs of goods and other expenses compare to other companies in the industry?
- Is the lease too expensive?
- Are supplies being wasted?
- Do actual expenses compare to budgeted expenses?

The business owner knows best where expenses can be trimmed from the operation. In addition to controlling expenses, the owner should always be looking for ways to increase profits, sell surplus inventory or assets and maintain an effective receivables collection program.

Types of Security Requested By Lenders

When providing financing to a small business, lenders require security to ensure that they are repaid. Often the value of the security is considerably more than the amount of the loan. This is because if the lender has to "realize" on the security and convert it into money, only a portion of the value of the asset will be obtained. As well, costs of hiring a lawyer, accountant, receiver or trustee may be involved. Your business may be evaluated by three different methods:

1. **Going concern value.** This is the most optimistic method, an estimate of the business based on its capitalized earnings. This method assumes that the selling price, sufficient to cover the loan, will be obtained if the business is sold as a going concern. This method gives no indication, of course, of the value of the assets if the business is not sold in this manner. Lenders would be interested in a going concern value if they have a debenture or General Security Agreement on the company.

2. **En bloc.** This is an estimate of a price at which the assets could be sold, without removal or alteration, if the business ceased to operate. The en bloc value is based on the purchase of all the assets, not just some of the assets, and on using the same location for operation.

3. **Current liquidation value.** This is the most pessimistic method of evaluating the assets of the business, based on what price the assets might be expected to realize in a forced sale or winding up of the business. Most lenders use this valuation in appraising the security for a loan, because they operate on the conservative premise that in a business problem situation, they cannot be assured of any higher value.

General Security Agreements (GSAs)

Wherever a borrower owes money, it can grant a security interest in any personal property it owns. It is not necessary to set out the obligations in the security agreement, which may be continual, or they may change from time to time. The nature of the personal property being secured can include accounts, equipment, inventories, tangible personal property (document of title, securities), intangibles (contracts, licences, goodwill, patents, trademarks, tradenames, industrial designs and intellectual property) and the proceeds of the sale of any personal property.

This type of document allows the lender to take continuing security over every facet of your business. You will covenant (promise) to protect the security, insure it and keep it in good repair. You will also agree to provide the lender with timely financial information and pay for the cost of preparing and registering the security, and any costs of the lender.

If you default, the lender will be at liberty to realize on the security. These events typically include default in payment of any loan, the death or winding-up or bankruptcy of the borrower, the seizure of security by another creditor and the impairment or destruction of some or all of the security. The lender will have rights to seize and sell the security, or appoint a receiver of the business, all at the cost of the borrower. The receiver may take over the business of the borrower, and sell off the assets or the business itself as a going concern in order to realize the monies necessary to pay off the debt.

Care should be taken if you are not incorporated. These documents do not distinguish between personal and business assets, and you could be pledging more assets than you need.

Specific Security Agreements (SSAs)

Modelled on general security agreements, this type of agreement secures only the assets listed. The rights given to the lender are not so wide as in the GSA. These provide security more like the old chattel mortgages and assignment of book accounts. The GSA is more like the old form of document called a debenture, which is still used in certain circumstances.

Registration

While these documents create rights and liabilities between you and the lender, it is necessary for the lenders to protect themselves from third parties who may loan you money on the strength of the same security, or who may buy the security from you. For this reason, most provinces have developed a personal property registry system where notice of the security is registered. The registration of this notice "perfects" the security, and provides the lender with the added protection.

After negotiating with the bank, request that the bank will confirm in writing that it is prepared to advance funds, under what circumstances and with what security. Discuss the implications of the letter with your accountant and lawyer, before agreeing to the terms outlined. Once you have signed, obtain copies of it for your lawyer as well as your own files. Never agree to provide security without fully understanding the nature of the security documentation.

Other Security Your Lender Might Require

There are many other forms of security that a potential lender or creditor might ask of you, depending on the lender's policy and your situation. Make sure you understand the nature of this security and negotiate a security package you feel comfortable providing. If you give too much security away the first time, you have nothing left to give later if you require more funds. Some of the most common types of security requested follow.

Guarantor

A guarantor guarantees the payment of a note by signing a commitment. Both private and government lenders commonly require a personal guarantee from directors of a corporation as security for loans. If the corporation defaults, the lender has the choice of suing the guarantor or the corporation or both. A guarantee is not requested of an individual debtor, as this person is automatically personally liable anyway. However, a lender may require a co-guarantor.

Try to negotiate a limited guarantee to cover the shortfall in the security, if other securities have been pledged. Be very careful not to sign a personal guarantee for the full amount of the loan if at all possible, or an unlimited guarantee. Request a written release of your guarantee as soon as the business has paid off its obligation or can carry the debt on its own security. Resist having your spouse sign a personal guarantee of your debts. If your spouse is not an officer or director of the company, your request is more credible. Marital tension is also a consideration. If you co-sign with others, remember each of you is liable for the full amount of the debt. Therefore, attempt to have the debt divided by the number of guarantors and then limit each guarantee to that portion. Also avoid signing personal guarantees on your corporate obligations to the landlord, leasing companies and general creditors. Remember, the main purpose of using a corporation is to avoid personal liability. Small business people are frequently too naïve and generous in giving out personal guarantees. Refer to Chapter 12 on Creditor Proofing Your Business.

Promissory Note
A promissory note is a written promise to pay a specified sum of money to the lender, either on demand or at a specified time in the future.

Endorser
Borrowers often get other people to sign a note in order to increase their own credit. These endorsers are contingently liable for the note they sign. If the borrower fails to pay off the loan, the lender expects the endorser to make good. Sometimes the endorser may be asked to pledge assets or securities as well, for example, a collateral mortgage on a home.

Demand Note
A demand note involves a written promise to pay the monies outstanding to the lender upon demand.

Mortgages (Conventional, Collateral, or Chattel)
A lender may require a mortgage against your property for the advancement of funds. It could be a conventional first, second or third mortgage against your property, or a collateral mortgage to a guarantee or demand note.

A chattel mortgage is on specific property other than land and buildings, such as a car or boat. The title of the chattel remains in the name of the borrower, but a lien against the chattel is placed in favour of the lender. The document you sign is generally called a specific security agreement (SSA) which itemizes the chattels pledged, and is registered in your provincial registry.

Assignment of Lease, Rents or Mortgage

The assignment of a lease is fairly common security in franchises, so that the franchisor can assume the lease if the franchisee goes out of business or defaults on the franchise agreement. The franchisor could then resell the franchise with a lease in place.

If you have rental income, a lender may ask you to sign a document that would not be used by the lender unless you were in default of your loan obligations. If you default, all rents would be diverted directly to the lender. The lender would notify the tenants and provide them with a copy of the assignment document.

You may have a mortgage that was given to you personally or corporately for security. In that event, the lender may want the mortgage assigned to them as security for your loan.

Assignment of Life Insurance

A lender may request that the borrower assign the proceeds of a life insurance policy to the lender up to the amount outstanding at the time of death of the borrower. Another form of assignment is against the cash surrender value of a life insurance policy. Banks generally lend up to the cash surrender value of a life insurance policy.

Assignment of Accounts Receivable or Contracts

A borrower may have to assign the business receivables or book debts to the lender to secure an operating line of credit or other loan. The borrower still collects the receivables; however, in a default, the lender will assume collection. The assignment is supported by a list of the business receivables every month. Generally, an SSA is signed.

Postponement of Claim

If you have a limited company and there are any loans from shareholders, the lender may ask for an agreement that the company will not repay the shareholders until the lender has been repaid in full. Don't sign this document without accounting and tax advice. The tax implications could be onerous. For example, you could be obliged to take out a salary, which is taxable, to meet your personal needs, rather than paying yourself back a part or all of the shareholder's loan, which of course, is not taxable in your hands.

Debenture

A debenture is a very powerful document to give as security, but it can only be given by a corporation. If you are in default, and the bank activates the debenture, it does so by appointing a receiver (usually a chartered accountant or certified general accountant). The receiver effectively takes over the corporation on behalf of the bank and sells either the corporation or its assets to pay the lender back its loan. Occasionally, you may be able to refinance the loan with funds from other sources, but once a receiver is appointed, your financial leverage generally is reduced, for obvious reasons. Debentures are still requested in some situations; otherwise, the lender will request a general security agreement, which is similar in protection to a debenture.

General Security Agreement and Specific Security Agreement
Discussed in detail earlier, the general security agreement is similar to a debenture. The specific security document covers items that were previously referred to as chattel mortgages or assignment of accounts receivable. Only the name of the documentation is changed, along with a different provincial registration.

Pledge of Stock or Bonds
The possession of stocks and bonds may be transferred to the lender, but title remains with the borrower. Sometimes referred to as "hypothecation agreements," assets pledged are itemized. The security must be marketable. As a protection against market declines and possible expenses at liquidation, banks usually lend no more than 75% of the market value of blue chip stock. On government or municipal bonds, they may be willing to lend 90% or more.

The lender may ask the borrower for additional security or payment whenever the market value of the stocks or bonds drops below the lender's required safety margin.

Warehouse Receipts
A warehouse receipt is frequently given to the lender as security which shows that the merchandise used as security either has been placed in a public warehouse or has been left on your premises under the control of one of your employees, who is bonded. The bank lends a percentage of the estimated value of only the readily marketable goods.

Section 427 *Bank Act* Security
Under s.427 of the *Bank Act,* a borrower can provide security for inventory and stock in trade. At the time the lender legally "activates" the security, the inventory is then controlled by the bank, subject to other rights that secured creditors under the *Bankruptcy and Insolvency Act* might have.

Floor Plan Contracts
In a "floor plan contract," either the manufacturer lends the items to the retailer, or the bank lends money for purchase of the merchandise on the condition that a trust receipt is signed showing the serial-numbered merchandise. This document requires that you acknowledge receipt of the merchandise, keep it in trust for the manufacturer or bank and promise to pay the manufacturer or bank as you sell the goods. This is often the only way that a small business could afford to have inventory such as automobiles, appliances or boats.

Be very careful when negotiating your security package. Lenders will usually ask for a lot more security than they really need for the loan. Find a lending institution that will accept a reasonable security package for your loan, appropriate for your circumstances and the realistic risks.

Summary

It is critical that you consult your lawyer and accountant before signing any security documentation. You may decide to negotiate the security documentation for the loan, revise and reduce your loan needs, or apply to another lender. The market is very competitive. There are many pitfalls for the unwary as well as creative financing alternatives to consider. Refer to Chapter 12 on Creditor Proofing Your Business to place financing risks in context.

Nine

Insurance

Introduction

Although it is possible to buy too much insurance, many people don't purchase enough or the right type of insurance. Considering the time, energy, commitment and resources that you are putting into your business, you want to minimize the risk inherent by making sure you have adequate insurance protection.

Organizing Your Insurance Program

It is important to consider all criteria to determine the best type of insurance for you and your business. Your goal should be adequate coverage. That can be achieved by periodic review of the risk you are insuring for, and by keeping your insurance representative informed of any changes in your business that could affect the adequacy or enforceability of your coverage. Such changes could include additional equipment purchases, extensions to your property, the business use of your personal car, or starting a home-based business.

The following advice will help you plan an insurance program:

■ Assess your business and identify the likely risk exposure
■ Cover your largest risk(s) first
■ Determine the magnitude of loss that the business can bear without financial difficulty, and use your premium dollar where the protection need is greatest
■ Insure the correct risk

Decide which of these three kinds of protection will work best for each risk:

■ Absorbing the risk (e.g., budgeting to cover loss or expense without getting insurance)
■ Minimizing the risk (e.g., reducing the factor that could contribute to the risks, rather than getting insurance)
■ Insuring against the risk with commercial insurance

Use every means possible to reduce the cost of insurance:

- Negotiate for lower premiums if your loss experience is low
- Increase deductibles as much as you can if you need the protection, but can't afford a low deductible premium
- Shop around for comparable rates and analyze insurance terms and provisions offered by different insurance companies
- Avoid duplication of insurance; have one agent handle all your business insurance if possible and practical
- Incorporate if necessary to further reduce personal liability
- Select an experienced insurance agency or broker. Refer to Chapter 1 on Legal and Other Advisors.

Regular reviews of risk exposure can help avoid overlaps and gaps in coverage, and thereby keep your risk and premiums lower. This is especially important if the business is growing. Reviews can also help you keep current with inflation.

Examples of Liability

Here are a few examples of liability you could be exposed to in your business and the insurance coverage that would protect you:

- **Case 1.** You provide a computer consulting service and a client who relied on your advice subsequently suffers a $100,000 loss. You are being sued for negligence. (Professional liability/malpractice insurance)
- **Case 2.** You operate a daycare business and while transporting children, your car is accidentally hit by another car and a child is injured. You are sued as the driver and car owner. (Automobile insurance)
- **Case 3.** You operate a catering business and someone cracks a tooth on a walnut shell in one of your muffins. He sues you for dental expenses. (Product liability insurance)
- **Case 4.** You operate a tailoring business, and a client slips on your stairs, breaks her leg, and is off work for two months. You are sued for damages. (General liability insurance)
- **Case 5.** You have expensive desktop publishing hardware and software in your basement. A fire breaks out, damages your equipment, and destroys all your clients' records. (Fire/business property/business replacement cost insurance)
- **Case 6.** You are a contractor, and while lifting a heavy object you injure your back. You are immobilized for three months and cannot work. You are the sole income earner and need income to meet your personal expenses. (Disability insurance)

Types of Insurance

The following brief overview is intended to alert you to the main types of coverage you may wish to consider, depending on the nature of your business.

General Liability
This type of policy covers losses that you would be liable to pay for causing bodily injury to someone (e.g., in an accident) or damage to the property of others. Make sure that your policy covers all legal fees for your defence and related costs. This policy generally covers negligence on your part that accidentally causes injury to clients, employees, or the public.

Business Property
If you are operating out of your home, your current basic homeowners' or apartment owners' policy may void any coverage of business-related assets. Request that coverage be added to include the business assets, or purchase a separate policy. If you own a computer, you may wish to get a special "floater" policy covering risks unique to computer owners, including power-surge and fire damage and theft of hardware and software.

Fire
This coverage enables you to replace or rebuild your office or home as well as replace inventory and equipment. Make sure your policy is a "replacement" policy.

Automobile
Automobile coverage insures physical damage to the car and bodily injury to the passengers as well as damage to other people's property, car or passengers. It also includes theft of your car. Make sure that your car is insured for business use. Otherwise, if the facts came out on a claim that it was being used for that purpose, your policy would be void and your claim disallowed.

Business Loan
Business loan insurance will cover the balance outstanding of a business bank loan, and is usually arranged through the bank at the time of the loan. In the event of your death or disability, the loan is paid off completely. You may be required to obtain this insurance as a condition of funding.

Malpractice
Also referred to as a professional liability insurance, this coverage protects you from claims for damages from your clients, arising out of negligence.

Business Interruption
Business interruption insurance compensates for lost earnings during a temporary cessation of business caused by fire, theft, flood or other disaster, until you return to normal working conditions. Check to make sure it covers the costs of temporarily renting other premises.

Business Continuation
Business continuation insurance provides for the transfer of a shareholder's or partner's interest in the event of that person's death.

Overhead Expense

Overhead expense insurance is purchased by professionals and business owners whose income would cease if they were temporarily disabled. In this event, the insurance would cover their fixed business overhead expenses. Other insurance would be needed for loss of income.

Key Personnel

Key personnel life insurance provides protection for the business owner against the death of a key person that could seriously affect the earning power of the business, including the owner, general manager or managing part ner. The purpose of the coverage, normally obtained by the company, is to cover temporary consulting expertise or hire a replacement with extensive industry experience.

Life

Term life insurance insures a person for a specific period of time or term, and then stops. Term life does not have a cash surrender value or loan value, as is found with a whole life plan. Term premiums are less expensive than whole life premiums. If you have a bank loan or personal or business obligations, consider term life coverage. Whole life insurance costs more as it includes a "term" component plus an investment savings component—you obtain interest on your investment part of your premium.

Leo and Arleen Consider their Insurance Options

Leo and Arleen are in their thirties, and have two young children. Leo is an architect and Arleen a management consultant. They both are self-employed, and depend on their combined incomes to cover the family's living expenses. They are managing to make their maximum RRSP contributions each year, but not any savings outside the RRSP.

Leo and Arleen are concerned that if either of them were to die prematurely, the family's financial health would be seriously jeopardized. They therefore decided to each take out $300,000 of term life insurance. They recognize that there will not be any cash value to the policies, the premiums will rise as they get older, and the coverage will terminate at a certain age, probably 65 or 70. In spite of these drawbacks compared to permanent insurance, they feel that term insurance gives them the maximum protection that they can afford for the next 15-20 years that the children will be financially dependent on them.

In addition, they took out disability insurance that would pay them $3,000 a month if they were not able to work in their professional fields.

Leo purchased his term and disability insurance through his provincial architect association group insurance plan, because the premium cost was significantly lower than those obtained privately. Arleen is undecided between her professional association, or a private insurance carrier. Although the group policy premiums were lower, the private coverage had more flexibility.

Buy/Sell

If you are considering or have a buy/sell agreement, consider where the company will get the money to buy out a deceased shareholder's interest. This is normally done with term life insurance. There are income tax advantages to using corporate life insurance to fund the share purchase. An experienced life insurance agent with experience in business insurance, can give you customized information. Also, speak to the company accountant.

Insurance options to fund a buy/sell for a deceased shareholder are as follows:

1. **Corporate-owned insurance.** In this example, the corporation insures the lives of the shareholders and receives the insurance proceeds on their deaths. These funds are then used to buy the deceased's shares, either from the estate or from the surviving spouse. In most cases, neither the deceased's estate nor the spouse will be exposed to tax on the purchase-back, if the insurance is structured properly.

2. **Criss-cross insurance.** With this type of policy, each shareholder of a corporation acquires a life insurance policy on each other's life. When one shareholder dies, the surviving shareholders receive the tax-free proceeds of the policy. The funds are then used to purchase the shares of the deceased from his or her beneficiaries or estate. The disadvantage is that the insurance cost on each shareholder can vary considerably, depending on their health and age.

3. **Split-dollar insurance.** A hybrid version of corporate and criss-cross insurance, in this example, each shareholder purchases a whole-life policy on the other shareholder. The cash value of the policy is assigned to the company, received when a shareholder dies. The surviving shareholders receive the face value of the policy minus the cash value. These funds are then used to purchase the shares. Most, if not all of the premiums are paid for by the company.

Home Office

It is important to recognize the potential risks of working from home and the policies available for protection against them. If you don't have insurance protection, you could be personally liable for all financial losses. Always advise your insurance agent that you are operating a business from your home. You will need extra coverage for any risk areas involved directly or indirectly with your business operation. Almost all homeowner policies exclude home businesses. However, the increased premium on your current home insurance policies will still be a saving compared to the higher insurance premium you would pay if your business was located in commercial premises. Use the same insurance broker for all your policies if possible, as you should be able to negotiate better rates. Ask for copies of the extra policy coverage for your file.

Employee

Employee insurance is usually taken out for employees by the employer as part of a group benefit package. Such plans usually include life, medical, dental and disability insurance.

Property

Property insurance covers destruction or damage to the insured property caused by perils such as fire, flood and burglary. Marine insurance protects goods during shipment. Boiler and machinery insurance covers damage and injury caused by explosion or other mishaps. Property insurance also covers items such as glass, and automobiles (from collision, theft, fire and vandalism).

Liability

Liability insurance covers any area in which the business, directors, officers, partners, employees or agents might be held liable for negligence, or some other act or omission. The most common type is general liability, which covers negligence causing injury. Other examples include:

- Product liability (purchased by manufacturers of a product)
- Errors and omissions liability (purchased by lawyers, accountants, architects, insurance agents)
- Professional liability (negligent advice given by professionals)
- Tenants' liability (purchased by a tenant of leased space)
- Employers' liability (purchased by employers; relates to worker safety)
- Officers' and directors' liability.

Disability

Good health is by far our greatest asset. With it, we can improve our financial net worth. Without it, only liabilities.

Statistics show that the chance of becoming disabled between 45 and 65 years of age for a minimum of three months is almost 40%. Almost one-half of those still disabled after six months, will still be disabled at the end of five years.

Depending on the disability, you might be covered by Workers' Compensation benefits, CPP benefits, or Employment Insurance disability benefits. You may have group or personal disability insurance benefits. Group and individual plans will only cover a portion of your gross earnings before you were disabled by injury or illness.

Definitions of disability vary. Whether or not you receive benefits may well depend on how the company defines disability. Carefully read the wording of your contract, as some are so restrictive that it might be almost impossible to be eligible for a claim. Most contracts define disability according to one of four types, from the least to the most restrictive:

1. **Own occupation.** Disability is defined as inability to work in your own occupation only. Prove that you are disabled from doing your own job and are under the care of a doctor, and you qualify for benefits. Even if you went to work in another occupation, you may still qualify for benefits. Individual insurance contracts may offer an "own occupation" clause to age 65.
2. **Regular occupation.** This type would provide coverage in the event that you are disabled and unable to work in your own occupation, provided that you choose not to work in an alternative occupation.
3. **Any occupation.** This would cover disability from any suitable occupation, based on your education, training and/or experience. Most, but not all, group insurance contracts specify an "any occupation" disability after the first two years of disability.
4. **Total and permanent.** Some insurance contracts require that you not only be totally disabled from working, but also that your disability must be permanent. Naturally, this insurance is high risk for you due to the severe nature of disability required before coverage commences. The insurance premium is lower as the risk is lower to the insurance company.

Out of Country Emergency Medical

If you are travelling outside Canada for business or pleasure for an hour, a day or a month, you need out-of-country emergency medical insurance. If you have a serious injury or illness in the US and require emergency medical attention, you will be financially devastated unless you have out-of-country medical insurance. Provincial health insurance plans vary by province, but each provides you with the necessary protection when travelling within Canada only. Coverage by provincial plans for hospital care outside Canada is nominal, e.g., $75 to $550 + Canadian funds per day, depending on your province. This is very low compared to medical costs in the US.

Check out as many comparable insurance programs as you can. Get confirmation in writing of any representations made by the insurance company. Keep copies of all correspondence, as well as receipts to be claimed for reimbursement. Remember to claim your insurance premiums for a tax credit on your income tax return under "medical expenses."

Here are the three common types of out-of-country emergency insurance plan options.

1. **Extended stay insurance.** This coverage is intended to protect you for the whole duration of your travel and the premium is based on the duration of your stay.
2. **Multi-trip insurance.** Designed for shorter-term stay coverage outside Canada, you arrange coverage for a maximum single duration stay (not exceeding 15, 30, 45, 90 days, etc.), as many times as you like within the length of your policy coverage. As soon as you return to Canada for at

least a day, the cycle starts again. The key benefit of a multi-trip plan is that it is available for spontaneous trips any time you cross the Canadian border. Obtain multi-trip plans through travel agents, banks and some credit card companies or insurers directly.

3. **Top-up insurance.** This plan provides additional supplemental emergency medical coverage to top-up an existing out-of-country medical plan such as that from an employer, union or credit card plan. Some plans don't permit top-ups. There is a risk that there could be a lapse in time periods between coverage, or disputes between insurers. For example, if your basic medical plan has a ceiling cap of say $50,000, and lasts for 14 days, and your top-up plan kicks in after that, what happens if you have a catastrophic injury just before the first plan lapses? You are only covered for $50,000. Your expenses could be $200,000. You would be out the difference. The top-up company could deem your illness as pre-existing, if you make a claim with your first insurer first. Coordinate a basic plan and top-up plan from the same insurer. Or, have one plan cover everything.

Workers' Compensation
If you have employees, make certain that they are covered by Workers' Compensation insurance to covers costs that may occur due to an injury to an employee. If you do not have coverage and your type of business requires it, you could be personally liable. *Note:* Some jobs, which have low injury risk, are exempt from Workers' Compensation regulations.

Surety and Fidelity Bonds
Bonding is a common requirement in business. A surety bond or guarantee bond is a contract between two parties and the bonding company relating to performance of a contractual obligation. Examples include following through on a bid, a performance of a construction contract, or supplying a product. The bonding company is called a surety and guarantees that the party meets its obligations. If the contractual obligations are not met, the bonding company pays out money as described in the bond agreement. A fidelity bond is purchased by someone who desires protection against the acts of others. An example would be protection against theft by a person cleaning a building under a maintenance contract.

Many insurance brokers also provide bonding services. Look in the yellow pages under "bonds—surety and fidelity." Obtain competitive quotations from at least three companies.

Summary
When starting a business, it is common for people to want to save on expenses whenever possible. With insurance, it is important to be realistic. Weigh the risks and potential business and personal financial exposure if you have no insurance or inadequate coverage. Look upon insurance premiums as an additional cost of doing business and budget accordingly.

Ten

Hiring and Firing Staff

Introduction

Besides help from a partner, spouse, business advisor or mentor, you may need paid staff to assist with the day-to-day operations. Your options include part-time, full-time, freelance, or sales agents. The latter two refer to a subcontracting arrangement with another entrepreneur.

Of the multitude of problems cited by business owners, personnel is identified as the greatest concern, with financing as a secondary concern. The most common difficulty was recruiting good people—professional and motivated. A business owner often overlooks the fact that employees do not necessarily share his or her interest, commitment and loyalty. Take care to ensure that the right people are screened, trained, and motivated to represent your business.

Strong people skills will play a large role in creating a welcoming atmosphere recognized by customers and staff alike. Be a model for your employees and present a consistent, favourable style of personal interaction with customers. If you are considerate and fair to your employees, they will respect and be proud of their employer, and speak well of the company both on and off the job.

Complying with Government Regulations

Ministry of Labour

Before hiring staff, contact your provincial Ministry of Labour office and request a copy of the current *Employment Standards Act* and a guide to the Act. The names of government departments and statutes can vary, depending on the province. These booklets are free, and cover topics such as: minimum wages, allowable deductions, hours of work, overtime, vacations and general holidays, severance pay, termination of employment, etc. These government standards will override any company policies you may set. It is important to keep that in mind in your dealings with your staff. If you follow these regulations, you can protect yourself from claims being made against you, such as wrongful dismissal.

Canada Customs and Revenue Agency (CCRA)

Secondly, you will have to contact the local CCRA office to request an Employer's Kit. You will be assigned an employer number to be used when submitting all records to CCRA concerning your employees' wages paid, deductions taken, and so on. The kit will include:

- **Information for the employer.** An instruction booklet will help you get started.
- **Tax exemption forms.** These forms are completed by each employee, and then referred to when making income tax deductions and completing the annual T4 summaries.
- **Current tables of provincial and federal income tax deduction at source.** These will be used at each pay period to calculate the income tax to be deducted from each employee's wages.
- **Current tables for calculating Canada Pension Plan (CPP) contribution and Employment Insurance (EI).** Similar to the income tax tables, this will be used at each pay period to calculate the amount of CPP and EI premiums to deduct from each employee's wages.
- **Remittance form.** This will be used on a monthly basis to report to CCRA the deductions made from employees' wages for income tax, CPP, EI and the employer's contribution to CPP and EI. It must be filed along with your cheque by the deadline in order to avoid heavy penalties.
- **Employer Guide—How to complete the Record of Employment.** This will be needed when terminating employment, and covers the necessary forms and the deadline for submitting them.

Workers' Compensation Board

Some businesses are required to pay monthly fees to the Workers' Compensation Board (WCB), while others are not. If there is a low risk of on-the-job personal injury (for example, service businesses such as lawyer's office, consultant, typing service), you may not be required to pay or, if you are, at a lower rate.

Human Rights Legislation

Check the provincial and federal human rights legislation that governs hiring practices for employers to prevent discrimination. The main areas usually covered include:

- Nationality, citizenship, race, colour
- Age, sex, sexual orientation
- Marital status, pregnancy/childbirth
- Religious or political belief
- Mental or physical handicap
- Criminal conviction.

If it can be proven that you have been discriminatory in your hiring, firing or other disciplinary practices, you may be subject to court action including heavy fines, as well an order to reinstate the employee.

Record-keeping

Government and Payroll Records

You are accountable to CCRA as well as your employees for the exact hours worked, monies earned and deductions taken. The following information should be detailed in a payroll journal:

- Employee's name, current address, birthday
- Employee's social insurance number and number of dependants
- Employee's date of employment and termination
- Employee's occupation
- Number of hours worked each day
- Wage rate and payment of wages
- Deductions made from wages
- Vacations and general holidays taken.

These records will be required when calculating the amounts to be paid to staff; when submitting the employer remittance form to CCRA, and on an annual basis when completing T4 summaries for each of your employees. As well, on the termination of each employee, a Record of Employment form must be submitted to the Canada Employment office for calculation of unemployment benefits. It is good practice to keep a separate file on each of your employees with further information.

Personnel Files

Set up a confidential file on each employee with a copy of the job posting, along with the employee's application form, résumé, letters of reference, notes from the personal interview and test results (if any).

Keep an ongoing record of the employee's performance. Admittedly, daily notes to the file may be too time-consuming but if you regularly document an employee's performance, your job will be easier when doing a performance appraisal, salary increment, or termination of employment. Examples of documents to include are:

- **Correspondence.** A copy of all correspondence of a personal or performance nature.
- **Illness record.** Dates and hours missed and reason.
- **Tardiness record.** Dates and hours missed and reason.
- **Exemplary performance.** Date and brief details of the achievement and benefits to the company.
- **Poor performance.** Date and brief explanation of the incident and the cost to the company. Also note any details about how the employee dealt with the matter, and discussions about future plans.

You may become aware of recurring or a pattern of incidents and need to refer to specific situations and dates when reprimanding an employee. You will avoid the trap of saying to an employee, "It seems your cash register till has been short rather frequently lately," without having any record of the amounts or the frequency. Only with a thorough "paper trail" will you have sufficient grounds for reprimanding the employee or terminating the employment. It is equally, if not more, important for your staff to be aware that you recognize and keep a record of their accomplishments also. Files of previous employees should be kept for a minimum of two years as you may need them for year-end income tax returns, inquiries from the former employee, or reference checks.

Personnel Policy

It is highly recommended that employers have a personnel policy manual. Written policies on sick leave, vacations, holidays, travel expenses, security and confidentiality can eliminate ambiguity and assist both you and your employees in resolving problems. Each employee should be given a copy and it must be adhered to by all personnel, including you, the manager.

Procedures

Once you have outlined the company policies, it is helpful to identify the techniques or procedures that will be used to carry out those policies, including:

- **Performance appraisal.** A brief written report will be prepared on each employee's work record after their first six months and on the yearly anniversary of the employment start date. The report will be discussed with the employee to acknowledge good work and point out areas that require improvement.
- **Wage review.** A review of each employee's wages will normally be carried out in conjunction with annual performance appraisals. The amount of the increase will depend on inflation, cost of living, comparable wages in a similar industry position, as well as market demand for individuals with a specialized skill set. The individual's performance rating, specific accomplishments and overall value to the productivity of the company will also count. Keep in mind the low cost of raising a person's salary, as opposed to hiring and training someone new.

Job Descriptions

The job description should state clearly the tasks for which the individual has the responsibility and authority to act independently. While this list may change from time to time, it is important to have a written job description for each position. The job description will be referred to:

- When recruiting and training new staff
- When reviewing employee performance and assigning pay increases
- When firing staff.

Job descriptions will eliminate misunderstandings regarding expectations that have not been clearly communicated. You will be in a difficult position with the

Labour Board when firing an employee for not meeting all the requirements of his/her position if the specific duties have not been clearly outlined in writing in the first place.

Disciplining and Firing Employees

Firing an employee is sometimes necessary in order to regain control of the efficient operation of your business. However, staff turnover is costly to any company. The time and costs involved in recruiting a replacement and retraining can be a major setback. As well, if the firing is not handled appropriately, a very resentful employee may speak poorly of you to your customers and competition, or perhaps initiate a wrongful dismissal claim against you.

If you practise constructive discipline techniques, a person whom you may perceive to be a problem employee may respond favourably to your consideration, and turn out to be a loyal, dependable employee. Staff turnover will be reduced and your business will have a much greater chance of success.

Constructive Discipline

Step 1: Evaluate the Situation

When a performance problem first arises, give careful thought to the situation, check out the facts, and plan a course of action.

What not to do—A situation can be worsened by overreacting, so avoid speaking or acting too quickly in a critical manner. Do not show heated emotion or anger. Blaming the employee in front of peers or customers is a serious mistake. Not only will you lose respect, but you could leave the door open for a labour relations claim.

What should be done—After your emotions are in check, speak with the employee in private. Use an "I" statement such as, "I feel disappointed about the manner in which that incident was handled." Ask for more information—there are two sides to every story. Listen for clues that will identify the root of the problem. Perhaps the employee has never been trained on aspects of your operation, or has been misinformed about procedures, or has handled matters that way at another company. Or perhaps the employee is preoccupied with a family, financial or health problem. All of these are forgivable—at least the first time.

If it appears that it was lack of information or training that caused the problem, be certain to say so to your employee. Immediately plan a time when you can provide the necessary training. Include other staff who may also benefit from the training session, even if it is a refresher. In this way, your staff will be able to pull together better as a team.

Before concluding, work out suggestions on how to handle a similar situation in the future. Document the correct course of action for your procedures manual and ensure the revised pages are circulated to all staff.

In some situations, it may be poor judgment rather than lack of training that caused the incident. Perhaps the employee was under the influence of alcohol while on the job. Even in this type of situation, it is important to check out any information that you may be lacking. It may be a special occasion such as the employee's birthday, and alcohol was consumed at lunch. Make the employee aware of the company policy and explain the negative impact it creates on customers and other staff. In a situation where the employee's negative attitude has created a problem, a time limit should be established for the employee to work towards correcting the negative behaviour.

Again, document the situation thoroughly, including suggestions for improvement. File your notes in the employee's personnel file. Many situations will end here, without any further discussion required.

Step 2: Constructive Discipline

Unfortunately, not all problems are dealt with as easily and quickly. Employee attitude problems tend to be the most difficult to correct, and sometimes it is necessary to terminate the employment. Your consistency in following through these subsequent steps of constructive discipline is crucial.

A second meeting is necessary if the problem recurs or a different situation arises, or if the agreed-upon time frame has not been met. Specifically referring to the suggestions for improvement made earlier, ask the employee if they have been practised, and if they proved helpful. Ask if the employee has any other suggestions. Stress the negative impact the behavioural trait has on the business, and the need for change. State that you want to help the employee make the desired change. Agree upon a time frame that the employee feels is fair for the problem to be corrected.

This time, you should document in a memo to the employee the discussions during your meeting, the agreed-upon suggestions and the time frame. Have the individual sign the memo. Again, place the memo in the employee's personnel file and note on your day calendar the date that was agreed upon.

Make interim check-ups on the employee, volunteering your assistance if required. Give positive feedback whenever appropriate.

Step 3: Resolution and Positive Feedback

Where an employee has made marked improvement and you are satisfied, the matter may be concluded. Have a brief meeting with the employee to relay your positive feedback and your appreciation for his/her efforts.

Encourage the employee to come to you at any time with any problems, and suggest that together you can work out a solution. In this way, you build loyalty with your employees. Be firm, but also fair and consistent in dealings with staff. Showing favouritism to one staff member can lead to the resentment and disloyalty of the others.

An employee's performance may slide back to its previous unsatisfactory level, and you may need to reopen the matter and set a new time frame for improvement. This time the period should be shorter, since you know the employee is capable of satisfactory performance.

An Alternative Step 3: Minimize the Damage

If the employee is unable or unwilling to change, plan to fire the employee at the earliest possible opportunity. Delay at this point will cause increased harm. If you have taken all the appropriate steps, you have acted responsibly as a manager to help the employee; however, you have a responsibility to your business and other staff.

Removing an Employee

While it isn't easy to fire someone, sometimes it must be done for the health of the business. When firing an employee, consider the following to determine the appropriate approach:

- Is the employee on probation?
- Has the employee been with the company a long time?
- Do you have an employment contract that has a termination clause?
- What impacts do provincial or federal employment standards legislation have on the issue?
- What does your lawyer advise you to do in your particular situation?

Firing for Just Cause

You can dismiss an employee without notice if there is just cause. Depending upon the facts, you can argue that the employee is not entitled to severance pay. If the fired employee sues you for wrongful dismissal, you will want to be certain you have kept a thorough record of all incidents leading up to the dismissal. Some of the most common reasons for dismissal with just cause include:

- Incompetence; insolent behaviour
- Serious misconduct, wilful disobedience, wilful neglect of duty
- Theft, dishonesty, fraud
- Intoxication on the job
- Cumulative effect: no one act would be sufficient, but when several acts are combined, could amount to just cause
- Chronic absence from work and/or lateness.

When dealing with dismissal decisions, it may be prudent to discuss the matter with a lawyer with specific expertise in labour law. An informed legal opinion might only cost $150 to $200 for a one-hour consultation, but could save you thousands of dollars, along with all the negative energy and wasted time.

Lay-off

When a staff lay-off is necessary, you are required to give reasonable notice or payment in lieu of notice, depending on your employee's length of service with the company. Your local employment standards office will be able to clarify the legislation in your situation. For a long-term employee, the general guide is from one week to one month's compensation for each year of service depending on responsibility. Examples of lay-off without cause include:

- Corporate reorganization due to company merger or buy-out
- Technological changes leading to redundancy
- Downsizing of operation.

Delivering the News

A firing or lay-off should be done in private and handled carefully, and unemotionally. The employee should be treated with respect and given an opportunity to provide an explanation, if appropriate. Tell the employee that he/she is fired within the first few statements made. Use "I" statements such as, "I am disappointed things didn't work out here." "You" statements tend to be accusational and may have to be defended later. Never lose your temper. An abrupt, heat-of-the-moment dismissal seldom stands up to outside scrutiny, and is usually noted with concern by other employees. The employee should be able to retain his/her dignity and understand completely the termination.

Be aware of the probation period as set out in your provincial labour standards legislation. In some provinces you will have to pay an employee who has worked more than three months the necessary severance pay and any outstanding vacation or holiday pay. A Record of Employment form will have to be completed and sent to the HRDC office within one week of termination.

Wrongful Dismissal

Unfortunately, too many managers are not committed to taking the time required to work with employees. Often they end up spending the time later defending their actions. If you fire for the wrong reasons, or without sufficient warnings, the fired employee could claim for an alleged:

- Breach of provincial or federal human rights legislation
- Breach of provincial or federal labour standards legislation
- Defamation of character (written or spoken)
- Wrongful dismissal.

Your main protection is careful recordkeeping. Complete itemized documentation of the employee's incompetence, misdeeds and failure to correct problems is required to defend against a wrongful dismissal suit.

> #### Jim could have Minimized—Or Prevented—A Lawsuit
>
> Jim had been in business about three years and had seven employees. The office manager had been with Jim since the beginning, but was going through some marital problems and having trouble concentrating. This resulted in Jim's workload increasing and caused tension between him and the manager. Jim had never discussed his frustrations with the office manager. In a fit of anger one day, Jim fired the manager. The manager went to a lawyer and sued Jim for wrongful dismissal.
>
> Jim could have handled the problem to minimize any legal comeback. First of all, he should have drafted a written job classification for the office

manager, setting out exactly his duties before the employment commenced. He should have met with the manager to discuss the issues, document the problems, and have the employee acknowledge receipt of the summary. This ongoing paper trail would show a pattern of fairness, and an attempt to deal with the problem in a pragmatic way. Finally, Jim should have spoken to a lawyer specializing in employment law before he took any steps to fire the employee, so as to minimize or eliminate any lawsuit, as the firing would have been done for "just cause."

Summary

Time invested in carefully selecting, training and managing staff is likely to reap the rewards of having reliable and competent long-term staff. This could turn the personnel issue from a "great concern" into a key asset of the company and enable you to spend more time on other aspects of the business.

By adopting a consistent, well-documented approach, you should minimize the risk, stress, cost and negative time and energy of dealing with legal or regulatory hassles. For further information on dealing with employees, including checklists and sample forms, refer to the book, *The Complete Canadian Small Business Guide*, 3rd edition, by Douglas and Diana Gray, published by McGraw-Hill Ryerson.

Eleven

Credit and Collection

Introduction
Most businesses rely on credit as their primary means of selling to customers. When extending credit, caution needs to be taken to ensure payment is received in a timely manner. Many businesses have fallen into disastrous cash flow problems because a large part of their sales revenue is outstanding and possibly uncollectible. Take time to carefully establish a credit and collection policy and procedure and follow through with its consistent implementation.

Methods of Payment
Depending on the nature of your business, you may depend upon cash and credit card sales only; other companies may extend credit and accept company cheques in payment. Regardless of preferred payment, a decision needs to be made on the methods of payment and the risks to be assumed with each.

Cash Payments
Other than retail establishments, few businesses receive cash payments. Those that do should train staff on the proper handling, recording and storage of cash to prevent losses and theft. Also, staff should be watchful for counterfeit bills which usually occur in larger denominations such as $20, $50 and $100.

Cheques
Cheques and direct wire transfers from one company's bank to the other are most common in business-to-business transactions. Amongst retailers that deal with the public, there is a move away from accepting personal cheques. This is largely due to the time delays for bank processing, as well as the high cost of dishonoured cheques.

Accepting Cheques
Studies show that small businesses suffer heavier losses from bad cheques than do large businesses. A properly structured cheque procedure will help reduce the

risk and administrative costs involved. Items to be covered in the procedures for staff include:

1. Closely examine a cheque before accepting it, to make sure that information on the face of the cheque appears to be valid. Watch for:
   - Cheque from a non-local bank
   - Inaccurate date or amount
   - Cheque that does not provide a customer's name and address
   - Cheque that is illegible
   - Cheques requiring two signatures
   - No computer code on bottom of cheque.

2. Obtain at least two types of proper identification from the person signing the cheque. Obtain information about that person sufficient to follow up if the cheque is not honoured.

   If you are exacting in your identification policies, the risk of forgery will be minimized. The following types of identification are frequently used:
   - **Current driver's licence.** If your province does not require a photograph on the licence, obtain additional photograph identification. Check that the address is current and the same as shown on the face of the cheque, and record the person's home and office telephone numbers.
   - **Bank credit cards.** Be certain to record the information exactly as shown on the card including name, card account number and expiry date.

3. An effective way of ensuring the proper verification is made on each cheque is to have a rubber stamp prepared and used on the back of each cheque. These rubber stamps can be made up at any stamp or stationery business.

4. Your policy might state that the supervisor or credit manager's approval is required before any cheque can be tendered. You may set a limit on the maximum amount of a cheque. You may have a policy that a cheque cannot be cashed for any amount more than the amount of the purchase. If the amount on the cheque is large, you may want to verify it. Have your bank contact the bank on which the cheque is drawn to see if there are sufficient funds. Have them inquire if the account is operating satisfactorily. You may wish to contract with a cheque verification service, located in the yellow pages under "cheque cashing protection services" or "cheque protection equipment."

5. Promptly follow-up on any returned cheques. A customer's cheque may be dishonoured because of intentional or unintentional error, insufficient funds, stop payment, no account or closed account, or forgery. Immediately contact the person, politely explain the situation, and ask for replacement payment. It is appropriate to charge a fee of $25 or more for returned cheques to defray the bank's charges and administrative costs. If the person does not promptly pay the outstanding amount, the cheque can be sent "on collection" to the customer's bank by your bank. The cheques

will be held there for up to three months, and as soon as a deposit is made, the funds will be withdrawn and sent to your bank.

Credit Cards

Credit cards are convenient for customers and guarantee payment for the business owner. The three basic types of credit cards are bank cards, membership cards and single firm cards. The credit cards issued by the major chartered banks include MasterCard and Visa. Membership cards include American Express and others. Single firm cards are those issued by department stores and gas companies. If you decide to become an authorized credit card merchant, you will need to contact the bank, membership card, or company representative. You would then display the credit card logos at your place of business, so that customers are aware of the acceptable methods of payment.

The credit card company will establish a floor limit beyond which telephone or computer authorization must be obtained from the credit card company before the transaction is completed. Bank credit card deposits can be made in the same manner as cheques or cash. In the case of membership cards, the merchant slip is forwarded to the member office and a cheque, minus the commission fee, is sent back, generally within a three-day turnaround. Many business owners have electronic processing, so that the funds go immediately into your bank account.

A fee or commission is charged by the credit card company for the convenience of using the service. The fee will generally range between 1% and 5% of the total sale. The average amount of purchases and the annual volume of credit card sales will determine the commission rate you will be required to pay. The higher the volume and sales, the lower the commission. Consider becoming a member of the retail merchant's association of your province, as one of the benefits is a reduced merchant commission. By using an automated authorization and deposit system, you can enjoy a low commission (approximately 1% or less) regardless of the volume of sales. The increased sales associated with credit card convenience and the reduced collection costs far offset the expense of the commission.

Benefits of accepting credit card payments include:

- **Easy processing procedures.** The forms and procedures of a credit card system are easy to learn and administer.
- **Immediate payment.** Credit card payments are equivalent to selling on a cash basis and provide you with instant working capital. With membership cards, there may be a delay of several days, before you receive payment in the mail.
- **Guaranteed payment.** As long as the merchant has complied with the verification authorization requirements, the merchant slip will always be honoured in full, minus the commission discount, regardless of whether a cardholder pays bills or not.
- **Lower operating costs.** You do not need an internal credit and collection system and there is no delay in checking on a person's credit or processing a credit application form.

- **Better competition with larger businesses.** In terms of attracting the credit card user, a small business that accepts major bank and membership credit cards can compete with larger businesses that have their own credit cards.

Credit Accounts

A credit account that you establish for your customers is based on the charge card concept. The customer makes a purchase and must pay the account in full within a 30-day period of the statement date. As long as the customer pays within the set time, there is no interest charged. The credit service is for a short term with a credit limit established at the outset of the relationship. This limit could be increased over time for a customer with a favourable credit history. A variation requires the customer to pay the full amount or a minimum percentage of the outstanding statement. The customer pays interest at whatever rate is established.

For high cost items such as furniture, equipment and machinery, a business may establish conditional sales contracts, more technically referred to as a specific security agreement (SSA), which is filed in a provincial registry. In this plan, the customer makes monthly payments on the purchase of a major expense item. The SSA protects the seller by maintaining title in the seller's name until the purchaser has paid for the item in full. A down payment of 10% to 20% of the item is usually required. Payments may be spread over 12 to 36 months and include principal, interest and service charge. Some business owners sell these SSAs to banks or finance companies in exchange for cash. The customer then pays the bank or finance company directly.

Granting Credit

- Credit is usually necessary to remain competitive and also has the following advantages: The majority of shoppers utilize credit to make purchases. Therefore, if you offer credit or accept credit cards, you are going to extend your customer base.
- The offering of credit increases the size of the average sale. Customers with credit are also more responsive to sales and displays.
- It is easier and more convenient for customers to purchase over the telephone, through mail order and Internet.
- Extending credit engenders goodwill for your business and builds customer loyalty.
- If your credit terms offer a more attractive interest rate, higher credit limits, or easier access to credit than your competitors, these factors could provide you with the competitive edge.
- The business will earn additional profit on the financing charges. Some businesses charge between 5% and 20% higher than conventional financing at a bank through loan or line of credit.
- By analyzing the information contained on your customers' accounts, you can obtain a profile of their purchase preferences, buying habits, times of

purchase and overall buying trends. This information could be utilized for sales promotions or advertising purposes, as well as direct mail campaigns.

Extending credit obviously involves additional direct and indirect costs and bad debt risks. These expenses would have to be deducted from sales revenue before arriving at your profit figure. Some of these disadvantages include:

- If your customers are slow in paying, then your working capital is reduced. Interest charges on your line of credit would reduce your overall profit.

- Studies show that there are a higher percentage of returns with credit sales than with goods sold on a cash basis. Frequently people buy first and decide later whether they really want to keep the items. If not, they are returned, sometimes many months later. This could result in a loss, as returned items may not be resaleable or could be out of season.

- There can be considerable operating and overhead costs associated with extending credit, including processing credit applications, bookkeeping, mailing out invoices and statements, and following up on overdue accounts. The cost of capital to finance the credit, personnel and collection agency fees or commissions are all hidden costs that need to be considered.

- Statistics show that despite the thoroughness of your credit application and screening, a certain percentage of customers are unable or unwilling to pay the amount that they owe. Bad debts will increase your operating expenses and in turn reduce your profitability.

Establishing Credit Policy and Procedures

Setting a Credit Policy

Once you have decided to extend credit, clearly establish your policy and procedures so that they are consistently followed by your staff. Clear procedures will also be helpful to fall back upon when a customer asks you for more credit or time than you are comfortable extending. A credit policy will keep you on track with your goals and minimize bad debt. When establishing your policy, consider your type of business, credit policies of your competition, market factors, economic and industry conditions, working capital requirements, financial position, cost of credit, credit record system required, credit terms needed and personnel required.

With a conservative policy, you would require a very detailed investigation of the applicant's application and creditworthiness before any credit is extended. You would be strict not only in the amount of risk you are prepared to accept, but the amount of credit that you would let each customer have outstanding at any particular time. Generally a small, safe amount is first granted, then increased as the customer's payment history becomes established.

Using a lenient approach, you may be more flexible on the amount of credit that you are prepared to extend and the amount of credit that any particular customer would have. You may require a minimal investigation of those customers you already know, or who have a very strong credit rating.

It is good business practice to start with a conservative approach to extending credit. In time, you may continue with a conservative approach, especially with new customers, or offer a more lenient policy for customers with a proven credit history.

Your credit policy and procedures should include the following issues:

- Credit and collection manager's role
- Credit application process
- Verification and approval of the credit application
- Establishing credit terms (due date, interest rate, deposits required)
- Amounts of credit to be extended
- Circumstances for credit privileges to be withdrawn
- Collection policy and follow-up procedures on overdue accounts
- Stage that overdue account is turned over to a third party for collection.

Learn from Nancy's Mistakes!

Nancy started a consulting business and within a year had a very large client and several smaller ones. The large client represented about 90% of her income. As she wanted to nurture the relationship with this key client, she was not very businesslike in her financial dealings. For example, she did not ask for disbursement costs in advance, but would carry them on her credit card until she was paid; she did not ask for a retainer or for progress payments on each project. The client was slow in paying, generally four months from date of invoice. One day, she heard that the client was going into bankruptcy. Nancy was just a general creditor, and ended up getting 10¢ on the dollar a year later. She lost about $100,000. As a result, Nancy had to sell her house and downsize into a condo.

With astute legal planning, Nancy could have avoided most of her business problems. There is an inherent risk in having just one major client for revenue. Pre-empt potential problems by anticipating them. Get an advance against anticipated disbursements, or charging expenses to the client's account. Ask for an initial retainer, e.g. 25%, and progress draws every month, with invoices paid within one month of receipt.

Characteristics of a Good Credit Manager

Once you have determined your credit policy, you will know whether you need to employ full-time or part-time assistance to manage a credit and collection function. Many small business owners feel uncomfortable performing the credit and collection function as this conflicts with a sales or public relations role they may also have. If this is the case, it is always best to assign the responsibility to someone who can follow through diligently.

Credit management requires sound judgment, tact, analytical and human relations abilities. The ability of a credit and collection person to interact positively but firmly with a prospective credit account customer or a collection problem is vital. Other traits such as courtesy, self confidence, and initiative are also important qualities. In addition, the credit manager should:

- Have knowledge of bookkeeping and accounting, in order to evaluate a customer's financial situation
- Be convincing and effective in verbal communication skills
- Show resourcefulness, adaptability, initiative and sound judgment in dealing with difficult situations
- Have the capacity to analyze problem situations realistically, and deal with customer relations firmly and diplomatically
- Be able to obtain and protect confidential information, and show fairness in dealing with people
- Have a sympathetic style in dealing with customers, and willingness to negotiate settlements, wherever possible.

Whether you are going to be performing the credit and/or collection function, or employ other people to do it, make sure that the person involved is properly trained for this important function. There are many educational seminars and courses that are offered on this topic through colleges and Dun & Bradstreet.

The Credit Application, Verification and Approval

The credit application form is the first step in the evaluation process of the applicant. You can obtain pre-printed application forms from your credit bureau, trade associations or commercial suppliers, then modify them to suit your needs.

Ensure the information provided by your customer on the credit application form is current, complete and signed. Investigate the credit information to confirm its accuracy. You may wish to use the assistance of external parties such as Dun & Bradstreet or the credit bureau. If the applicant is a corporation, the Better Business Bureau could advise you of any unresolved complaints.

In addition to evaluating the credit risk, make an assessment of the individual's character, reputation and style of doing business. If the applicant is a corporation, request a personal guarantee.

Once you have decided to accept or reject the application, confirm that in writing to the applicant. Your letter should confirm the credit limit you have granted, the penalties for late payment and when the payments are due. If you are rejecting a credit applicant, the letter could simply read, "Upon assessing credit information supplied from the customer and through other investigation, we find that the applicant does not conform to our policy requirements at this point. However, the applicant's interest in applying for credit is appreciated."

Monitoring Your Accounts Receivable

Establishing Effective Records

Before you start extending credit, you must establish an efficient record-keeping system. A record-keeping system has to accurately record all changes in a customer's account and indicate any arrears. Your system should track individual customer information, overall accounts receivable information and aged accounts receivable analysis.

An individual customer record should include all essential details on the account status. Some small businesses use a ledger card system. However, there are numerous inexpensive computer software programs. MYOB and Simply Accounting are easy to use and effective for tracking historical trends. A record should include the account number, billing date, account limit, customer's name, address, business and residence phone numbers, authorized users of the account, any special restrictions or specialized requirements, the terms and conditions of sale and a cumulative record of transactions. The record of transactions would show the date, the item, any debits (charges), any credits (payments) and running balance. Using this type of current information, you or your staff can make decisions on whether you should extend further orders to the customer.

Most small businesses now use a computer software program for all the record-keeping purposes. A paper-based ledger system is not as efficient or effective, and also takes more time. An aged accounts receivable general ledger is a summary of the amount of money owed to your business and how long the amounts have been outstanding. The ledger should be updated on a weekly, biweekly, or at least a monthly basis. Most banks require an aged list of receivables on a monthly basis to support an operating line of credit.

Warning Signs

To keep your accounts receivable as low as possible, someone should be specifically designated to monitor accounts. Here are some of the warning signs that can indicate potential bad debt losses:

- Customer delays in providing concrete information about his/her business
- Customer's order much smaller or much larger than you would expect to receive in normal circumstances
- You have heard from reliable sources that your customer's business has been refused other trade credit
- Customer fails to take advantage of discounts for prompt payment
- Customer frequently or unexpectedly delays in paying the accounts on time
- Customer has sent you an NSF cheque, a post-dated cheque or a cheque with an error without promptly notifying you
- You have been requested to accept the return of merchandise for full credit
- You have seen signs that your customer is having financial difficulties or is laying off staff
- You have noticed from the cheques you have received from your customer that they have changed their bank from the bank noted on the credit application
- Your attempts to contact your customer by phone or letter have been ignored.

If you have noticed any of the foregoing warning signs, take prompt action. You may wish to do an immediate credit bureau or Dun & Bradstreet credit check or have your bank make an inquiry of your customer's bank, as to the satisfactory operation of their account. You may decide to suspend further credit privileges and start collection procedures.

Analyzing Effectiveness of Credit Policy

There are three main measurements of the effectiveness of your credit and collection policy: the average collection period, the aging of accounts receivable and bad debt ratio.

1. **Average collection period.** This calculation compares total accounts receivable with average daily credit sales. Divide the credit sales within a short period of time (for example, within the last month, but no more than three months) by the number of business days during that period. If you have established your terms of credit at thirty days, then that is the figure to use. Your collection period should not exceed your normal selling terms, if you are running an efficient operation. Compare this figure with previous figures and with published industry averages.

2. **Aging of accounts receivable.** This is a more accurate measure of the extent to which your accounts receivable are being paid in accord with the terms of your credit. When aging your accounts receivable, amounts outstanding are classified under categories such as under 30 days, 31 to 60 days, 61 to 90 days, 91 to 120 days, and over 120 days. The aging process can be done on a weekly or monthly basis. The outcome will show the condition of your receivables as of that date.

3. **Bad debt ratio.** Divide your bad debts by the total credit sales to get your bad debt ratio. Compare it with figures from previous periods and with published industry bad debt statistics.

Collecting Overdue Accounts

The more stringent that you are on your credit policy, the less time you will have to spend on your collection policy. If you are stringent on both your credit and collection policies, you will minimize bad debts and keep your receivables low. There are two main categories of delinquent customers—those who are willing but unable to pay, and those who are able but unwilling to pay. The challenge is to find out which category your delinquent accounts fall under.

Your collections policy should detail the steps that your firm will follow from when a customer account is first discovered to be delinquent until the account is collected internally, or assigned to a third party for collection.

Although you want to be consistent in your collection procedures, you also have to take into account individual differences that will alter your particular technique; for example, how long the account has been past due, the amount of the account and why the customer is not paying. Probably 95% of customers want to maintain their credit record and continue doing business with you. You want to maintain their goodwill so that they will refer other business, and continue doing business with you.

Customers become delinquent in their payments for the following reasons:

- **Overextended.** This customer may be overextended because of seasonal overbuying, receivable delays, or excessive use of credit. You may eventually receive all your money, but you should ascertain the problem immediately and monitor the account on a regular basis. For example, you may accept monthly, post-dated cheques from the customer so you can ensure that the cheques are processed. You may require that ongoing orders be paid for on a COD basis.

- **Personal misfortune.** Some customers may have some temporary difficulty because of personal illness or disaster. Attempt to be compassionate, but be realistic in your expectations of regular repayments. You may require that ongoing business be done on a COD basis.

- **Negligence or forgetfulness.** Some customers have the money to pay you, but are inefficient in their administrative bookkeeping, and do not handle their accounts properly. They may just deal with the large bills first or the small bills first, or wait until they are pressed before they pay. This type of debtor needs to be reminded on a regular basis. If the collection procedures are consistent, they will continue to pay. You might decide it is too frustrating to monitor this customer, even though they have the ability and eventually do pay.

- **Intentionally slow.** Some businesses use trade credit for working capital, and extend their credit privileges to the extreme. They pay only when they are dealt with in a serious fashion, such as a threat to cancel credit. Look for a consistent pattern on the accounts receivable ledger and decide whether you really want to do business with this type of customer.

- **Customer misunderstands terms of the credit agreement.** Possibly your customer did not fully understand when and how much they were supposed to pay. Good communication should resolve the matter.

- **Customer believes that the bill is incorrect.** Your customer may feel that there is an error in the bill and, until it is corrected or explained, does not want to pay on the account. This could be a bluff but it could be a legitimate concern. Clarify the situation and provide an adjustment if necessary.

- **Dishonesty.** There are customers who intend to abuse their credit privileges. Watch for threats to stop doing business with you, excuses for temporary setbacks which are not true, repeated broken promises to pay, attempts to evade answering direct questions. Take immediate action.

Maintain positive and regular contact with your customers. Customers who are made to feel embarrassed because they are in arrears with your firm could cease doing business with you. If an account was not seriously overdue, this could be a greater loss to the business. If there is no regular contact, customers who abuse their credit could assume that it could be a long time before you attempt collection action.

Collection Process

Keep in mind that you not only want to recover the money owed to you, but you want to retain your customer's goodwill. Whenever you are communicating with the customer, reflect an attitude of fairness as well as firmness. Collection involves distinct, graduated procedures with the content and timing of messages carefully calculated. Your style and tone of collection technique will reflect the customer's credit history with you, the importance of the customer's ongoing business, your assessment of the customer's viability and sincerity, the circumstances causing the customer's delay, your standard industry approaches, and the type of company that you operate. Here are some stages of collection that may be appropriate for your type of business.

Reminder Statement

Once the credit period has expired (usually 15 or 30 days, depending on your internal risk policy), you may send a duplicate copy of the statement with a pre-printed rubber stamp message or a stick-on reminder that the account is 15 days overdue. If you are a member of your local credit bureau or Dun & Bradstreet, you can purchase adhesive stickers for invoices that serve as a reminder. You may also wish to obtain pre-printed four-step and multicoloured collection letters from various companies offering these services. In addition, you can get software programs with sample forms.

In the reminder stage, give your customer the benefit of the doubt. Your customer may have been on holiday or sick, or there could be employee turnover in the payable department. Keep a friendly tone. Send out the reminder promptly after the payment is overdue, within a few days, or at the most a week. If your customers perceive that you are well organized and carefully monitoring your accounts, they will take you more seriously.

Make sure you check with the credit record system *first* (computerized or manual) to see if the payment is still outstanding. Possibly it has been paid but not yet fully recorded. If it is your policy to charge interest on overdue accounts, and this has been agreed to in writing, then the interest should be shown on the statement. A computerized system with regular input of accounts receivables paid will increase the efficiency of your collection system.

Inquiry Stage

If your customer has not responded to your reminder letter, you may wish to send out a follow-up letter. This letter could have a sticker attached stating that the account is now thirty days overdue. In this inquiry stage, you want to determine why payment is late, but the tone of your letter is friendly but firm without any accusations. Address the letter to the appropriate individual; refer to the trade customer's credit application form to determine who is responsible for accounts payable.

Planning your Collection Calls

You can make an unlimited number of local phone calls without adding to your phone bill, whereas each letter you write increases your out-of-pocket collection expense. In many cases, it is far more practical to phone your customers than to send delinquency letters. The steps in the telephone-collection process follow.

1. **Pre-call planning.** In preparing for the telephone call, determine the problem, and find the solution that will return the account to a current status as soon as possible. Ideally this will take just one phone call. By anticipating problems, you can maximize the productive outcome. Be familiar with the file, and ensure that it is accurate. Ask yourself:
   - Was the account rendered to the customer on time and is the amount correct?
   - Has the customer moved from the most recent address on your files and has the new address been noted?
   - Was the merchandise returned and a proper credit made?
   - Has the customer ever complained or inquired about the billing or the terms of the credit relationship?

2. **Collection call.** While you may prepare for the telephone conversation, you cannot predict the outcome. You can do your best to control the tone of the call to ensure that it meets your objectives.
   - Make sure that you speak to the correct person.
   - Respect your customer's right to confidentiality, and do not discuss financial matters with unauthorized personnel.
   - Once you are speaking to the correct party, identify yourself and your firm and state the reason for the phone call.
   - If the customer doesn't offer a reason, ask why the account has not been paid. Wait for a response. Listen carefully to the answers and note them on your records.
   - Ask the customer how and when he or she intends to repay you. This shows that you wish to retain the customer's goodwill and business, assuming of course that you do.
   - If you have conducted yourself with courtesy as well as being firm and fair up to this point, the customer will likely want to cooperate. If a customer is angry at your approach, they may look for excuses to avoid paying you.
   - Make payment arrangements with the customer. Obtain a commitment with the customer over the phone relating to dates and amounts of payment. Record this discussion in your notes. If possible, have the customer restate the accepted plan.

- Thank the customer for his or her cooperation, to reinforce the importance that you place on positive communication and an ongoing relationship. Tell the customer to forward the funds directly to the attention of a specific person in your firm, normally the person making the call.

3. **Follow-up.** After your call, make sure that you record the exact date and amounts agreed upon. Outline the various problems or excuses that you encountered in the phone call.

   - Sometimes it is necessary to confirm in writing the verbal arrangement to ensure that the customer does not forget the terms. If there is a lot of money owing to you by a trade creditor, it is particularly important to confirm it. If it is a consumer credit matter with a small amount owing, then the letter may not be necessary. Your policy and judgment will dictate your procedures.

   - If the debtor receives a confirmation letter within a few days of your phone call, it shows that you are organized in your recordkeeping. It also restates the verbal agreement, reminds the debtor of the obligation to pay, confirms the details of the agreement such as the amounts to be paid and dates, and provides you with a written record of the telephone conversation.

   - Be certain that the tone of the confirmation letter is polite and the letter is short and factual. Keep in mind that you want to assist your customer through any cash flow problems and maintain business in the future.

   - If the customer does not comply with the terms of the new payment agreement, make sure that you follow up with a phone call immediately. Studies show that approximately 50% of customers who promise to pay require a follow-up stimulus before they meet their obligations. If the payment is substantial and comes from a trade customer, you may wish to thank the customer for their cooperation after receipt and processing of the payment.

Research has shown that the most productive time for making collection calls to people's homes generally is between 8:00 and 10:00 am, and 4:00 and 8:00 pm. Keep in mind that if you make calls any earlier or any later, it could be construed by the customer as harassment. The law is specific in not permitting anyone to threaten or harass debtors over the phone. Make sure that your staff is aware of provincial and federal regulations that affect the collection process. For example, most provinces have a *Debt Collection Act*, which regulates debt collectors. In addition, most provinces have a *Consumer Credit Reporting Act* which sets out what information you can obtain about debtors. The *Orderly Payment of Debts Act*, or equivalent, sets out the means by which a consumer creditor can restructure their creditor repayment obligations through a provincial government department.

Have your lawyer advise you on the proper approach, to keep within the law. By being a member of the credit bureau and taking courses on credit and collection, you will obtain information to assist you in the collection function.

Using Outside Assistance

If after all your efforts you are unable to collect the amount owing by the customer, you can write off the debt, or turn it over to a collection agency or a lawyer. At this point you have lost your profit. At best, you may only be able to recover a portion of the expenses that you have incurred.

Collection Agents

In most cases, professional collection agencies make money only if they actually collect money from a customer. Therefore, collection agencies tend to take whatever actions will secure the quickest response from the delinquent customer. Collection agencies charge different fees, a percentage of what is collected, depending on whether it is a consumer or a trade collection. The consumer collection rate is normally 50% of the amount collected. The following scale of charges is typical for collecting commercial debts, but comparison-check, as every agency has their own fee policy.

- Accounts less than $100—50% commission
- Accounts more than $100 but less than $500—18% commission
- Accounts more than $500 but less than $2,000—15% commission
- Accounts over $2,000—10% commission
- Accounts forwarded to an out-of-town collection agent—25% commission
- Where the creditor accepts returned goods in settlement of an account, the collection agent will receive 15% of the value of those goods.

The following terms are fairly standard in a collection agency agreement. The creditor is asked to agree to the following:

- To assign the account to the collection agency
- To advance actual court costs on all cases in which legal action is taken (usually refunded from the first monies collected on the account)
- To report to the collection agent every payment made directly to the creditor by the debtor, on any of the accounts assigned to the collection agency (the creditor is to give full credit for such collection to the collection agent, when payment is made directly to the creditor)
- To pay all commission fees due to the collection agent no later than the tenth of the following month
- To leave the account in the hands of the collection agency for at least 12 months; the collection agent will return all accounts upon request after that if they are not in the actual process of collection
- The collection agent will not be responsible for any account becoming barred by the Statute of Limitations while in the hands of the collection agent. In

other words, if there is a two-year deadline for commencing a lawsuit, and the collection agent fails to do so, it cannot be held liable.

Consider the image problem that your business will suffer if the agency uses improper collection tactics. Understand the collection agent's policy. Some firms do not charge a fee for collecting an account if it can be collected within ten days after a demand letter or phone call. The credit bureau in your community and Dun & Bradstreet have extensive collection resources that can be customized for your needs. Most of the major collection firms have automated collections. The collection agency should maintain a personalized and sensitive service using firmness and tact. The range of some of the automated collection services include the following:

- **On-line computerized collection system.** Automatic procedures continually monitor the account through to recovery. Some systems automatically calculate interest up to the date of collection at the rate you specify, can combine multiple debtors, produce computer-generated trust accounting, and computer-generated progress and account status reports on request.
- **Computer-to-computer.** This system has the ability to accept accounts for collection directly from your computer.
- **Account control.** This computer system tracks account progress and presents your debtor files to actual collection agents for action on a controlled basis. A paperless office means there are no misplaced files and more effective collections.
- **Automatic forwarding.** While control of your accounts is always maintained locally, claims are promptly routed through other cities in Canada, the United States, and throughout the world as your debtor changes location.
- **Customized reports.** Status reports on your accounts are system-generated automatically or available with same-day delivery.
- **Accounts receivable program.** This service combines a pre-collection service with a regular collection service. At specific intervals, for example, ten-day intervals, a collection letter printed on the collection agent's letterhead is system generated, advising your debtor to remit payment to you directly. If this approach is successful, no recovery commission is generally charged. If unsuccessful, the account is automatically placed as a consumer collection or commercial collection.

There are distinct benefits to using a credit bureau or Dun & Bradstreet. Debtors would realize that it could quickly show up on their personal or business credit record, affecting one's credit reputation and ability to borrow funds. The next time that a creditor or bank does a search, the claim would show up.

Lawyers
Depending on the amount owing and whether or not it is a trade customer, you may decide to instruct your lawyer to attempt to collect the account. The lawyer

may request a percentage of the amount collected (contingency fee) or an hourly bill-out rate. Lawyers will generally charge between 25% and 50% of the amount collected, plus any out-of-pocket disbursements (expenses). The lawyer would draw up a contract with the creditor, or confirm the arrangement in a letter of confirmation. Frequently, the legal implications of being contacted by a lawyer will persuade a customer to pay. The customer knows that litigation will result in legal fees.

Most lawyers do not take on a collection matter on a fee contingency basis. The downside risk is greater than the upside potential.

When you select a lawyer to do collection work for you, retain one who is experienced in doing litigation work as discussed as in Chapter 1 on Legal and Other Advisors.

Suing in Small Claims Court

Suing in small claims court can save the expense of using a lawyer or a collection agent. Many provinces in Canada have a ceiling up to $10,000 that can be claimed in small claims court. Small claims court is informal, and is designed for the layperson. Obtain further information on small claims courts by looking in the blue pages of your phone book under provincial courts. Free publications, sometimes available from provincial small claims court offices, set out the procedures, and you can purchase or borrow books from the library on how to conduct yourself in small claims court.

If you are suing in small claims court, or if you are having your lawyer sue in a higher level of court, it is important to understand the litigation steps. Other than small claims court, the procedures are technical and formal, and that is why you need a lawyer. For further information on the litigation process, refer to Chapter 16.

Summary

You need to be very careful when extending credit. It does not take many bad debts to occur before you have lost your profit margin for the year, if not worse. This chapter covered the types of credit and collection issues and options that you have available. For various credit and collection checklists and sample forms, refer to the book, *The Complete Canadian Small Business Guide*, 3/e, by Douglas and Diana Gray, published by McGraw-Hill Ryerson.

Twelve

Creditor Proofing
Your Business

Introduction

This chapter will raise your awareness of the proactive steps you should consider to protect your business and financial interests. You want to minimize your risks in case your business runs into difficulties. It will also give you a starting point for discussion with your legal and tax advisors. The options outlined in this chapter, if done properly and with professional advice, will give you enhanced peace of mind. This will help balance the predictable stresses and uncertainty that comes with running your own business.

What does Creditor Proofing Mean?

"Creditor proofing" refers to conducting your business affairs in such a way that legally minimizes your personal and business risk in a doomsday scenario. The term "creditor proofing" is somewhat of a misnomer, as you may not be able to totally eliminate risk, but you can minimize it substantially.

The rationale behind a defensive creditor proofing philosophy, in the context of this chapter, is very simple. You have a legitimate right and responsibility to minimize your business and personal risk exposure. As a small businessperson, you are embarking on a venture and adventure which is inherently high risk. Statistically, four out of five small business start-ups don't survive the first five years. There are many reasons for this high failure rate, both internal and external. After reading this book, following its cautions and getting the right professional advice, you should fall into the 20% of businesses that succeed beyond five years.

Starting and managing a small business is a major life commitment. It is immensely consuming, stressful and demanding of your personal and business time, especially during the start-up years, but also on an ongoing basis. There are many personal sacrifices. At the same time, you are helping to stimulate the local economy, create employment, and increase the tax revenue to the government.

You do your best in good faith in your business dealings. However, if events occur which you can't anticipate or control, you want to maintain your core sense of security. That means those things that matter most to your sense of personal well being—your partner, children, family, friends, home and a sense of financial security.

Sadly, many small business failures are avoidable. Many business failures result in personal bankruptcy and marital distress and divorce. By being focused and proactive about setting up protective strategies, you can minimize the downside personal risks.

Don't Try To Do It Yourself

Creditor proofing involves many strategic, tactical and legal issues. It would be foolish to try to accomplish these protections yourself. The paperwork has to be done correctly to be enforceable. Also, you need to know what you can and can't do and why. You want to make sure that the legal and tax decisions you make can withstand retroactive scrutiny from attack. Timing is also an important issue as you don't want to just start out your business with the appropriate protections. You want to monitor your business protections on an ongoing basis, as circumstances arise. You should have a risk assessment check-up at least once a year.

How to select the right lawyer and accountant for your needs was covered in Chapter 1, Legal and Other Advisors. You need to get information customized to your situation.

Timing is Everything

When it comes to protecting your assets, timing is essential. You don't want to be in a position where the strategic decisions you have made can be overturned by a creditor. That would defeat the whole purpose of creditor proofing. For example, a creditor could claim that you purposely moved personal or business assets around, or set up various corporate structures, to avoid paying creditors. The primary test is whether your corporation was insolvent at the time, for example, in arrears or unable to pay its creditors in a timely manner. There are particular retroactive time periods for a transaction to be challenged, overturned or reversed, for example, under federal bankruptcy and insolvency legislation, and provincial legislation relating to fraudulent conveyance of assets or fraudulent preference of creditors. As a general rule, transactions can be looked at for at least one year back. Your lawyer can give you more information.

Do a Risk Assessment

Your business risks are not static. They are always in a state of flux, as that is the nature of business and business cycles. That is why a regular check-up with your lawyer is essential, to pre-empt problems before they occur. A few conversations with your lawyer will help you develop a general sense of when you need to discuss risk issues, so that you can recognize the warning signs.

In any business, you need to do a SWOT analysis regularly—an objective and detailed analysis of the business' **S**trengths, **W**eaknesses, **O**pportunities and **T**hreats. Under the categories of potential threats, consider the impact on the business of the following. There may be no impact or it may be mild, major, serious or fatal.

- Competition enters your market area thereby eroding market share, and you don't have the resources to compete
- Lender interest rates increase, due to market changes, changed lender criteria or re-assessment of your business risk
- Difficulties with the lender or inability to get more funds; change of lending officer, resulting in a personality conflict with new lending officer
- Lender calls in or reduces the line of credit or calls the demand loan
- Location problems with office building or mall empties out resulting in reduced customer traffic, or building and general area deteriorating and becoming unattractive
- Landlord refuses to renew a lease or increases the rent dramatically on renewal
- Employee turnover problems or problem employees
- Theft or shoplifting
- Collection problems with major customers
- Sued by client or customer for breach of contract or product liability
- Insurance company denies claim for loss
- Conflict with investors
- Health, injury or disability problems
- Marital or business partnership problems
- Arrears owing to landlord and landlord threatening to send in a bailiff and locking the doors or seizing assets
- Arrears owing to lender and lender threatening to call the loan, exercise on security and seize assets
- Lender or other creditor garnishing money from company account
- Business failing due to internal management problems
- Business failing due to external problems, such as major supplier or customers' business failing
- New technologies making your business obsolete or unsustainable financially
- Client alleging breach of contract for failure to meet the quality or timeline expected
- Underestimating a fixed price contract and then running out of money before completing it
- Employee lawsuit due to claim for wrongful dismissal
- Customer claiming negligence or misrepresentation
- Motor vehicle accidents causing injury to yourself, your employees or others
- Claims for infringement of trademark or other rights of another business
- Fines by Workers Compensation for workplace injuries or non-compliance
- Fines by municipal, provincial or federal government for non-compliance with regulations

- Actions by creditors for personal guarantees you signed or collateral security you pledged
- Lawsuits by creditors, investors, clients, customers, employees, or government departments.

As you can see, there is no shortage of business risk issues to reflect on and deal with proactively and protectively.

Types of Creditors

Different categories of creditors, such as statutory creditors, secured creditors or unsecured creditors, have different legal rights in terms of claims against your business assets. Refer to Chapter 17 on Bankruptcy and Insolvency for more detail. Directors of corporations can also be exposed to personal liability. Refer to Chapter 2 on Business Structures for a discussion of directors' liability.

Statutory or Preferred Creditors

Various federal government departments such as Canada Customs and Revenue Agency (CCRA) are statutory or preferred creditors. This would include arrears of personal or business income tax owing, or employee payroll tax deductions at source or EI and CPP deductions at source, that were collected but not remitted, and GST/HST collected and owing but not remitted.

Under federal bankruptcy legislation and provincial legislation, there could be protection to employees for arrears of salary and holiday pay, up to a limit. In some situations under the federal *Bankruptcy and Insolvency Act*, landlords can have priority ahead of secured creditors for up to three months rent.

Under provincial legislation there is preferred creditor status in most situations. For example, provincial sales tax collected and owing, and claims under *Workers Compensation Act*. Also, claims for employee salary arrears up to a certain limit.

Secured Creditors

These are creditors who have secured their credit by some form of security. For example, a bank could be secured by business inventory under a section of the *Bank Act*, a lender could also have security by means of a General Security Agreement, or Specific Security Agreement, covering various specific or general assets. A lender could have a mortgage on the business property or a collateral mortgage on your home to secure a promissory note. Generally, creditors who are secured are paid off in full, in order of priority of when they filed the security. A leasing company is a secured creditor, as it keeps title to the car or equipment until it is paid for in full. A landlord could be a secured creditor for certain assets under the *Rent Distress* or *Commercial Tenancy* provincial legislation.

Refer to Chapter 8 for a discussion of other types of security that creditors could have. Also, refer to Chapter 17 on Bankruptcy and Insolvency.

Unsecured Creditors

The most common type of creditor, sometimes referred to as general creditors, this category includes any creditors that do not have security. This includes lenders who are not secured for a personal line of credit, trade creditors and suppliers. Utility companies for electricity, telephone, gas and cable would also fall under this category. The same would apply to anyone holding a court judgment, or who had a legal claim for a breach of contract.

Creditors under this category get paid only after everyone under the previous two categories are paid off in full. What is left goes into a general pool, and is paid to creditors on a pro-rata basis. That is, a percentage of their claim relative to the total amount owing to all the general creditors. Frequently, there is nothing left for general creditors in practical terms, or maybe just five cents on the dollar, after all administrative and legal expenses are paid off. That is why you want to be a secured creditor if at all possible. Conversely, you don't want to give out security if you are a debtor if you can avoid it.

Limiting Your Business Liability Exposure

There are many ways of minimizing the risks to your business. Here are the key ones to discuss with your professional advisors.

- **Separate your personal and business assets and liabilities.** Make sure you have a separate bank account set up for your business activities. Whether you are operating a part-time business out of your home, or a non-incorporated business, you want to demonstrate the separation between the business and personal aspects of your life. Have separate cheques and records. You don't want to cause confusion with your creditors.

- **Incorporate your business before you start.** The problem with a partnership and proprietorship type of business that, in law, you and your business are deemed to be one and the same. This means a creditor can go after your personal assets. This is high risk, as all your personal assets could be seized and sold if there was a judgment against you.

  The alternative is to incorporate your business. As discussed in Chapter 2, in law you and your incorporated business are deemed to be separate legal entities. For maximum protection, incorporate before you start your business, as the potential risk starts the moment you provide the service or sell the product. Some accountants tell clients that they don't need to incorporate for tax reasons until a certain profit level is earned. However, the compelling legal reasons for incorporation at the outset is more critical than tax considerations in most cases.

  To get the maximum protection from your corporation, always sign all documents in the corporate name, as an "authorized signatory."

- **Never have oral agreements.** Always make sure all your business dealings are clear and put into writing to eliminate the risk of uncertainty. For example, if you died or were incapacitated, how would anyone know what the deal was otherwise? Over time, people can innocently and honestly forget the details. Others could exploit the lack of paperwork for their own interests. If a lawsuit occurred, it is almost impossible to reconstruct and prove the facts, when there are differing and sometimes self-serving recollections of the bargain. This type of uncertainty puts your business in jeopardy; it also wastes a lot of time, energy and money.

■ **Limit the liability in your contracts.** You can include in your contracts that your potential liability is limited to the amount that you received under your contract, or a fixed amount, e.g. $5,000. Don't be exposed to open-ended liability for client financial damages or losses.

■ **Obtain adequate insurance protection.** Refer to Chapter 9 on Insurance for a discussion of the various types of insurance to consider as part of your risk assessment.

■ **Have a tight credit and collection policy.** Refer to Chapter 11 on Credit and Collections. A few bad debts could wipe out your profit for the year. This could mean that you expended your time and life energy for free. A sloppy credit and collection approach could result in the death of your business.

■ **Be careful about pledging corporate security.** Don't pledge any of your corporate assets to a creditor without first discussing the matter with your legal and tax advisors. You want to know the implications and alternatives. Also, your lawyer might negotiate a better deal for you in certain situations.

■ **Make sure you have a shareholder's agreement with buy-sell clause.** If you go into business with other partners, make sure you have a shareholder's agreement at the outset—during the honeymoon phase of your relationship and before reality sets in. See Chapter 2 for more information on including a buy-sell clause. This deals with the formula for you to get out of the business relationship, or to get your partner out.

■ **Utilize a holding company to protect business profit.** This strategy involves setting up a separate corporation that holds the shares of your active corporation business, hence called a holding company. When your active business makes extra money over its needs, it can declare dividends from time to time. This money will go to the holding company, as it holds 100% of the shares of the active business. If your active business was ever sued, the money is protected in the holding company, assuming the appropriate legal steps were taken. The holding company could lend money back to the active company in exchange for security on assets or other tangible security, just like any secured creditor. You could own 100% of the shares of the holding company, which in turn owns 100% of the shares of the active company. The purpose of this exercise is to insulate each company from the other.

■ **Utilize a sister corporation to own and lease assets.** Utilizing a sister corporation involves incorporating a third company that buys all the necessary equipment, furniture, etc. that your active company needs. This company then leases the assets to your active company. In this scenario, your active company would not have any tangible assets of worth, as all the key assets are leased. Your leasing company could have obtained a loan from the holding company that was secured by the assets. If your active company were sued, the creditor would not be able to seize any assets. The holding company and leasing company are separate entities in law, and are not owned by the active company, even if you personally are the sole shareholder of both. Also, the creditor does not have any legal contractual relationship or rights relative to those other companies.

- **Make sure you have a will.** If you die and have a will, the shares in your company will become an asset of your estate. If your spouse is the beneficiary of your estate, then he or she takes over the shares and the company. This should facilitate a smooth transition. If you have partners, you want the shareholder's agreement to deal with what happens to the deceased's shares on death—who gets them and when and how. Estate planning to protect your business investment is discussed later in this chapter and also in Chapter 14.

Limiting Your Personal Liability Exposure

In addition to protecting the company from creditors, you also want to protect yourself and your family. Here are some techniques to discuss with your lawyer.

Protecting the Family Assets

Jane had always wanted to operate her own construction business. She owned a house, had three children and wanted to protect her hard-earned assets from business risk. After getting advice from a business lawyer and tax accountant, she decided to structure her business in a strategic way before she started. She transferred her home over to her husband's name, who was not involved in the business or any business, incorporated the company and acted as the sole director and officer of the company. *The Family Relations Act* in her province would have deemed the family home as a 50/50 asset regardless of whose name it was in, in the event of a divorce. Whatever happened to the business, she did not want to put the family home or assets at risk. She had a firm policy of never signing any personal guarantees for the company, or pledging her family assets, thereby insulating herself personally from exposure. As part of her strategic estate planning, she updated her will, and ensured that her insurance policies and RRSPs were left to designated beneficiaries. Nearly all her money would thereby bypass her estate, leaving very little for any potential creditors.

- **Don't sign or limit personal guarantees.** There is no point in going to the effort of incorporating a company, if you nullify the personal protection by signing a personal guarantee of the corporate debts. Don't sign personal guarantees at all, for example, to suppliers, trade creditors, landlords, etc. Alternatively, only do so for a bank if absolutely necessary, and then limit the amount of liability. For example, if the company is borrowing $45,000, and there are three partners, agree to be liable for a maximum of one-third only. Get legal advice before you sign any personal guarantee to a lender. Remember that the marketplace is very competitive. Use that knowledge as leverage when paying one creditor over another.

- **Don't pledge personal security.** Adopt a policy of not pledging any personal security, for example your personal car, house or life insurance policy, under any circumstances.

- **Transfer property and other assets to your spouse.** You can transfer the ownership of your home and other personal assets, such as your car, to your spouse. That way, the assets are not in your personal name. In the event of a marital break-up, the matrimonial home is deemed to be owned 50/50 in most situations anyway. Also, under the family relations legislation of most provinces, family assets are combined for calculation purposes and then divided in half. Speak to your lawyer about the laws in your province.

- **Be aware of director liability.** If you are a director of a corporation, you do have liability risk particularly under government legislation. Refer to Chapter 2, Business Structures, for a more detailed discussion. Therefore, if you are a director, consider not owning any personal assets of consequence, to limit the potential risk.

- **Don't have spouse as guarantor or director.** To limit the family's risk, you don't want to ask your spouse to act as a director or guarantor.

- **Don't have joint accounts.** If you have a joint account, and a creditor garnishees your bank account, they will seize all the funds in that account. By having separate accounts, you separate that risk.

- **Consider spousal RRSPs.** If your spouse is earning less than you are, you may wish to contribute to his or her RRSP, as a spousal RRSP. You get the RRSP tax deduction, but your spouse gets the money in his or her RRSP account. Therefore, if a creditor tries to collect on your RRSP with a court judgment, there will be less money available. If an RRSP is collapsed to pay the creditor, there will only be the amount left after federal tax is taken off the RRSP amount. This fact gives room for your lawyer to negotiate with the creditor for some creative compromise settlement—for example, a maximum of 50 cents on the dollar, with flexible payment terms over time, interest-free. Your lawyer can negotiate on your behalf if you are too emotionally involved. Also, your business lawyer will have experience negotiating and have more credibility in the eyes of the creditor.

- **Consider RRSPs with insurance companies.** If you have an RRSP, RRIF or non-registered investments with an insurance company, under certain circumstances, creditors are not able to collect on the RRSP. Check with your financial and tax advisor.

- **Sign business documents as authorized signatory of corporation.** In order to get the full protection of your corporation, always make it clear that you are signing on behalf of your corporation. That way, no one can try to claim that you were signing in your personal capacity.
- **Consider allocating CPP primarily in spouse's name.** Another income splitting option, which also has the effect of putting more money in your spouse's hands, is to apportion a certain percentage of your CPP to go into your spouse's name. You are entitled to start taking out your CPP at age 60, at a reduced amount. This approach means that there is less money available for creditors from your personal income. Get tax advice on the appropriateness of this option.
- **Lend money to your corporation and become a secured creditor.** You could lend money as a creditor to the company and take back security, like any other creditor could. This could be in the form of a General Security Agreement, Specific Security Agreement, Assignment of Receivables, mortgage on the business property, etc.

  If your company wants to borrow money from a lender, and the lender does not want to be secured behind your security, then you can subordinate or postpone your claim to that of the other secured creditor. However, your security document remains registered. In addition, you can also have umbrella security from the company that covers you for any future loans that you give the company, under the same security document that you have registered. You don't need to keep registering security each time you advance a loan.
- **Consider a personal management company for services.** Rather than drawing a salary as an employee of your own company, you may wish to have a management consulting agreement with your own company as an independent contractor. You might consider a separate corporation as your personal management corporation. There are various tax and other considerations for this approach.
- **Make sure you have a will.** The legal and financial nightmare your family will have to deal with if you don't have a will, will not be the type of legacy you want to be remembered for. Refer to the next section and Chapter 14 on Estate Planning.

Limiting Your Estate Liability Exposure

What if you are still running your business when you die? The business could cease to function, as you are the key person. The business goes under, and creditors start looking for assets. If you are liable under a personal guarantee or as a director, then the creditors could claim from your estate.

Here are some options to discuss with your professional advisors to minimize the risk to your estate.

- **Make sure you have a will.** A current will that has been drafted with your lawyer and accountant is the first step. Refer to Chapter 14 on Estate Planning.

- **Make sure you have a shareholder's agreement with buy-sell clause.** The need for this protection was covered earlier in this chapter.
- **Designate beneficiaries of your insurance policies.** By designating beneficiaries in your insurance policies, the money bypasses the will completely and is therefore not part of your estate. It goes directly to your designated beneficiaries tax-free. Your personal creditors can only claim from assets in your estate.
- **Designate beneficiaries for your RRSPs and RRIFs.** By designating a beneficiary for registered retirement plans, you bypass your will and your estate. The money goes directly to the beneficiary and is unavailable to creditors. You can also designate beneficiaries for your non-registered investments.
- **Consider the use of trusts.** If you set up a *living trust* while you are alive; it bypasses your will and therefore your estate, on your death. A *testamentary trust* is set up through your will, and takes effect after your death. Both types divert assets out of your estate, away from creditors of your estate.

Keeping Peace in the Family

In a worst case scenario and your business goes under, ensure that your relationships with your friends, family and relatives survive the business ordeal through the following suggestions.

- **Secure loans from family and friends.** If you borrow money from friends and family, consider securing them with security such as a mortgage or General Security Agreement or Specific Security Agreement. That way they are a secured creditor like any secured creditor.
- **Consider loans plus equity.** You could structure your loans from family and friends to include an equity (share) feature as a value-added incentive.
- **Consider a convertible option from loans to equity.** You could give an option to your family or friends who are loaning money, to be able to convert those loans in part or in full to share equity if they wanted to do so later. That is, after the company has proven itself to be viable.
- **Don't ask family or friends to sign personal guarantees or co-sign.** If you ask family, friends or your spouse to act as a guarantor, or to co-sign a loan, and the loan is called, you will regret it. The relationship may not survive the financial loss, depending on the amount and related circumstances.
- **Don't ask family or friends to act as director.** Being a director carries a lot of potential liability to a lot of different categories of creditors. Depending on the business, the risk could be very high. Directors don't generally consider being sued personally and having all their personal assets at risk. That process does not engender the continuation of a meaningful relationship.
- **Don't ask spouse to consent to collateral mortgage.** Don't ask your spouse to agree to a collateral mortgage on your house, no matter how immune you think you might be to the statistical reality of business failure. Ask yourself how the quality of your marital relationship will be affected in a business downside situation, and the bank starts action to foreclose on the house?

- **Don't assign life insurance proceeds.** If you assign your life insurance proceeds to secure a loan and you die, your creditor could get all the money, leaving nothing for your family. If a creditor insists on insurance and you have tried all alternatives, most banks will offer special loan insurance. A monthly insurance premium is added to your loan, and if you die, the loan is paid off in full.

Document Everything

You want to make sure that you have all the documentation necessary to protect your strategic plans, in a timely manner. Your legal and tax advisors can assist you in ensuring that all the paperwork is in order. Never rely on verbal deals or assurances.

Summary

This chapter covered a range of options to explore with your professional advisors. It also demonstrated the complexity involved in the total strategic and protective picture. You need this knowledge to make the right business decisions and to plan proactively. Timing is everything. Work in an integrated way with your experienced legal and tax advisors. Don't consider any of the options in isolation; they need to be considered in context.

Thirteen

Tax Planning

Introduction

Proper tax planning is critically important to the entrepreneur. In addition to personal taxes, the taxation of the business and treatment of the relationship between the owner and the business must be thoroughly considered. Tax laws and regulations are increasingly complex and constantly changing, making it difficult for the small business owner to keep current, let alone understand the relevant tax laws. In addition, you need to integrate your tax and estate planning, covered in the next chapter.

Taxation and record-keeping are closely related. If Canada Customs and Revenue Agency (CCRA), formerly Revenue Canada, requires an audit, you will need to produce thorough records for review. Obtain the services of a professionally qualified accountant from the outset, and throughout the life of the business. Make sure your advisor has special expertise on the subject of small business taxation if you are going to rely on that advice. Refer to Chapter 1 on Legal and Other Advisors.

Tax Effects on Different Legal Structures

If you are the sole proprietor of your business, your salary (if included as an expense) and the profits that you earn in your business constitute your personal income and are taxable as such in that taxation year. When you file your personal income tax return, you have to complete the Statement of Income and Expenses, obtained on request from CCRA. It outlines the basic sources of income and type of expenses and allowances.

If your business is a partnership, all partners are taxed on their salaries and their share of the profits, whether withdrawn or not. The same Statement of Income and Expenses form is used for a partnership, although you must also provide the percentage share of profit or loss that is being declared.

A corporation files a corporate tax return, which is separate and distinct from the individuals involved in the company. It is therefore not filed with the personal income tax return, as with a proprietorship or partnership.

A corporation in Canada is entitled to a small business tax deduction, assuming various conditions are met, such as generating an active business income. This deduction, which is approximately one-half the regular tax rate, is designed to help Canadian-controlled private companies accumulate capital for business expansion. Many provinces also allow a provincial tax rate reduction as well as other incentives. An active business, as the name implies, is one in which people are actively generating income, rather than passively receiving income.

Tax Planning Strategies

There are many ways of reducing, eliminating or delaying tax on your business income. Discuss these strategies with your accountant.

$500,000 Lifetime Capital Gains Exemption

The *Income Tax Act* provides a special "exemption" of up to $500,000 of the capital gain arising on the disposition of shares of a "small business corporation." (This exemption is reduced to $400,000 for anyone who took advantage of a different $100,000 lifetime capital gains exemption that was eliminated in 1994.)

In order to qualify for the exemption, your business must carry on an "active business" primarily in Canada. Furthermore, at least 90% of the assets of the company must be used in the active business. This active business test means that investment holding companies generally do not qualify.

The ability of a person to utilize the $500,000 exemption is limited where the person has a "cumulative net investment loss" as a result of claiming tax shelter deductions or certain investment expenses in earlier years' tax returns.

Speak to your tax advisor to see how you may be able to utilize the capital gains exemption. For example, there are ways of "locking-in" or "crystallizing" your capital gain, prior to actually selling the business.

Estate Freezing

Estate freezing is a tax planning strategy that "freezes" the value of a person's ownership interest in a private company. Usually, this is done to limit the future, presumably higher, capital gains tax that will be imposed on the death of the individual, to the tax that relates to today's value of the business.

Typically, a freeze involves the current owner of the business exchanging his or her common shares for special preferred shares that are redeemable, and have a fixed redemption amount. Such a share exchange qualifies as a rollover for Canadian tax purposes, thereby avoiding any immediate capital gains tax. However, tax is deferred, not eliminated. Any unrealized capital gain that is currently reflected in the owner's common shares (e.g., the excess of the current *fair market value* over the *adjusted cost base* for the shares) is merely shifted to the new preferred shares. They are *freeze* shares because they cannot go up in value beyond the fixed redemption amount.

When a freeze is carried out, it is customary for new common shares of the business to be issued to the chosen successor(s). Sometimes, a discretionary family trust is utilized, if the business owner has not yet made up his or her mind as to which child or children should take over the business. Under the new share ownership structure, the future growth in the value of the business will accrue to the benefit of the common shareholders (e.g., the children). This could occur through direct ownership of the common shares, or by virtue of them being named as beneficiaries of a trust that owns the common shares. In either case, when the current owner dies, only the shares that were frozen will attract capital gains tax in his or her final income tax return.

This strategy assumes that the new common shareholder, e.g. the child, will outlive the parent. However, sometimes estate freezes backfire because the child who acquired the growth shares under the estate freeze dies before the parent who froze the shares in the first place. Capital gains tax then becomes payable on the child's common shares of the business (assuming they have gone up in value since the freeze).

Utilizing the Spousal Rollover

One way to postpone capital gains tax on your death would be to leave your shares in the family business either outright, or in trust for your spouse. If you die before your spouse, no capital gains tax on your shares of the business would arise on your death. Instead, capital gains tax would be postponed or rolled over until the death of your spouse, or until the business is sold.

Family Farming Business

Farming businesses are afforded different and far more generous tax treatment. For example:

- If property that is used in an active farming business (e.g. the land) is transferred to a spouse, child, grandchild, or great-grandchild of the business owner, the transfer is generally considered to take place at "cost," not *fair market value*. Thus, no capital gain has to be reported.
- Farming businesses are also eligible for a $500,000 lifetime capital gains exemption, similar to the one for "small business corporations." This exemption will save capital gains tax if the family farm business is being sold to a non-family member, and the above-mentioned "intergenerational exemption" does not apply.

How to Pay Yourself

With smart tax advice, you can take money out of your business in a mix of different ways to minimize or delay the tax hit. Here are some common techniques:

- **Salary.** If you take a salary, you are taxed based on a graduated marginal tax rate. Depending on your income, this could have a considerable tax impact, not necessarily in your best interests.

- **Dividends.** In this example, you would receive money when your corporation declares dividends, at any time throughout the year that your accountant feels is advantageous to you. You are taxed at a lower rate for dividend income than salaried income.
- **Draws.** In this example, your accountant shows a draw at the end of the year, which has to be taken out within six months of the company's fiscal year-end. However, you don't need to declare the drawn amount until the following tax year, effectively deferring tax for a year.
- **Capital gains.** The value of your shares at the outset of your business operation and at the time of sale determines the capital gains. You are taxed on 50% of the gain. There is currently an exemption for this gain, up to a ceiling of $500,000 as mentioned earlier. You would not be receiving this tax-free financial benefit until you sell the business. Ask your accountant about the benefits of "crystallizing" your capital gain before a sale of your business.
- **Holding company.** You could hold the shares in your corporation through a personal holding company. When dividends are declared, the money goes to your personal management company, rather than to you personally. In effect, your holding company is like a bank. You can take out whatever you want, depending on your needs and optimal tax timing. It also is a technique for protecting company assets from creditors. Refer to Chapter 12 on creditor proofing your business.
- **Management contract.** You could incorporate a company and have an exclusive contract to manage your operating company. That way, your management company is a revenue buffer because business income is taxed at a more favourable rate. You can take out the money from your company as your needs dictate and when it is advantageous from a tax standpoint.
- **Paying family members.** Employing family members to help you in the business is a classic way of income splitting. As the marginal tax rate for each person is lower than if all the money were paid to one person, there are aggregate tax savings.

Expenses

An expense is tax-deductible if its purpose is to earn income; it is not of a capital nature; and it is reasonable in the circumstances. A capital expense means an asset that is depreciated over a period of time according to the Capital Cost Allowance (CCA) class interest deduction. The allowance must not exceed the maximum rate allowable in any year. The percentages range from 5% to 100% depreciation in a year. Obtain a copy of these CCA categories from CCRA upon request.

Your accountant will advise you as to which categories of expenses are deductible in your particular business and which are not. Also, if some of the expenses are related to personal use, you are supposed to deduct that portion from the business expense. Reasonable remuneration paid to spouses for service rendered to the business is also deductible. The Statement of Income and Expenses form from CCRA outlines some of the expenses to consider. Your accountant may suggest other expenses that you could be eligible for.

Tips on Maximizing Write-offs

It's not what you make, but what you keep—after taxes. While some business expenses are fully deductible that same year, others have to depreciate over time. CCRA allows you to go back three years and carry forward up to seven years any legitimate business expenses you incur. You then offset those expenses against income. Get in the habit of keeping receipts for everything. Your accountant can advise you later as to what expenses can be used and in what portion or fashion, depending on changing tax laws. In addition to obvious expenses such as supplies, rent or lease payments, or bad debts, review the following key areas to make sure you are getting the maximum benefit:

- **Home/apartment.** If you operate from your home, CCRA states that the area designated as your "business location" must be used exclusively and regularly for business-related purposes. This can include a work area, an office area and storage space. If you do have clients coming to your home, claim a separate reception area and washrooms for business use, if that is the case, or else a portion of "common area" (personal and business) usage for business purposes.

  To calculate the percentage of home-office use, divide the total house or apartment square footage by the overall square footage used for business-related purposes, or calculate the number of rooms used of the total rooms in the house—whatever formula works to your advantage. Don't forget to also take a portion of the "common area" used for business purposes (e.g., the hallway and stairs). Also, don't forget to include any remodelling and decorating costs involved in converting a room. These improvements are considered allowable expenses.

  In addition, you can claim a portion of all the house-related expenses for your home-office use: mortgage interest and property taxes—or rent—plus insurance, maintenance costs, and utilities (electricity, water, heating, and telephone). If your total house expenses are $25,000 per year for all of the above, for example, and 25% of the square footage of your house relates to your home office, the deductible expense against business income would be $6,250 per year.

- **Car.** If you have one car and use it 50% of the time for business, claim half of all your car-related expenses (e.g., gas, oil, maintenance, insurance and interest on car financing costs) as business expenses. Maintain a mileage logbook to support your business usage claim. For a jointly used car (personal and business), you may consider charging a per-kilometre charge instead. If you have two cars and use one exclusively for business, you can claim 100% of that car's expenses. Be sure to claim depreciation of 30% on your car and deduct the appropriate portion each year from income. If you lease your car, the maximum write-off is $800 per month. Whatever price you pay for your leased car, the maximum CCA value is $30,000.

- **Furniture and equipment.** Your office furniture, computer hardware, printer, software and other equipment have to be depreciated over time, using the capital cost allowance formula, which allows for a portion (from 20% to 100% per year) to be deducted each year.

- **Salaries.** Salaries paid to your children, spouse, relatives or others to perform work for your company are also deductible business expenses. However, the amount you pay them should be reasonable in the circumstances.

- **Entertainment.** Entertaining existing or potential customers/clients for promotion or prospecting purposes is another deductible expense. You can claim as an expense 50% of the cost of the entertainment, including tips and taxes.

- **Education.** Your professional or business education, such as books, seminars, conventions or conferences, provides other opportunities to claim deductions against your business income.

- **Trade shows.** Any expenses relating to trade shows that you attend for your business purposes are deductible. To find out about upcoming trade shows or conventions, check with your chamber of commerce or government small business centres.

- **Travel.** If you travel for business-related purposes, you can write off all or a portion of expenses such as airfare, transportation, car rental, hotel and a portion (50%) of your meal costs.

Remember to obtain tax advice prior to starting your business and on an ongoing basis from a Chartered Accountant or Certified General Accountant. Advice customized to your specific circumstances is essential. The rule of three—that is, having an initial consultation with at least three accountants before selecting your advisor—is important. In most cases, the initial consultation is free. Ask in advance before making an appointment. Put your questions in writing so you don't forget. Ask about incoming splitting, fiscal year-end, business structure options and ways of maximizing deductions and minimizing taxes.

Don't Lose out on the Advantages of a Home Office

Mary had always wanted to be her own boss. At the age of 50, she accepted an attractive early retirement package from her employer. Mary considered various small businesses, but finally decided to start an interior design business out of her home. She worked very hard and made good money, but she was frustrated at having to pay the taxes she did. Mary had not obtained any tax planning advice, and was not taking off all her home office and business-related expenses.

Had Mary obtained professional tax advice at the outset, she could have netted a lot more "take home" after-tax income. She may still be able to claim some or all of the expenses that she missed, as the Canadian Customs and Revenue Agency allows you to send in an amended return. In addition, you can carry forward losses up to seven years in the future. Legitimate home office expenses include a percentage of the house expenses relating to home office use, for example, insurance, property taxes, utilities, mortgage interest and maintenance. If the home expenses were $30,000 in total and 20% of the home square footage was used as an office, the deduction would be $6,000 from business income.

Goods and Services Tax

The GST, which is administered by CCRA, came into being on January 1, 1991. Its purpose was to replace the 13.5% sales tax on manufactured goods with a 7% goods and services tax. You are not obligated to apply for a GST registration number if your gross sales do not exceed $30,000 a year. However, if you are paying out GST on your purchases and want to get a portion of it back, you need to register. The basic premise is that there is an input tax credit for GST you paid that you can offset against GST you collect. You either remit the difference if you owe money to CCRA or request money from CCRA if there is an overage of money owing to you. For further information, contact your local CCRA office (blue pages of your phone book) and obtain their current publications for small business and the GST.

HST means harmonized sales tax. Some provinces combine their tax with the federal government's so that only one tax is charged. The parties involved then split the collected tax based on an agreed formula.

What is a Business Number (BN)?

The BN is a numbering system that simplifies the way businesses deal with government—one business, one number. The BN includes the four major business categories of dealing with CCRA—corporate income tax, import/export, payroll deductions, and goods and services tax/harmonized sales tax (GST/HST). You can register for a BN by contacting CCRA by phone, mail or fax.

Each sole proprietor, partnership or corporation will get one BN. Sole proprietors will get one BN for all their businesses. If you change the legal basis under which you carry on a business, e.g., your unincorporated business becomes a corporation, or your corporation merges with another to form a new corporation, you will need a new BN.

If you are a sole proprietor or a partner in a partnership, you will continue to use your SIN to file your individual income tax return, even though you may have a BN for your GST/HST, payroll deductions and import/export accounts.

Who has to Register?

There are two important factors to consider when determining whether to register for and charge GST/HST:

1. The nature of the goods and services you will sell or otherwise provide
2. Whether your annual world-wide GST/HST taxable sales, including those of any associates, are more than $30,000 in the immediate preceding four consecutive calendar quarters or in a single calendar year (alternatively, you may project that your future income will exceed this figure, if you are just starting out).

For further information, contact your professional accountant or CCRA.

Tax Avoidance and Evasion

CCRA does not object to a taxpayer openly arranging financial affairs within the framework of the law so as to keep taxes to a minimum. There is a distinction, however, between legitimate tax planning and tax evasion. When attempting to reduce taxes, be certain to obtain professional tax advice to ensure that your approach is within the bounds of legitimate tax planning. If a taxpayer deliberately conceals income or attempts to evade the payment of taxes by misrepresentation, conspiracy, or some other means, this will be deemed to be an offence and is liable to criminal prosecution. This will result in severe penalties—heavy fines and in some cases jail sentences. In a proprietorship or partnership, you would be personally liable; in a corporation, the directors and officers of the corporation could be deemed liable.

Why Record-keeping is Necessary

Records must be kept in any type of business regardless of how small your small business is. Business records are continually generated and include bank deposit books, delivery slips, invoices, receipts, sales slips, contracts, and numerous other documents. It is critically important that systems be developed for recording and filing the various records in order that they can be retrieved efficiently.

Many business owners use computer software programs for maintaining many financial records, rather than using a manual system approach. Check with your accountant and software retailer for recommended small business software. In Canada, the most popular small business software is MYOB, Simply Accounting and Quickbooks.

Examples of typical financial records include:
- Sales journal
- Cash receipts journal
- Accounts receivable ledger
- Accounts payable journal
- Cash disbursements journal
- Credit purchases journal
- Credit sales journal
- Payroll journal
- General synoptic ledger.

Some of the non-financial records include those relating to personnel, equipment, inventory and production. Many federal, provincial and municipal government departments and agencies have set rules and regulations relating to the keeping of records for a small business. For example, Statistics Canada requires that information be supplied upon request. CCRA requires the payment of income tax by the business, as well as deductions at source, by the business, of employee taxes and contributions to Employment Insurance and Canada Pension Plan. GST documentation has to be kept. More detail on employee records and government requirements is covered in Chapter 10 on Hiring Staff.

Some other external reasons for keeping records are as follows:

- Raising financing and attracting potential investors
- Selling a business
- Creditor and supplier requirements
- Insurance company requirements for a loss claim.

Internal reasons for maintaining records include:

- Keeping you better informed about the financial position of your business
- Making it easier to complete accurate income tax returns with supporting receipts for expenses
- Eliminating most of the problems that might be encountered if tax returns are audited
- Providing the basis for evaluating the condition and effectiveness of equipment
- Reminding you when creditor obligations are due
- Demonstrating good management skills and effective time management
- Providing an opportunity for comparing budget goals with historical records and future projections
- Permitting an accurate basis for ratio analysis in comparison with industry averages
- Providing the basis for preparation of financial statements and other documents required to obtain credit or financing.

The *Income Tax Act* requires that you keep your records in an orderly manner at your place of business or your residence, as this material may be requested at any time by CCRA for review or audit purposes. You are required to maintain business records and supporting documents for at least seven years from the end of the last taxation year to which they relate. If you filed your return late for any year, records and supporting documents must be kept for seven years from the date you filed that return. The following books and records, or computerized version of them may not be destroyed for two years from the day an incorporated business is dissolved, and six years from the last day of the related taxation year in the case of the termination of an unincorporated business:

- General and private ledger sheets
- Special contracts and agreements

- General journal, if essential for understanding the general ledger entries
- All corporate minute-book records.

Other books and records must be kept for seven years unless CCRA grants permission to destroy them earlier. This would apply to:
- Original books of entry such as cash, purchase and sales books or journals (except the general journal), inventory and production records, and payroll and distribution sheets
- Sales invoices, statements, purchase and expense vouchers
- Payroll time and rate cards.

Many people prefer the convenience of e-filing their tax returns. This is a very easy method and saves you sending in attached documents, unless they are subsequently requested.

Summary

This chapter discussed basic tax considerations and tax strategies. Tax laws are constantly changing so you need to rely on current and accurate information. Customized feedback from a professional accountant can maximize your take home income and minimize your tax payable.

Fourteen

Understanding
Estate Planning

Introduction

Your will is the most important document you will ever sign. With very few exceptions, everybody should have a will. As a business owner, a will is the only legal document that can ensure that your assets will be distributed to your beneficiaries, instead of by a government formula, in a timely manner and with effective estate planning. Your will takes effect only after your death and is strictly confidential until that time.

There are no estate taxes or succession duties in Canada, but estate planning can minimize the amount that is taxed in other ways. Part of estate planning also includes having a power of attorney and possibly a living will. For a more detailed discussion of estate and tax planning, refer to the book, *The Canadian Guide to Will and Estate Planning*, by Douglas Gray and John Budd, published by McGraw-Hill Ryerson.

Why You Need a Will

It is estimated that only one out of three adults has a will, which means that when the other two-thirds die, the government has to become involved. Some people just procrastinate by nature or have busy lives and simply never make getting a will done a priority. Others do not appreciate the full implications of dying without a will or even think about it. And some people simply resist the reality that they are mortal. Preparing a will and dealing with estate planning issues certainly faces the issue of mortality in a direct way.

Of those that do have a will, many do not modify it based on changing circumstances. People first think of their will when they marry, have children, the first time they fly without their children, or upon news of the sudden death of a friend or relative. Once completed, they forget about it. Not updating your will can be as bad as not having one and could cause the beneficiaries a lot of grief, stress, time and expense. Your marital status may have changed, assets increased or decreased, or you may have started or wound-up a business, moved to a new province, or a new government tax or other legislation could be introduced which should prompt you to revisit your estate plan. Other people do their own will, and make serious mistakes.

What is Estate Planning?

Estate planning refers to the process of preserving and transferring your wealth in an effective manner. From a tax perspective, your estate objectives including a properly drafted will include:

- Minimizing and deferring taxes
- Moving any tax burden to your heirs to be paid only upon future sale of the assets.

There are various techniques to attain the above objectives, including:

- Arranging for assets to be transferred to family members in a lower tax bracket
- Establishing trusts for your children and/or spouse
- Setting up estate freezes, generally for your children, which reduce the future tax they pay on assets of increased value
- Making optimal use of the benefit of charitable donations, tax shelters, holding companies or dividend tax credits
- Taking advantage of gifting during your lifetime
- Minimizing the risk of business creditors encroaching on personal estate assets
- Having sufficient insurance to cover anticipated tax on death
- Avoiding probate fees by having assets in joint names or with a designated beneficiary.

What's in a Will?

Depending on the complexity of your estate, your will could either be simple or complex. A basic will contains:

- Name and address of person making the will (the testator)
- A declaration that the document is their last will and testament and it revokes all former wills and codicils (a supplementary document which may change, add or subtract from the original will)
- Appointment of an executor (person or an organization who will administer your estate) and possibly a trustee (required where you have included trust provisions in your will)
- Authorization to pay outstanding debts including funeral expenses, taxes, fees and other administrative expenses before any gift of property can be made
- Disposition of property and cash legacies to beneficiaries, or a gift of part or the entire residue of your estate (what is left after all debts, funeral and administrative expenses, taxes and fees have been paid and specific property gifts and cash legacies distributed)

- Attestation clause which states that the will was properly signed in the presence of at least two witnesses who were both present at the same time, and who both signed in your presence and the presence of each other.
- Appointment of a guardian for infant children.

Special Provisions

Consult a lawyer who specializes in wills and estates to assist you in identifying and preparing special provisions for your situation. A few of the many special provisions include:

- **Alternate beneficiaries and 30-day survivorship clause.** Where spouses die together or within a very short time of each other, if they have wills leaving everything to each other without naming alternate beneficiaries, the situation is similar to not having a will at all. Although uncommon, you still should provide for the possibility that your spouse may not be able to benefit from the estate. A 30-day clause provides that in order for your beneficiaries to benefit from your estate, they have to survive you by 30 days. If it is impossible to determine who of a married couple died first, it is presumed that the younger spouse survived the older spouse.
- **Trusts.** If you want to give someone a gift but do not want him or her to have direct control of the property, you can set up a trust provision in your will to manage the gift. Trusts are discussed in more detail later.

Funeral Instructions

Some people detail in their will their instructions regarding funeral arrangements and the disposition of the body. These instructions are not legally binding on the executor, for various legal reasons. Inform your executor and immediate family of your funeral arrangement wishes. Your will is generally not located and read until after the funeral has already occurred. Your comments in the will should simply reinforce what you have stated verbally.

What Happens if there is No Will?

If you don't have a will, or don't have a valid will, the outcome could be a legal and financial nightmare and emotionally devastating ordeal for your loved ones. This is compounded greatly if you have a business. Not having a will at the time of death is called being intestate. Under provincial legislation, the court will appoint an administrator. If no family member applies to act as administrator, the public trustee or official administrator is appointed. Your estate will be distributed in accordance with the legal formulas of your province, which are inflexible and may not reflect either your personal wishes or the needs of your family or loved ones.

While the law attempts to be fair, it does not provide for special needs. A home or other assets could be sold under unfavourable market conditions in order to distribute the assets. Your heirs may pay taxes that might easily have been deferred or reduced. There may not be sufficient worth in the estate to pay the taxes. Your family could be left without money for an extended period, and your assets may be lost or destroyed. There may be a delay in the administration of your estate and added costs such as an administrator bond (similar to an insurance policy if the administrator makes a mistake).

If you die without a will appointing a guardian for your young children, and there is no surviving parent who has legal custody, provincial laws come into effect. The public trustee becomes the guardian and manager of the assets that your children are entitled to. The provincial child welfare services assume their care, upbringing, education and health. A relative or other person can apply to the court for guardianship but it is up to the court's discretion.

If you have minor children and are separated, divorced or living common-law, dying intestate can result in a bitter legal custody battle. A guardian could be appointed who you personally would not have approved. The whole experience could be unpleasant, costly, protracted and traumatizing to the children.

Is Your Will Valid in the US for US Assets?

In general terms, if you have a valid will that is legally enforceable in your province, it would probably also be valid in the US state that you have assets. Possibly you own recreational property or are thinking of buying property in the US for business purposes.

There could be a serious problem if you have two wills, one Canadian, one American. Because they are different legal jurisdictions, there could be a challenge about the contents of the will by a beneficiary (or someone who would like to be one), in one will jurisdiction but not in the other one. Standard boilerplate will clauses often state that the most recent will automatically revokes any and all previous wills. If you inadvertently included that clause in a US will, it could automatically nullify your Canadian will!

You could instruct your Canadian lawyer to include specific terms in your Canadian will relating to your US assets and have affidavit attestation of the witnesses of your will at the same time. All this must be done in conjunction with feedback from a US lawyer expert in will matters in the state that you own assets. Another option is to have a US lawyer transfer your US assets into joint names, with right of survivorship, so that those assets would automatically go to your surviving spouse. Consider having your US property in a living trust or revocable trust. This bypasses your estate, and therefore probate procedures, as the trust is not in the deceased's name, but a trustee's name. Your lawyer will help you assess the options in your situation.

Preparing a Will

There are basically three ways to prepare a will: writing it yourself, having a lawyer do it for you, or having a trust company arrange a lawyer to do it for you. The advantages and disadvantages of each are outlined following:

1. Self-written Wills

This is the poorest choice, because the inadequacies of a self-written will could result in a legal, financial and administrative nightmare for your family, relatives and beneficiaries. How you expressed your wishes may be legally interpreted differently than what you intended. Worse still, a clause or the whole will could be deemed void for technical reasons. Some people draft a will from scratch or use a "standard form" of will format purchased in book or stationery stores. The risk is very high and it is false economy as depending on your situation, you could have a lot to lose.

2. Lawyer-prepared Wills

In almost all cases, wills should be prepared by a lawyer familiar with wills because he or she is qualified to provide legal advice and is knowledgeable on how to complete the legal work.

Depending on the complexity of the estate however, you may also need to enlist the expertise of the other specialists, including a professionally qualified tax accountant or a financial planner. Refer to Chapter 1 on Lawyers and Other Advisors to assist you in finding professional assistance.

The legal fee for preparing a will is very modest, generally between $100 to $300 + per person. If your estate is complex, this fee could be higher because of the additional time and expertise required. A "back-to-back" will is a duplicate reverse one for husband and wife and is generally a reduced price.

Key Reasons for Consulting a Lawyer

To reinforce the necessity to obtain a legal consultation before completing or re-doing a will, just look at some of the many reasons when legal advice is specifically required because of the complex legal issues and options involved:

- You own or plan to own a business, or part-own a business with partners
- You are separated from your spouse but not divorced
- You are divorced and want to re-marry
- You are divorced and paying for support
- You are living in, entering or leaving a common-law relationship
- You are in a blended family relationship
- Your estate is large and you need assistance with estate planning to reduce or eliminate taxes on your death
- You have a history of emotional or mental problems such that someone could attack the validity of your will on the basis that you did not under-stand the implications of your actions
- You want to have unbiased, professional advice rather than being influenced by or under duress from relatives
- You want to live outside of Canada for extended periods of time, for example retire and travel south in the winter (your permanent residence at the time of your death has legal and tax implications)

- You own or plan to own foreign real estate
- You have a will that was signed outside Canada or plan to do so
- You want to forgive certain debts, or make arrangements for the repaying of debts to your estate should you die before the debt is paid
- You want events to occur which have to be carefully worded, such as having a spouse have income or use of a home until he or she re-marries or dies and at that time the balance goes elsewhere
- You want to set up a trust
- You want to make special arrangements to care for someone who is incapable of looking after himself or herself or unable to apply sound financial judgment (a child, an immature adolescent, a gambler, an alcoholic, a spendthrift, or someone with emotional, physical or mental disabilities or who is ill)
- You wish to disinherit a spouse, relative, or child because of a serious estrangement or the fact that all your children are now independently wealthy and don't need your money
- You have several children and you want to provide one specific child with the opportunity to buy, have an option to buy, or receive in the will a specific possession of your estate.

As you can see, there are many reasons to consult with a legal expert for a will customized for your needs.

3. Trust Company

A trust company can offer extensive services in terms of will and estate planning, generally in conjunction with a lawyer of your choice, or they could recommend one. Always obtain independent legal advice. A trust company is invaluable when a trust is set up as part of your estate planning, as well as to act as your executor. Needs vary and after obtaining advice, you may not require a trust company.

Selecting an Executor or Trustee

Your executor acts as your "personal representative" and deals with all the financial, tax, administrative and other aspects of your estate. You grant your executor the power to convert any part of your estate into money as he or she thinks best in order to wind up the estate. It is difficult to find a layperson or family member who could adequately fulfil all the qualifications that might be required. Not only can the process be time-consuming and complicated, it can also expose the executor to personal legal liability if errors are made. The executor is accountable to all beneficiaries.

Selecting an Executor

There are two kinds of executors. The professional executor is a lawyer, accountant or trust company staff. The other type is the inexperienced layperson, generally a relative or family friend.

Many people consider being asked to be an executor an honour, a reflection of the trust in the relationship. However, conflicts can and do occur between executors and beneficiaries. The executor may be perceived as overzealous or indifferent, authoritarian or showing favouritism, lacking necessary knowledge or making decisions too hastily. An executor can retain a lawyer or a trust company as an agent. You can also name more than one person to administer the estate, referred to as co-executors. They have equal rights and responsibilities for the administration of the estate. For example, you could consider having a spouse and a trust company as co-executors. If you are naming an individual, make sure you have an alternate executor in case the first one is unwilling or unable to act.

Selecting a Trustee

Trusts operable during your lifetime are generally called *inter-vivos* trusts. A trust that is operable upon your death as outlined in your will is a testamentary trust. You would need to have a trustee manage either type, both discussed later in this chapter.

You may wish to appoint a trustee to manage a portion of your assets for an extended period of time. If you are selecting a layperson to be the executor, you may not want the same person to be the trustee to prevent a potential conflict of interest. Trustees are normally responsible for taking in and investing money, selling assets and distributing the estate proceeds in accordance with the trust terms. The trustee must maintain a balance between the interests of income beneficiaries and beneficiaries subsequently entitled to the capital. In addition, a trustee should maintain accounts and regularly issue accounting statements and income tax receipts to beneficiaries, make income payments, and exercise discretion on early withdrawal of capital, to meet special needs. Finally, the trustee makes the final distribution of the trust fund in accordance with the will. You can see why trust companies perform a vital role. An individual may not have the long-term continuity required, due to death or lack of interest or ability. Selection of the right executor and trustee will enhance the smooth disposition of your assets and reduce your family's stress. Use professionals to act as an executor or trustee, or appoint a family member to be a co-executor or co-trustee if the circumstances warrant. Remember to short-list three prospects and/or trust companies before you decide who to select to act as your executor and/or trustee.

Benefits of Using a Trust Company as an Executor and/or Trustee

- **Experience and expertise in will and estate planning.** The trust company's broad expertise enables it to administer the estate economically and efficiently. Part of estate planning involves establishing objectives for estate distribution taking into consideration any legislation concerning provision for dependants and minimizing or providing for all payable taxes.
- **Continuity of service.** The appointment of a trust company ensures continuity of service during the full administration of the estate. This is particularly

important if the estate involves a trust responsibility, which might have to be administered for many years (e.g. young children).

■ **Accessibility.** One trust officer is assigned to a specific estate and is personally responsible for providing customized and responsive service.

■ **Full attention to the needs of your estate.** If a layperson is your executor, his or her attention to the executor duties could be influenced by other personal interests, age, ill health, procrastination or excessive stress due to the demands of fulfilling expectations in an area where they have no experience.

■ **Provide portfolio management.** A trust company can provide expertise in cash management or operating a business.

■ **Ensuring control when that is important.** A professional, neutral and experienced executor or trustee can exercise control when for example, releasing funds to an adult child who lacks financial responsibility. Another example would be the management of a business until the appropriate time to sell it. Trust companies can competently deal with any situation that might come up.

■ **Confidential nature of the estate administration business.** Trust company staff is trained to treat the estate administration and related client business in the strictest confidence.

■ **Sharing responsibility.** If you decide to nominate a layperson as a joint executor, the trust company assumes the burden of the administration but works with your other executor to make joint decisions.

■ **Financial responsibility and security.** Most trust companies in Canada are well established and backed by substantial capital and reserve account. Reputable trust companies also strictly segregate estate assets from the general funds. Also, a trust company is covered by insurance if there is a mistake or oversight due to negligence or inadvertence.

■ **Funding capacity.** A trust company can work with your family to provide for their immediate financial requirements and needs immediately after your death.

■ **Specialized knowledge.** Due to the increasingly complex nature of tax and other legislation relating to an estate, as well as a wide variety of options, a trust company employs specialists in business, tax, legal, insurance, investment and other areas. In major decisions, a trust company will utilize a variety of senior specialists to arrive at a group decision.

■ **Fees and savings.** Most trust companies will enter into a fee agreement at the time that your will is prepared. Trust company fees are determined by legislative guidelines and the courts in most provinces; however, a separate agreement can deal with additional fees. The same guidelines also apply to a private executor. There can also be savings due to efficiency by having an experienced trust company perform the executor duties. This would not, of course, include fees involved in ongoing estate management, or the maintenance of trusts set up during the will planning process and included in the will. Obtain quotes from the trust company.

- **Avoiding the possibility of family conflict.** In any family situation, there could be personality conflicts, friction over control, power, money, distribution of family possessions or assets, resentment due to past financial favours to certain children, forgiveness of loans to others, or unequal distribution of the estate to family members etc. A trust company acts as a neutral, objective catalyst in pre-empting or resolving potential disagreements.
- **Peace of mind.** There is a great reduction in stress to know that the estate will be administered competently, professionally, promptly and in accord with your stated wishes. An experienced trust company can provide this peace of mind and feeling of security.

Selecting a Guardian

If you have children, it is in your children's best interests to thoroughly plan for their upbringing and care in the event of your death. When you appoint a guardian, you are really just making a request, as your wishes are not legally binding as children are not property and therefore cannot be willed. The law attempts to determine what is in the best interests of the children. If the guardian is willing and able to perform the responsibilities, the courts will generally uphold your wishes. Make sure you name an alternate guardian in case the first one is unwilling or unable to assume the responsibility, or predeceases you.

Discuss with, and obtain the consent of, the main and alternate guardians before naming them in your will. Leave with your will, in your safety deposit box, a letter detailing your wishes with regards to raising your children. This would include fundamental issues such as religion, education, values and general up-bringing. Discuss these issues with the guardian.

Appointing different people to be the trustee and guardian of the children should eliminate any potential conflict of interest. The trustee is responsible for protecting the child's inheritance. A guardian frequently attempts to obtain more funds for the upbringing, health and education of the child. One way of making sure there is sufficient money for the trust is to purchase life insurance.

Understanding Trusts

Trusts are a very common way of dealing with a range of personal choice, family or business options. Basically, a trust is a legal structure whereby a trustee deals with property or assets, e.g. cash, stocks, bonds, etc. over which the trustee has control, for the benefit of persons called beneficiaries. The trustee could also be one of the beneficiaries. Although the trustee has legal title to the trust property, beneficial ownership rests with the beneficiaries.

A trustee only derives certain limited powers by provincial statute. Therefore, your will should specify exactly what powers you want to give to your trustee in carrying out the provisions of the trust. For example, if you do not want your trustee restricted in the type of investments of trust funds, you must provide your trustee with expanded investment powers in your will.

Living Trusts

There are a number of creative ways that you can use a living trust, including the following examples.

Family Trust

This trust would involve having some of the shares in a company owned by a spouse held in the name of a family trust. These shares could be non-voting shares. This family trust could be comprised of your spouse and children. The monies that would go to the trust by means of dividends could then be distributed through dividends to each of the trust members. If the members of the trust were not receiving any other income, they could each take out $23,756 of dividend income each year tax-free. If the family members were minors and if the trust were formed properly, the normal CCRA policy of attributing income to a minor to the parents for tax purposes (the attribution rule) would not be applicable.

Unfortunately, in the February 1999 Federal Budget, the government clamped down on income splitting arrangements by introducing a special "income splitting" tax. This tax will apply at the top marginal income tax rate to individuals under 18 years of age who directly or indirectly receive taxable dividends on shares of Canadian private corporations and foreign corporations. This special tax will also apply to some business income allocated to a minor from a partnership or a trust. Get customized feedback from your tax accountant.

Estate Freeze

If your company or other assets have shown a consistent pattern of growth over time, which you anticipate will continue, an estate freeze using a corporation set up for the purpose, along with a living trust agreement could be an effective strategy. This technique freezes the value of your assets as of the effective date of the agreement. All future capital gains will accrue to the benefit of your beneficiaries, e.g. children.

Providing for Family Members with Special Needs

If you have family members who are not able to handle their own affairs, due to mental or physical incapacity, or other reasons, a living trust could be established to provide for their financial needs for their life. On the recipient's death, the residue of the funds in the trust could be left for some other purpose, e.g. a charity.

Passing on the Business to the Next Generation

Donny and Johnny operated a successful travel agency. After many years of hard work, it became clear that their two children would succeed them in the business. The children had natural business aptitude, plus a strong work ethic inherited from their parents. They also liked the free and low-cost perks and familiarization trips. Based on feedback from their professional advisors, Donny and Johnny decided to do an estate freeze. They converted their common shares into preferred shares at the fair market value, and then issued new common shares in equal portions to their two children. This process effectively "froze" the capital gain in the parents' hands at that point in time, with the children's portion starting at zero. As the parents were still actively involved in the business, they prepared a management agreement, giving them exclusive control over the day-to-day operation of the business. The parents could also issue one common voting share in the new company, with the children having all the other non-voting shares. In that scenario, the children would have the equity position, but the parents would have the control.

Donny and Johnny also made sure their wills were current, and that their insurance policies and other investments went to their children as designated beneficiaries, thereby bypassing the will and probate process.

Giving to Charity

You may wish to set up what is referred to as a "charitable remainder trust." In this situation, you could assist your charity of choice by means of donating a residual interest in a trust to the charity. The common format is for the capital in the trust to go to the charity on your death, and in the meantime, you receive the income earned from the assets in the trust. It is possible that the trust could be structured so that you receive a non-refundable tax credit when the trust is established, representing the projected fair market value of the residual interest (the "remainder"), e.g. the capital available on your death. If the capital is not going to be eroded during your lifetime, it is easy to project the remainder.

Managing Retirement Needs

With the advances in medical science and people being more aware of healthy living and eating, the average life span has increased immensely over the years. It is not uncommon for people to live into the 80's and 90's.

However, with aging, many people do not feel comfortable managing their own affairs. Possibly their children do not have money management skills, are very busy or live out of town. For these reasons, many people consider the benefits of a living trust, managed by a trust company and a responsible family member, as co-trustees. Assets are set aside and put into the trust. Normally it is structured so that the parents receive income for life, with the capital distributed to the children and/or grandchildren on the death of the surviving parent.

The trust could also have a provision stating that the capital of the trust could be used under certain conditions, such as greater financial needs dictated by health. For example, paying for a long-term care facility in a retirement home.

Keeping a Gift Confidential

For a variety of reasons, you may wish to keep your gift confidential. By transferring assets to a living trust, the assets no longer become the property of the owner's estate on death. Therefore, the probate process does not cover them. The assets would therefore not be included in the public record when the will is probated.

Payments for Divorce Settlements

Sometimes divorce settlements where children are involved can be contentious. There are a lot of issues than can arise. On the one hand, the spouse who is the primary caregiver needs to be able to rely on regular support payments for the children. On the other hand, the spouse who is paying the support wants to make sure that money is going for the purpose intended. As lump sum support payments can be a source of disagreement, one way around the issue is to put available capital into a living trust agreement for the benefit of the children. The children would continue to get the support payments under the trust until they reached the age of majority, e.g. 19.

Testamentary Trusts

Testamentary trusts, created in your will, include the spousal trust, trusts set up for minor children or grandchildren, providing for family members with special needs, discretionary trusts for children who are spendthrifts and gifts for charities. Here are some examples.

- **Spousal trust.** In this situation, you set up a trust to provide income for the life of your spouse, with the capital remaining at death to go to the children or grandchildren. This type of trust is common when a spouse is ill or incapacitated or lacks financial expertise. A variation of this format, if there are no children or grandchildren, is to leave the capital to charity, on the death of the surviving spouse.
- **Trusts for minors.** This is probably an obvious one for most people. You may probably already have in your will that in the event that both parents die at the same time, or when the surviving parent dies, that a portion of your estate shall be held in trust for minor children or grandchildren until they reach a certain age. In the meantime, the trustee can encroach on the capital for specific needs of the children. Many people then arrange to have the money disbursed over various time periods as the children mature. For example, one-third at age 19, one-third at age 25, and one-third at age 30.
- **Trust for charities.** You may wish to set up a trust that provides family members with income for life, but on their death the remaining capital in the trust is distributed to a charity of your choice.
- **Spendthrift trust.** There could be a situation where you have a child who has a history of financial irresponsibility. One solution is to set up a trust to control the funds or assets that the child would otherwise receive. The

trustees would have the power to distribute as much of the income as appears reasonable for the child, with any excess income being re-invested in the trust. There could also be powers to use some of the capital of the trust, necessary in extenuating circumstances. On the death of the child, the capital in the trust could go to the grandchildren, for example.

- **Special needs trust.** If you have a family member who is physically or mentally challenged and not able to manage his or her own affairs, you may want to consider a trust. That way, you would have the assurance that the needs of the child would be looked after from the interest on the capital of the trust, with encroachment powers on the capital in extenuating circumstances. Any excess interest would be re-invested in the trust and added to the capital. If it appears that the trust would be operating for an extended time, it is prudent to consider the benefits of having a trust company as trustee or co-trustee.
- **International trust.** There could be situations where it would be to your distinct advantage to establish an international trust if considerable assets are involved, e.g. over $500,000 and the circumstances make such a choice attractive. This type of trust should be considered when close family members are living outside Canada that you want to gift money to, or you anticipate receiving money from close relatives outside the country.

The purpose of the international trust is to either provide tax-sheltered income to non-residents of Canada, or receive tax favoured inheritances or gifts from non-residents of Canada. As you can appreciate, there are technical tax and legal issues involved with Canada and the other country involved. You need to seek highly specialized legal and tax advice before considering this option.

Fees and Expenses

The main fees associated with probating a will or settling an estate or dealing with a trust are as follows.

Executors/Administrators Compensation

In most cases, an executor or administrator is entitled to a fee for his or her time and services, normally 3% to 5% of the value of the estate. The beneficiaries or court have to approve the accounts prepared for compensation and the amount comes out of the estate. An executor who is also a beneficiary could be denied a fee unless the will makes it clear that the gift to the executor is given in addition to, not instead of, executor's fees.

Legal Fees

Legal fees are considered a proper expense and may be paid out of estate funds, subject to approval of the court or the beneficiaries. A lawyer may charge a fee for itemized services rendered, or a lump sum fee of generally up to 2% of the value of the estate for certain basic services. This is a maximum percentage, not a standard rate. If any legal issue arises, such as the validity or meaning of a will, or where an application to the court is made, legal fees will be extra and are normally billed out at the lawyer's hourly rate, usually between $150 to $200+ an hour.

Probate Fees

Also known as court fees, probate fees are established by provincial legislation and paid to that government. They do not form part of the executor's compensation nor do they include legal fees. The probate fees can range from low to high depending on the province. The value of the estate is used as a base when determining the probate fee.

Trustee Fees

These would generally be negotiated separately, especially if a trust company is involved, and confirmed in writing.

Additional Fees and Costs

If a beneficiary of the estate feels that the administration fee charged by an executor is excessive, he or she can ask the executor to "pass accounts" in a court of law. The executor must present an accounting of the work done to the court and ask a judge to set the fees. The final fee may be higher or lower than the fee that the executor initially requested. When there are infant beneficiaries, the executor may be required to pass accounts because minors cannot give their approval for the actions of the executor. If the executor or beneficiary believes the legal fees are excessive, they can be challenged. This is called "taxing" a lawyer's account, generally in front of the registrar at the courthouse. Check the procedures in your community.

Living Will

A living will is designed for those who are concerned about their quality of life when they are near death. It is a written statement of your intentions to the people who are most likely to have control over your care, such as your family and your doctor. Have a copy of the living will where it can be readily obtained, such as in your wallet. Give a copy to your spouse and family doctor. You should also review your living will from time to time.

The purpose of a living will is to convey your wishes if there is no reasonable expectation of recovery from physical or mental disability. Such a will requests that you be allowed to die naturally, with dignity, and not be kept alive by "heroic medical measures." In some provinces, a living will is merely an expression of your wishes and is not legally binding on your doctor or the hospital. Other provinces have officially endorsed the concept through legislation, if your written instructions are correctly done. For further information contact the Joint Centre for Bioethics, University of Toronto (416) 978-2709, Web site: *www.utoronto.ca/jcb*.

Power of Attorney (PA)

Many lawyers recommend a power of attorney (PA), sometimes referred to as an "enduring" PA, at the same time that they prepare a will. The purpose of a PA is to designate a person or a trust company to take over your affairs if you can no longer handle them due to illness or incapacitation, for example. Another reason is that you may be away for extended periods on personal or business matters. A power of attorney is important if you have substantial assets that require active management. You can grant a general PA over all your affairs, or a limited one specific to a certain task or time period. You can revoke the power of attorney at any time in writing. A PA is only valid in your province. You would need to have a separate PA if you own assets in the US or elsewhere.

If you do not have a power of attorney and become incapacitated, an application has to be made to the court by the party who wishes permission to manage your affairs. This person would be called a committee. If another family member does not wish to perform this responsibility, a trust company can be appointed, with court approval. Committee duties include filing with the court a summary of assets, liabilities and income sources, with a description of the person's needs and an outline of how the committee proposes to manage the accounts and/or structure the estate to serve those needs.

Summary

A will should be customized for your specific needs and updated on a regular basis. As a will is a legal document, the wording and necessary clauses to reflect your wishes should be approved by your lawyer. The consequence of not having a will is not the legacy most people would choose to inflict on their family. There is no logical reason not to have a will and a power of attorney, both integral parts of estate planning.

Fifteen

Intellectual Property

Introduction

Intellectual property refers primarily to patents, trademarks, copyright and industrial design. Whereas all refer to rights granted for intellectual creativity, the public is sometimes confused by the different forms. Patents are for structure and function, whereas copyright refers to literary, dramatic, artistic or musical works. Industrial designs are the shape, pattern or ornamentation applied to an industrially produced object. A trademark is a word, picture, or symbol, or combination of these, used to distinguish goods or services by one person or organization from others in the marketplace.

The laws governing these areas are federal statutes and include the *Patent Act*, *Copyright Act*, *Trade Marks Act* and the *Industrial Design Act*. Statutes are constantly being revised to reflect changing circumstances, including more efficient legal administration. For this reason, obtain the assistance from professionals in advance. Legislation governing intellectual properties is administered and regulated by Industry Canada, which has branches throughout Canada. Consumer and Corporate Affairs has an excellent series of free booklets on intellectual property available on request. Their Web site address is ***www.ic.gc.ca***. They also provide general information over the phone (blue pages of the phone book). Information is also available at ***cipo.gc.ca***.

As a business owner, you may want to protect your rights to your inventions. Alternatively, you may want to purchase or become a franchisee of the inventions of others. You could also manufacture the inventions of others without legally having to pay a fee to the inventor, if that person lost or abandoned the patent rights or never registered them in Canada.

Patents

On the average, a patent grants its owner a legal right to exclude others for 18 years from making, selling, or using the invention. Patents are granted for products, compositions, apparatuses and processes, or for improvements in these that are new, useful, and not obvious. Only an inventor, assignee or other successor may obtain a patent for the invention. A patent is not renewable.

Protecting Joe's Invention

Joe was a creative thinker who was always inventing product ideas. One day, Joe came up with a brilliant idea for a dog collar with a built-in global positioning system locator. That way, the owner would always know where the dog was hanging out. He thought that dog owners would go to any expense to keep track of their dog. He called the device the "Muttlocator." However, Joe wanted to protect his product from others that might try to "rip him off." He didn't know what steps to take.

Joe could look in the Yellow Pages under "patent" lawyers or attorneys. He could also phone the local lawyer referral service to ask for a lawyer in intellectual property. The lawyer will review Joe's idea and give advice on patenting the product, if it is truly unique and patentable. Also, the lawyer could suggest applying to trademark the name. Both these steps take time. It is the nature of business that competitors will try to replicate a successful or unique product. Therefore, planning for a rapid national marketing campaign or joint venture opportunities would be prudent. Test market initiatives are essential to estimate interest and demand.

Patent Office

The Canadian Patent Office, part of Consumer and Corporate Affairs Canada, is under a larger agency called the Intellectual Property Directorate. In addition to protecting the inventor's rights, the Patent Office also promotes economic activity and technological development by making information available to the public. The Patent Office grants patents for inventions if, in law, the applicants are entitled to it. It also records assignments of patents, maintains search files of Canadian patents and provides a public research room.

Benefits of Patented Information

More than 70% of all patented information and data on new technologies throughout the industrial world is available only in patent literature documented at the Patent Office. Knowledge often makes a difference between success and failure to a small business. Keeping aware of new technology is very important when:

- Launching new products
- Capturing or increasing market share
- Finding the best suppliers of new technology
- Reducing costs
- Raising productivity
- Challenging foreign competition
- Avoiding legal problems associated with the use of already patented inventions.

Obtaining a Patent

The minimum cost of preparing and filing one patent in Canada is typically around $2,500, if a lawyer is retained. If the invention has no commercial feasibility, the money could be wasted. Ask yourself these questions:

- Is there an existing or potential market for the invention?
- Who are the potential purchasers and how much would they are prepared to pay for it?
- Where will the invention be sold or assigned, and who will negotiate the transaction?
- What is the cost to manufacture the invention, and who would do it?
- Where will you obtain the necessary financing to commercially exploit your invention?
- Do you have the necessary business contacts and expertise required to market the invention in a commercially successful fashion?

Three key criteria of the invention have to be present to be granted a patent:
1. **Novelty.** The invention has to be new. Under the legislation, a patent will be granted to the inventor who is the first to file an application. Publication or use of the invention in Canada or elsewhere before the patent application is filed is a bar to obtaining a patent in Canada. The Patent Office allows a one-year "grace period" to the inventor to file the application, if the invention has been disclosed. Under the old Act, patents were given to the first investor, irrespective of filing dates, and the "grace period" was two years and applied to everyone.
2. **Utility.** The Patent Office will not issue a patent on something which doesn't work or which has no inherent or disclosed use.
3. **Inventive ingenuity.** An invention must be a development or an improvement that would not have been obvious beforehand to people of average skill in the technology involved.

Registered Patent Agents

Although any Canadian can personally file a patent application within Canada, the preparation and successful acceptance of an application requires an extensive knowledge of patent law and Patent Office practice. It is highly recommended that inventors consult a registered patent agent to prevent delays. If the patent is eventually obtained, it may not adequately protect the invention.

A registered patent agent must pass an examination in patent law and practice before they are permitted to represent inventors. A patent agent generally has a thorough knowledge of patent legislation in most foreign countries, as well as Canada. Patent agents are not necessarily patent lawyers. You can find the names of patent agents and patent lawyers in the Yellow Pages under "Patent attorneys and agents—registered;" the lawyer referral service in your area; and in a list of registered patent agents available from the Patent Office. Get at least two professional opinions before making your final decision.

Trade Secrets

Before you decide to patent, consider the advantages of not patenting your technology. Some companies prefer to keep their inventions a trade secret. They believe that the advantages of nondisclosure outweigh the benefits of patent protection. An inventor who has not obtained a patent, however, runs the risk of a competitor buying the product on the open market and copying it. The competitor could even apply for a patent on an improved and patentable version of the product, thereby inhibiting the inventor from marketing the invention.

Patent Protection Outside Canada

A Canadian patent does not provide protection in other countries. A patent application must be made in each country that you intend to sell, assign, or manufacture the invention. Patent laws vary and some countries have no patent laws at all.

In most foreign countries, if you advertise or talk publicly about your product, display it at a trade show, or allow publication of its description anywhere in the world, you would be prevented from obtaining a patent. You would not be able to prevent others from copying your product.

Assigning or Licensing a Patent

Once you have a patent, you have the exclusive right to make, use or sell the product, or sell or license exclusive rights. The legal agreement to transfer rights is either an assignment or a licence.

An assignment permanently transfers all or part of the interest and ownership rights in the design from the holder of the patent to another party, called the assignee. The arrangement must be in writing and the Patent Office must be formally notified. Licensing allows the owner of the patent to retain ownership, but temporarily allows the licensee to use the patent, subject to the conditions set forth in the licensing agreement.

Before starting any discussions with domestic or foreign companies concerning assignment or licensing agreements, it may be necessary to openly discuss technology that has not been patented in either Canada or the foreign country. In such a situation, the parties should sign a confidentiality and nondisclosure agreement (NDA); otherwise, premature disclosure of unpatented technology could result in forfeiture of the right to protection.

Patent owners may require employees to sign a confidentiality agreement, as well as a provision that any new innovations or intellectual property derived by an employee belong exclusively to the employer. Have your lawyer customize it for you. If any of the above agreements were breached, the person asserting the intellectual property rights could sue in court. The claim would be for financial damages, as well as request that the court prohibit the other party from using the intellectual property in any fashion. It could be difficult and very expensive to enforce the contract outside Canada.

Trademarks

A trademark is registered for a period of 15 years from the date of registration. It is renewable every 15 years upon paying the required registration fees. A trademark is a word, logo, symbol or design, or a combination of one or more of these features, that is displayed for identification purposes to the public. The display can be on commercial goods or their labels, or in advertisements. The purpose of the trademark is to indicate that the goods or services meet the same standard of quality as others associated with the same trademark. It can also infer that the product is approved or sponsored by the company or individual associated with the trademark.

In general, the first person to use the trademark in Canada is entitled to register the mark. It is possible also to establish priority based on future intention to use the trademark. In practical terms, rights in a trademark are created through its use. A trade name is a name under which a particular business is carried on, sometimes the same as a corporate name. A trade name can be registered under the *Trade Marks Act* as a trademark only if it is also used as a trademark.

Under the *Trade Marks Act* there are three main types of trademarks:

1. **Certification mark.** A type of trademark used to distinguish goods or services that meet a defined standard, for example the woolmark label used on clothing.
2. **Distinguishing guise.** The shape or design of the product or packaging that effectively distinguishes the product from others. In order for a distinguishing guise to be registered, it must be proven that it has become distinctive through usage.
3. **Ordinary trademarks.** A distinctive single word, a group of words, a slogan, a design or picture used in association with goods or services, to distinguish them in the marketplace. A trademark often stands for consistency of quality and advertising is frequently used to reinforce this image. A trademark can therefore become a very valuable asset.

Differences between Registered and Unregistered Trademarks

It is not mandatory to register a trademark, but it is advisable in many situations. If a trademark has not been registered, the holder has what are called common law rights. The owner of the unregistered trademark must rely on the courts to determine what is appropriate in the circumstances.

The main advantages to registering a trademark include:

- A registered trademark would alert parties who might be contemplating the same or confusingly similar mark to the possibility of conflict. An unregistered trademark would not show up in the trademark registry.
- A registered trademark can usually be protected throughout Canada. An unregistered trademark can be protected only in the specific area that it has established a reputation and goodwill.
- A registered trademark allows the owner to commence trademark infringement proceedings in the federal court of Canada or a provincial superior

court. The owner of an unregistered trademark would not have the same legal enforcement options.

- A registered trademark may provide legal protection against a non-competitor, if its use by the non-competitor devalues the goodwill of the registered trademark owner. The owner of an unregistered trademark normally can commence an action only against a competitor.
- A registered trademark, after five years, can be deemed to be incontestable in most circumstances. The owner of an unregistered trademark would have no such automatic right.
- A registered trademark is entitled to be licensed to other parties, who are called registered users. The owner of an unregistered trademark would have difficulty in maintaining the distinctiveness of the trademark if another party was given a licence to use it.
- A registered trademark usually entitles the owner to register the mark in other countries, a feature not usually possible with unregistered trademarks.

Obtaining a Registered Trademark

Generally, a trademark can be registered if:
- It cannot be confused with a trademark already registered.
- It is not a prohibited mark, for example, the Royal Arms, crest, flag or emblems of a federal, provincial or municipal governmental body, or the symbol of the Red Cross. Scandalous or obscene matter or portraits or signatures of living individuals are also prohibited from registration.

Registered Trademark Agents

As with registering a patent, it is prudent to use a registered trademark agent to file your application. See the earlier section on patent agents for more information on finding a professional to assist you with this process.

Trademark Registration Process

Conduct a registrability search in the Trademark Office to determine whether there is an existing or pending registration of the same or similar marks before you apply. A conflict could prevent registration of your mark. The legal costs and search fees involved are reasonably low. A search cannot assure that the trademark will be registered, as it is merely a list of names that have not been thoroughly checked by a trademark examiner.

The initial NUANS search will scan the database in Ottawa that currently has over three million corporate names, trademarks and business names. The report will list all similar names. If it passes the initial search, then the next step is a manual search of the documents in the Trademark Office in Ottawa. Your agent normally does this.

Registering a Trademark Outside Canada

A registered trademark gives its owner the exclusive rights to its use in Canada only. If your products or services are sold in other countries, you should consider registration of your trademark in those countries. Otherwise you could lose your trademark rights completely in those countries. You are required to apply for registration within six months of the date of the filing of the Canadian trademark application.

Assigning or Licensing a Trademark

The rights to a trademark registration or pending application, with or without the goodwill of the business, can be assigned or licensed to another party. Any changes in the ownership or assignment of a registered trademark should be registered with the Trademark Office.

It is very common for trademark rights to be licensed to a third party by means of a registered user agreement. The agreement outlines the conditions of the licence, including quality control, nature of use, duration and fees. If the terms are breached, the licence can be cancelled. Manufacturers and the franchise industry often license registered users. If the franchisor allows the franchisee to use a trademark without being registered as a registered user, the trademark protection could be lost and anyone could use the name.

Copyright

Copyright means that the owner has the exclusive right to copy his or her work, or permit someone else to do so. It generally includes the sole right to publish, produce, reproduce, perform, translate, adapt, convert, publicly present, broadcast or record the work, or any substantial part of it.

Copyright applies to all original literary, dramatic, artistic and musical works, including books, writings, musical works, paintings, sculptures, photographs, motion picture films, encyclopaedias and dictionaries. Copyright also applies to mechanical devices such as records, cassettes, and tapes.

Copyright usually lasts for the lifetime of the author plus a period of 50 years after his or her death. For photographs, records, tapes and other manufactured devices that are protected by copyright, the right exists for 50 years from the making of the original device, or master copy. The author owns the copyright, unless he or she was employed by some other person to create the work, in which case the employer is the owner. A copyright could also be sold or assigned to another person, covered later in this section. If the author dies, the copyright will form part of the estate.

Differences between Copyright and Industrial Design

All literary, dramatic, musical and artistic works are subject to copyright protection, regardless of the quantity in which they are reproduced. However, artistic works that are used as models intended to be reproduced in numbers greater than

50 are protected only by the *Industrial Design Act*. Examples would include dolls, toys and pendants.

Acquiring Copyright

Copyright in Canada is automatically acquired upon creation of an original work by a Canadian citizen or a citizen of a qualifying foreign country. Although voluntary registration is not required to obtain basic protection, it is advisable. On registration of the copyright, certification is issued providing evidence that the person registered is the copyright owner. This certificate can be used in court to establish ownership.

Advantages of Copyright Registration

Registration provides legal credibility that the person registered is in fact the owner of the copyright. Other practical and legal benefits to copyright registration follow:

- A registered copyright provides the owner with a basis for commencing a successful action for copyright infringement. The copyright owner could sue for an injunction restraining any further infringement, as well as claim financial damages. If the copyright was not registered at the time of the infringement, the defendants could claim that they had no reasonable basis for knowing that the copyright existed in the work. Then, the copyright owner would only be entitled to a court injunction to stop further infringement.
- If the copyright is registered, it can provide very important negotiating leverage and credibility in the sale or licensing of the rights.

Copyright Registration Process

Anyone can register a copyright, and the procedures within Canada are fairly simple. Forms can be obtained from the Copyright Office or any branch of Consumer and Corporate Affairs Canada (***www.canada.gc.ca***). There is a one-time registration fee and processing takes approximately two months. You may wish to retain a lawyer or other qualified professional to prepare and file the documents for you, depending on the complexity of the work.

Copies of the copyright work are not required by the copyright office. However, if you have released a sound recording manufactured in Canada with some Canadian content, or if you have published a book in Canada, you are required to send one copy of the sound recording and two copies of the book to the National Library of Canada within one week of publication.

Copyright Protection Outside Canada

It is not necessary to make any indication on a book that it is copyrighted. However, to retain copyright protection under the provisions of the *Universal Copyright Convention* in countries that require registration, all copies of a work should be marked with a small c in a circle ©, and include the name of the copyright owner and the year of first publication. The United States requires this format. It may be advisable to register your copyright in the other countries concerned, depending on the circumstances. Obtain the advice of a lawyer specializing in copyright matters. In the United States, a complete copy of the work must be submitted to the United States copyright office with the copyright application. In addition, a copyright infringement action in the United States cannot be commenced unless the copyright has first been registered in that country.

Assigning or Licensing a Copyright

A copyright can be sold, assigned, or licensed in whole or in part. To be valid, however, any assignment must be in writing and signed by the owner. Register the assignment or licence in the Copyright Registry to eliminate any confusion with the public. It also protects the rights of the original owner or assignee or licensee.

An assignment is a sale of rights that involves a transfer of ownership. A licence does not involve a transfer of ownership and is temporary. A licence is usually based on a fee or royalty paid to use a work, under certain conditions.

Industrial Design

An industrial design is any original shape or pattern applied to an article of manufacture, such as the shape of a table, decoration on a spoon, or the pattern of fabric. An industrial process must make the article. The industrial design must be registered in the Industrial Design Registry within one year of first publication, public use, or sale in Canada.

An industrial design registration lasts five years, and may be renewed. Once the registration has expired, so does the protection and anyone may use or sell the design in Canada.

Differences between Industrial Design, Copyright and Patent

Protection provided by the *Industrial Design Act* is frequently confused with protection under the *Copyright Act*. Many designs, being works of art, are automatically protected under the *Copyright Act*. But once the original artistic work is used as a model to produce more than 50 articles or sets of articles, the artistic work then becomes an industrial design. This design can be protected only under the *Industrial Design Act*. Since the legal distinction is a fine one, seek specialized legal advice.

You may be able to patent details of the construction, mode of operation, or functioning of an article as an invention under the *Patent Act,* but it cannot also be part of an industrial design registered under the *Industrial Design Act*.

Assistance from Patent Agent or Lawyer

Although you are entitled to apply on your own to register an industrial design, it is not advisable. If it is not done properly, potential legal problems could impair your protection. You can contact a lawyer or a patent agent in the Yellow Pages under "Patent attorneys and agents—registered," or obtain a list from the Patent

Office or Consumer and Corporate Affairs Canada. Obtain three professional opinions before selecting your advisor.

Industrial Design Registration Process

Only the author of the design may register it, unless it was created in the course of employment for someone else. In that event, the employer is the owner, and the only one authorized to request registration. Rights acquired by registration become part of the author's estate and are passed on to the beneficiaries.

Industrial Design Protection Outside Canada

Registration in Canada does not provide any protection outside Canada. Protection can only be obtained in foreign countries by filing for registration in each country. Most countries, under the *International Convention*, allow the applicant to use the filing date in Canada as the filing date of the subsequent foreign country application, as long as the latter is filed within six months of the Canadian application date.

Assigning or Licensing an Industrial Design

Once your design has been registered, you may assign or license a design to anyone else. The arrangement must be in writing and the Industrial Design Office should be notified in writing.

An assignment means permanently giving up all or part of your interest in your design. A licence temporarily permits someone to make, use, and sell your design under very specific terms. Obtain the advice of your lawyer, as there are many potential pitfalls. Read the other sections of this chapter relating to patent and copyright before speaking with your professional advisor.

Summary

At some point in your business, you may want to register your rights to your intellectual property. Conversely, you may wish to licence the use of someone else's intellectual property, or at least ensure that you don't inadvertently infringe on someone else's intellectual property rights. Seek advice from a lawyer specializing in intellectual property.

Sixteen

Litigation and the ADR Process

Introduction

At some point in your small business career, the odds are very great that either you will be suing someone or someone will be suing you. This chapter should raise your awareness of the litigation process, as well as the Alternate Dispute Resolution process. About 95% of all litigation is settled before trial, either by a negotiated settlement, or because one side discontinues the action. For information on selecting a lawyer, refer to Chapter 1 on Legal and other Advisors.

The Courts

Law is based on provincial and federal statutes as well as the common law. Common law refers to previous court decisions primarily from Canada or England. In Quebec, the law is governed by the *Quebec Civil Code*, as well as other provincial legislation. The names of the various levels of courts, the pre-trial steps, and the terminology might vary from province to province, but the concepts and procedures are similar.

Although some provinces only have three levels of courts, most have four governed by provincial legislation. These are Small Claims Court, County Court, Supreme Court and Court of Appeal. The federal government has the Federal Court of Canada and the Supreme Court of Canada.

Small Claims Court

Small claims court is designed for the layperson to present a claim without hiring a lawyer. The monetary limit normally ranges from $3,000 to $10,000. A guidebook is generally available from the court that explains the step-by-step procedures when making a claim. There are also books available in libraries and bookstores on small claims court procedures. You may find it helpful to attend the court as an observer to familiarize yourself with the process.

County Court
County court normally has a monetary ceiling of $25,000 to $50,000, although this can vary between provinces. The conduct of action is formal, technical and requires representation by a lawyer.

Supreme Court
Supreme Court has unlimited monetary jurisdiction; it can hear any claim of any nature. Again, the legal process is formal and technical, and a lawyer is required.

Court of Appeal
If you believe the decision at the Supreme Court was legally flawed or handled unfairly, you can appeal the decision to the Court of Appeal. Approximately 30% of judgments appealed to the Court of Appeal are overturned.

Federal Court
The Federal Court hears matters relating to federal government legislation. An example, under the *Income Tax Act*, is your company being sued for arrears of taxes.

Supreme Court of Canada
Canada's court of last resort hears appeals from provincial courts of appeal, whether governed by the common law or by the *Quebec Civil Code*. The Supreme Court of Canada is selective, simply because of the workload involved. One criterion for appeal is that the legal issues have a national implication or impact.

The Litigation Process
Although you may have very good grounds for suing someone, it may be more beneficial to you to settle the matter out of court. You and/or your lawyer may wish to hold a "without prejudice" meeting, or exchange "without prejudice" correspondence with the other party in the dispute. The term without prejudice means that any information discussed in the meeting or correspondence would not be permissible evidence in court. Therefore, both parties may participate in full and open discussions in an attempt to reach an amicable settlement. Your accountant may attend as well, if there are financial considerations involved.

After assessing the situation, you may conclude that it is not worth suing, because the other party has little or no money. You may be suing a corporation with liability limited to the assets of the corporation. However, by the time the trial date arrives, the assets of the corporation may have been pledged as security or to raise money to pay the lawyer to defend the lawsuit. The debtor may have adopted some of the "creditor proofing" strategies outlined in Chapter 12 of this book! Litigation can be extremely expensive, time-consuming, full of risk of losing the case or losing money, and stressful. The following steps will help you understand the process. Small claims court involves a simplified or condensed version of these steps, to expedite the process.

Writ of Summons and Statement of Claim

The writ is the document that initiates the formal legal process. The statement of claim is the document in which the plaintiff (the person suing) sets out all the facts, allegations, nature and amount of the claim.

Both documents are filed in the appropriate court. Copies are delivered to the defendants (the individuals or companies being sued), which may take several weeks and is usually done by a private process server, or a provincial sheriff.

Appearance

An appearance is a short document filed in the court office within 14 days by the defendant's lawyer. It simply acknowledges receipt of the writ and statement of claim, and states that a defence will be filed. A copy of the appearance is served on the plaintiff's lawyer.

If no appearance is entered within the limited time, the plaintiff's lawyer can initiate steps to have a judgment entered in default of appearance. A judgment is an order by the court to the defendant to pay the plaintiff the amount of the claim. A default judgment can be removed, but an application to the court has to be made and reasons given for failure to file the appearance on time.

Statement of Defence

The defendant states the intention to defend the action, and replies to the claim in the statement of defence. The statement of defence generally must be filed within 21 days of receipt of the statement of claim. If the statement of defence is not filed within the time required, the plaintiff could enter a judgment in default of defence. Again, this default judgment can usually be set aside by the court if an application and an affidavit are filed swearing that the defences that you have in the case have merit.

Where there is more than one defendant, no conflict between the defendants' stories and no conflict over liability, it may be prudent to present a joint statement of defence. This approach can result in substantial savings in legal fees.

Summary Judgment Application

After reviewing the defendant's statement of defence, a plaintiff may decide to make a summary judgment application to the courts. A judge will award a summary judgment when the evidence clearly shows that there are no merits to the defence. A successful summary judgment application terminates the legal proceedings, and the plaintiff is awarded a judgment against the defendant.

Counterclaim

Sometimes a defendant, in preparing a defence, may counterclaim against the plaintiff for monies allegedly owed or financial losses suffered (damages) by the plaintiff. A counterclaim is, in fact, a separate lawsuit against the plaintiff based on the same facts. For instance, if you have refused to make final payments on equipment that was delivered late and the supplier files a lawsuit against you, you may enter a counterclaim for damages due to the late delivery. Your counterclaim may equal the plaintiff's claim, or could also exceed it.

Defence to Counterclaim

Where a counterclaim has been filed, the plaintiff has to file a defence to the allegations raised.

Third Party Claim

In some situations, a third party may be involved and be brought into the action by the defendant. The defendant's lawyer may file and serve on the third party a third party notice. The third party then has to file a defence and serve it on the plaintiff and the defendant.

Discovery of Documents

Discovery of documents means that the parties in the litigation exchange, through their lawyers, a list of the evidence, including letters, plans, diagrams, manuals, contracts, agreements, receipts, and other documents relating to the case.

Copies of the documents will then be supplied to each side on request. Both sides then review these documents in preparation for the examination for discovery.

Examination for Discovery

An examination for discovery is an interview of both parties by both their lawyers in order to collect the relevant facts and evidence. The examinations take place under oath and are reported word for word by a court reporter. A copy of the transcript can be later entered into court as evidence. Each party has the opportunity to become familiar with the opposing side's case and possibly build a basis upon which to negotiate an out-of-court settlement. Examinations for discovery are an essential part of the pre-trial process. Although the pleadings—that is, the initial stages of litigation including the statement of claim, defence, counterclaim, defence to counterclaim—allege various facts, they are not made under oath. The facts alleged could have substantial merit, or no merit. The examination for discovery, conducted under oath, clarifies how much merit the pleadings have. Approximately 75% to 80% of settlement negotiations that result in a compromise resolution before trial occur after the examinations for discovery.

Discovery by Interrogatories

If a one-on-one examination for discovery is not practical, for example, if one party lives in another country, the discoveries are done by written examination. Interrogatories are a list of typed questions posed by each party to the other. Similar to the examination for discovery, they are usually done well before the trial and after the defence and other documents have been served. Questions have to be answered in writing. These answers to interrogatories, usually in a typed reply, are sworn under oath and can be used as evidence or for cross-examination at trial.

Trial Date Set

The plaintiff's lawyer sets the trial date based on an agreement between the lawyers as to the duration of the trial. If there is a disagreement, a trial date will be set based on the lawyer who suggests the longer duration. Generally, the longer the length of trial, the longer the wait before a trial date. The waiting time for trial could be anywhere from six months to three years or longer, depending on the backlog, complexity of trial and other factors.

Pre-trial Conference

At any time after a trial date has been set, either party can request of the court that a pre-trial conference be held. The conference is attended by a judge and the lawyers for the parties, and considers clarification of the legal issues and any other matters that might help in settling the dispute.

Trial

The trial is held before a judge alone unless the legislation in your province allows for a jury to be requested by one of the parties. The plaintiff presents its case first, then the defendants all together or each in turn. Witnesses may be called or subpoenaed as well to give evidence on facts. Both sides give and are then cross-examined. Expert witnesses may be called. For example, if a claim is being made for damages (financial losses), a professional accountant may give expert testimony.

In the final stage of the trial, the lawyers present legal arguments in an attempt to persuade the judge and/or jury that the evidence and applicable laws call for a verdict in favour of their client. It is in these arguments that past cases that have a bearing on the present case are often brought forward. This is called referring to the common law or court case law. These cases generally come from Canada, the United States, or England.

Judgment

The judge or jury has the responsibility to determine the extent that each party contributed to the overall problem and the amount to be paid. One or more of the defendants may be held fully or partly responsible. Or, the plaintiff may have contributed to the problem. If the defendants have put in a counterclaim and the courts uphold the counterclaim, then a set-off will occur against any claim in favour of the plaintiff.

The judge will present an opinion on the case and state the judgment to be awarded and court costs, if any. The losing side is usually obliged to pay court costs to the other side, based on a specified tariff schedule. If the court awards party-party costs, this is a lower tariff schedule than solicitor-client costs. The court has the discretion to grant the higher level of costs if the circumstances justify it. The highest level of court costs generally only represents between 15% and 35% of the actual amount of the winner's legal costs.

Appeal

After the judgment is rendered, one or more of the parties may decide to appeal either the finding of liability, or lack thereof, and/or the amount of the damages awarded. A notice of appeal must be filed within a limited time after judgment. Appeals are heard before a panel of senior judges, and are concerned primarily with errors in the interpretation and application of law, as opposed to the interpretation of the facts and evidence. Only evidence or law introduced at trial can be part of the appeal. It is not a "new" trial. Like the trial process, the appeal process can be lengthy, expensive, unpredictable and stressful.

Examination in Aid of Execution

The party who has been awarded the judgment is entitled to examine under oath the person or company on which the judgment was obtained in order to determine the assets of the judgment debtor. Then procedures can commence to collect the amount of the judgment.

Execution of Judgment

Execution of a judgment can include garnisheeing bank accounts and accounts receivable, seizing assets such as cars, boats and equipment, and commencing action on any real estate owned by the debtor. If the assets are already pledged as security to other creditors, there may be very little, if any, equity remaining.

Settlement

Negotiations to reach a compromise rather than proceeding to trial can be conducted at all stages of the litigation process. After the examination for discovery, negotiations usually occur in earnest, as the bargaining positions become clear.

The courts encourage out-of-court settlements by providing a procedure whereby a party may make a formal offer to settle. If this is done within a limited time prior to the trial and the outcome of the trial is at least as favourable to the offeror as the terms of the offer, the party who failed to accept the offer is penalized by the court by having to pay a higher percentage of the offeror's legal expenses. The offer is open for acceptance until it is either formally withdrawn or the judgment is rendered.

Legal Fees, Expenses and Court Costs

Say you wanted to sue a debtor for $30,000 and retained a lawyer on an hourly bill-out rate of $150. The defendant files a defence and a counterclaim against you for $30,000, claiming a set-off for sloppy and incomplete workmanship and delays. You believe the defendant is bluffing and has no merits to the defence or counterclaim, so you proceed down the litigation road.

Pre-trial procedures go on for a year and then there is a further one or two-year wait before trial. At the trial you win on your claim and are awarded court costs. The trial lasts a week, and there are many witnesses and documents.

Figure 16.1 gives a breakdown of the legal fees and disbursements (out-of-pocket expenses) that you could have incurred. GST/HST is extra, and in some provinces, you would also have to pay PST on legal fees. Monies would be payable from the commencement of the court action.

FIGURE 16.1 ■ *Legal Fees and Disbursements for One Legal Action*

LEGAL FEES	$150/hour	Amount
■ The initial client meetings, obtaining instructions and reviewing of documents	15 hours	$ 2,250
■ Drafting writ of summons and statement of claim, reviewing defence and counterclaim, drafting defence to counterclaim and other documentation	15 hours	$ 2,250
■ Demanding discovery of documents, preparing list of documents, reviewing lists from defendants, obtaining copies of documents from defendants, preparing and photocopying all plaintiff's documents to supply to defendants	10 hours	$ 1,500
■ Preparing for examination for discovery, including reviewing all documents, meeting with clients, preparing list of questions to ask or to anticipate; approximately 1½ days' preparation (average for each day of discovery); therefore 8 days of discovery × 1½ = 12 days × average of 8 hrs/day = 96 hrs	96 hours	$ 14,400
■ Attending at examination for discovery; 8 days of discovery × 8 hrs/day = 64 hrs	64 hours	$ 9,600
■ Preparing for trial, including examining witnesses, reviewing documents, reviewing examination for discovery transcripts, reviewing the law that has been researched; average 2 days' preparation for each day of trial, 5-day trial × 2 = 10 days' preparation × 8 hrs/day = 80 hrs.	80 hours	$ 12,000
■ Researching case law and statute law	25 hours	$ 3,750
■ Attending at trial for a 5-day trial × 8 hrs/day = 40 hrs	40 hours	$ 6,000
Total Legal Fees		**$51,750**

DISBURSEMENTS
- Filing and serving of writ and statement of claim $ 100
- Photocopies $ 1,000
- Court reporter fees and transcripts of examinations for $ 2,000
  discovery
- Long distance telephone calls, fax charges, etc. $ 200
- Miscellaneous $ 200
- Total Disbursements $ 3,500
  Grand Total of Fees and Disbursements paid by plaintiff $55,250

FINANCIAL OUTCOME OF TRIAL
- Court costs by tariff schedule in favour of plaintiff based $15,000
  on party-party costs loser (defendant) has to pay
- Judgment against defendant for amount of claim $30,000
- Plus interest as determined by the court from the $ 6,000
  date the money was owing (varies depending on prime
  rate of interest, but say 10% for example purposes)
  2-year period from date debt owing before
  trial = approx. $3,000 per year × 2 years = $6,000
  Total of Judgment on Debt Owing plus Interest and Court Costs $51,000

Net Loss by Plaintiff

The plaintiff (the "winner") was awarded judgment on the $30,000 plus interest and court costs. When the plaintiff subtracts these amounts from the total financial outlay, there is a net loss of $4,250.

After looking at the preceding example, you might have considerable anxiety when contemplating suing or being sued. In the example given, even though the case was decided in the plaintiff's favour, the plaintiff was still out of pocket. As well, for a two-year period the plaintiff had to deal with the risk, uncertainty, anxiety and frustration of the litigation process. Consider the following:

- Was litigation worth the frustration and risk?
- What if the defendant succeeded in the counterclaim?
- What if the court did not award costs to either party?
- What if the defendant was a corporation, and by the time the trial commenced, it had no assets, and you had no personal guarantees?
- What if the defendant's assets were pledged as security to creditors or to the bank for a loan to pay the legal fees?
- What if the defendant corporation went into bankruptcy just prior to or after the trial?
- What if just prior to trial your lawyer required another retainer and you did not have sufficient cash flow and therefore had no choice but to discontinue the case?

- What if the defendant's counterclaim against you showed up in a Dun & Bradstreet or credit bureau record and because of it you could not obtain further credit?
- What if the non-payment of the $30,000 debt plus the extensive legal fees caused your business to go under because you could not collect on the debt? If you had signed personal guarantees for your corporate liabilities, you may have additional legal problems.

Until or unless you receive a judgment at trial, you would not be entitled to examine the debtor under oath as to the debtor's assets. You would have no idea if the company was pledging its assets, selling off its assets, or ready to go under prior to or shortly after trial.

Some lawyers are more efficient than others in litigation. Make sure that your lawyer is a skilled litigator and attempts to resolve the matter by out-of-court settlement, if at all possible.

Legal Strategies and Tactics

It is common for settlements to be made not on what is fair, in the opinion of one or both parties, but what is economically and pragmatically expedient. Understand these realities before getting involved in litigation.

The civil litigation process is adversarial in nature. Each side will exert their best efforts to convince the court on the merits of their respective positions. At the same time, the goal is to try to diminish the merits of the other side's case. The reality might be somewhere in the middle, or may be weighted on one side or the other.

Consider the following strategic approaches and note that they have very little to do with the facts or dispute at issue. They have a lot to do with tactics. Lawyers differ in their desire or attempt to find a basis for settlement. Some of the strategies are listed here:

- A defendant may counterclaim when you may feel the allegations are totally without merit. However, a counterclaim could affect your credit standing and reputation because most litigation matters show up in the credit bureau or Dun & Bradstreet records. In addition, a counterclaim makes the overall litigation far more complicated than if a simple defence were filed.
- A defendant may attempt to delay the pre-trial proceedings by being slow in responding to the various stages. This could cause a lot of stress and interfere with the momentum of the action. The longer the delay, the more likely that one side is prepared to settle. People's priorities change and litigation is very stressful.
- One party may attempt to frustrate the other by bringing on various motions (heard in front of the chambers judge) on procedural matters. This causes legal costs to escalate, and can further delay the litigation process.

- One party may wish to delay the trial date as long as possible. The more complex the legal issues become, the more likely the trial date will be set further away. For example, one lawyer may state that it will be a two-day trial, in anticipation of an early trial date. The other lawyer may assert that the trial will take five days. A trial date would therefore be set based on a five-day duration, which could be a two-year wait. After two years, the person who wanted a shorter trial may have run out of financial resources or the will to continue, and would be more receptive to an out-of-court settlement.
- One of the parties in the action may have almost unlimited financial resources enabling them to continue indefinitely. If this is asserted at the early stage of litigation, this can compel the other party to settle; otherwise, this party could end up in a serious financial situation.
- If you sue someone in a different geographic area than where you reside there would be additional costs for legal fees for two lawyers and for travelling for the examinations for discovery and the trial. Additional costs for the witnesses' travel, accommodation, and other financial losses while at trial are also possible. These factors go a long way toward providing leverage to one party to effect a settlement.
- Another tactic is to garnishee the account of the party that you are suing, as soon as you commence an action. Some provinces permit garnisheeing before judgment, and others only after. Garnisheeing is only allowed if, for example, you have a fixed debt that is owing to you.

If you are suing a trade creditor and you have the address of the company's bank from the credit application form, you could garnishee the account for the debt. This would provide very effective leverage on which to negotiate a settlement as it means that the defendant does not have those financial resources to use for legal fees. You would know that there is money available to you if you succeeded at the trial.

Avoiding the Pitfalls of Litigation

As in any game, litigation is inherently an adversarial process; if you don't know how to play it well, or retain a lawyer who does, the odds of "winning" are not in your favour. No matter what debt, breach of contract or negligence is causing you to consider suing, keep the following pitfalls foremost in your mind.

Avoid Lawsuits Based on Emotion

You might feel that you have been wronged and you are naturally very upset. Your decision to sue however, should be based on hard-nosed business realities. Maybe there is not much money involved but it is a matter of principle. Give yourself some time, maybe several months, to see if the intensity of your emotions subsides. The litigation process itself has enough negative emotion associated with it.

Frank Sues Out of Anger—And Gets Nothing

Frank extended supplier credit to Art for $40,000 of product. Art operated through an incorporated company and did not sign a personal guarantee. Art was having financial difficulties and delayed paying Frank. Frank was very aware that the industry was having a difficult time. However, Art offered to pay Frank $30,000 within a week if Frank would settle for that as payment in full of the debt. Frank got angry, refused the offer, and sued Art for the full $40,000. Six months later and about three months before the trial date, Art's business went under and Frank never received a penny. All the creditors were secured against Art's assets. Frank was just a general creditor and there was no money left in the company.

Frank was naïve and acted out of emotion, not pragmatic reality. If he had received legal advice and taken into account the overall industry downturn, he should have settled and called it a day. Not only did Frank lose out on the $30,000, he also paid out $10,000 in legal fees.

Have Realistic Expectations

Many people assume that if they are right, they will "win" at the end of the day. However, very few issues in law are black and white. The litigation process is inherently unpredictable. In addition, when you factor in legal fees, even if you win, the court costs you are awarded only amount to about 15% to 35% of your legal fees, so you still lose financially. And then you have the challenge of attempting to collect on the judgment.

Assess the Defendants' Assets

You could "win" at trial, but still be a big time loser. The defendant could have no assets in their name or have all their assets leveraged up with debt at the time you commence an action or by the time you get a judgment. A corporate entity could be a hollow shell without any net worth.

Do an objective risk assessment of the realistic potential of collecting on a judgment. You could be throwing good money after bad. The negative learning experience could be seen as a cost of business, and you could then commit to changing your business practices to pre-empt a recurrence.

Weighing Potential Gains vs. Losses

Realistically assess the relative pros and cons of litigation, in money and lost productivity. Can you afford the fight to the end? Have you obtained three written quotes as to the cost of the complete pre-trial and trial process? Is it going to cost more than the amount you are claiming? What if you lose? You will be out not only legal fees, but court costs as well. What if the defendant counterclaims against you and wins?

Consider a Settlement

Settlements occur all the time. Only about 5% of lawsuits ever end up at trial, with the exception of small claims court. Even small claims court has a settlement hearing process before trial, in many provinces. Settlements allow both parties to strike a deal and get on with life, saving a lot of court time. Because of the uncertainty of the trial process outcome, settling for 20, 30, 50 or 70% of the original claim is better than the risk of getting nothing and being out legal fees as well.

Don't Sue Too Early

Don't commence your action before you have all the facts. Ideally, you want to have all your arguments included in your claim, to show your opponent that you have done your homework.

Don't Sue Too Late

If you wait too long, you could miss a statutory time limit to commence your action. Different actions and different provinces have different time limits.

Get Expert Legal Advice

Before you make any decisions, have a minimum of three lawyers give you objective feedback on your chances at trial, how long it will take and how much it will cost. You need a benchmark for comparison and to make sure that the advice is consistent, and if not, why not. Refer to Chapter 1 on Legal and Other Advisors. A few consultations will enhance your knowledge and increase your confidence in your final decision. Then, sleep on your dilemma for a few weeks or a month. See if you have the same opinion at the end of that time.

Alternative Dispute Resolution

Using the legal process to resolve a conflict should be a last resort. Apart from the time and costs involved, the relationship will probably be damaged beyond repair. If the parties get to the point where they communicate only through their respective lawyers, it is inevitable that there will be at best a winner and loser, or two losers. It is doubtful that it will be a win-win, which is obviously the best outcome.

The first step to resolving a dispute is obviously for both parties to sit down together and attempt to work out a solution that is mutually acceptable. If a dispute cannot be resolved at this level, the alternative dispute resolution (ADR) approach is gaining favour in many types of business conflicts. Trained professionals can provide mediation and arbitration services for business disputes including mediating contract interpretation, disputes or negotiations, or providing a written opinion proposing a pragmatic, equitable and reasonable resolution of conflict. Mediation is an informal resolution facilitation service. Arbitration is more formal and is generally governed by the provincial *Arbitration Act*, which sets out procedures and protocols.

Mediation

Mediation is gaining popularity because it has several advantages over arbitration. First, the mediation process leads the parties to a mutually acceptable resolution—a win-win—without the mediator providing an opinion as to the merits of the claim. The mediator should have some knowledge of the legal issues or business concepts under discussion.

Including mediation clauses in business contracts will become more common as business owners realize its advantages. Clauses will detail provisions such as allocation of costs, agreement for each party to invest a minimum time, and selection criteria for the mediator.

Most larger cities in Canada have business mediation services available. Look in the Yellow Pages of your phone book under "mediation services" or visit the Canadian Dispute Resolution Corporation's Web site at *www.cdrc.com* for links.

Arbitration

If the mediation process does not resolve the issue, the next step is arbitration. The wording of a business contract between the parties usually states that arbitration is binding upon the parties, ruling out an appeal process. The agreement also provides a method of selecting an arbitrator that is acceptable to both parties and also covers the issue of fees.

Check in the Yellow Pages of your phone book under "arbitration services" to find an arbitrator in the larger cities. Or visit the BC International Commercial Arbitration Centre's Web site at *www.bcicac.com* for links.

Effective business management and controls may avoid many potentially litigious situations. A good level of communication between customers and suppliers, careful documentation of terms and conditions of verbal agreements and timely follow-up on problem situations will reduce potential risks.

Summary

This chapter demonstrates why you want to do everything possible to avoid litigation. By following the tips and cautions throughout this book, and avoiding the pitfalls that abound in business, you can minimize your chances of experiencing the litigation process first-and. Don't feel overwhelmed by the experience. By selecting the right business lawyer, you are maximizing your chances at business success.

Seventeen

Bankruptcy and Insolvency

Introduction

Most business owners do not know the process or implications of business distress including insolvency, bankruptcy and receivership. Considering that approximately four out of five small businesses cease to operate within three to five years of start-up, the odds are very high that one of your suppliers or customers may fall upon such hardship. By understanding insolvency, bankruptcy and receivership, and your rights and remedies, you can protect yourself.

Historical Causes of Financial Difficulties

Financial factors that may result in insolvency, bankruptcy, or receivership may include the following:

- Poor budgeting of income and expenses
- Misuse or overuse of credit
- Employment problems such as lack of work, irregular employment, or seasonal employment
- Partnership disputes
- Personal guarantees of corporate debts called
- Marital problems
- Family tragedy such as loss of home, death, or disability
- Loss of second income from spouse or from part-time employment
- Physical, emotional, or mental health problems
- Dependence on alcohol or drugs.

The main reasons for business difficulties include incompetence, lack of experience, neglect, fraud and disaster.

Incompetence

Incompetence is by far the largest single factor in business failure. It can also be the most difficult to detect and correct. Researchers have identified several guidelines to indicate when incompetence is present, only one of which may be required before the business actually fails:

- **Undercapitalization.** The business starts out with inadequate financial resources to meet reasonably projected needs and contingencies.
- **Excessive expenses.** It is very common for start-up businesses to spend more money than is really required, especially during the first few years. Careful cash flow management is essential.
- **Inventory problems.** Being overly optimistic about trends and sales requirements is also common. Too much money could be tied up in surplus inventory that may not move as quickly as projected. Not having enough stock of other items could cause loss of customer loyalty.
- **Receivables problems.** Companies in the first few years of operation tend to allow liberal credit and are careless with their collection procedures. Receivables increase in amount and age, thereby limiting use of those funds as working capital.
- **Excessive fixed assets.** A small business might invest too much money in fixed assets that are unproductive capital allocations, for example, expensive furniture could cost three times as much as basic start-up items that the company could have purchased or leased. The business could then be short of working capital or security leverage at the bank.
- **Poor location.** A poor location may cause a business to fail before potential customers know it exists. Careful market research could avoid this situation.
- **Competitive weakness.** Due to insufficient planning and poor research of the competition and the needs of the marketplace, your business may not have the uniqueness necessary to attract a clientele base.
- **Low sales volume.** Many small business owners are overly optimistic initially and delude themselves into thinking that they will generate far more income than the circumstances would indicate. Possibly cash flow projections were not done, or they were not based on realistic research.

Lack of Experience

- **Lack of management experience.** Many small business owner-managers lack any managerial experience or training. The owner may have little knowledge of, or dislike certain areas, for example, bookkeeping or sales, and therefore let those important areas go unattended. The expense for a part-time or full-time manager may be hard to justify at that stage of the business.
- **Unbalanced experience.** This occurs when the small business owner has excellent skills in certain areas and little or none in others.
- **Lack of specialized expertise in the business.** Some small business owners have no specific experience or background knowledge of the industry sector of their new business. Without at least a working knowledge of the service or product to be sold, decision-making will not be based on any realistic foundation. It will also be difficult to build customer and staff confidence.

Neglect

Neglect of the needs of the business is frequently caused by bad habits, lack of confidence, marital or partnership difficulties, fatigue, or poor health. Outside consulting assistance would help identify any bad management habits. The other factors are more difficult to cure and could lessen the owner's interest in the business because of distractions. In these situations, the solution may be to sell the business or the owner's interest to another partner or shareholder.

Fraud

Fraud accounts for a very small number of business failures. Where bankruptcy is imminent, owners may defraud the business by taking assets out before it goes under, thereby defeating creditors' access to the company assets. False financial statements may be prepared in order to deceive Canada Customs and Revenue Agency (formerly Revenue Canada), the bank, or other creditors, or to convince suppliers to extend further credit. Inaccurate financial data may be used to sell the business for an inflated price. Premeditated overbuying occurs when a company intentionally overbuys on credit terms, then has a sale of the items to convert to cash before putting the business under. The suppliers are left with a large debt, which they would be unable to collect.

These examples involve a deliberate intention on the part of the small business owner to financially benefit at the expense of creditors in an illegal fashion; they do not refer to poor business management. If a creditor believes a criminal fraud has taken place, it can be reported to the police. In addition, under provincial legislation, a creditor could commence action alleging a civil fraud. Under the federal *Bankruptcy and Insolvency Act*, a creditor could also allege improper acts and request the trustee in bankruptcy to review them.

Disaster

Disaster accounts for a very small portion of the reasons for business failure, and includes employee fraud, burglary, floods and fire. Good insurance coverage may help to recuperate the financial losses incurred. However, unless you carry coverage for loss of income through business interruption, the time delay to rebuild the business may be too great to endure.

It is important for the businessperson to understand the reasons why businesses fail. Incompetence, which accounts for approximately two-thirds of business failures, can sometimes be corrected through candid personal and business assessment before the business commences. One must have the desire and ability to recognize and compensate for deficiencies.

Other causes of financial difficulties in business include failure to realistically self-evaluate; failure to establish, review and revise goals; failure to anticipate obstacles or to learn from experience. A lack of sustained commitment is also a factor.

Insolvency

Many businesses could be technically insolvent from time to time but not become bankrupt or suffer other business failure. The insolvency state could be a temporary one, for example, due to overdue receivables and cash flow problems. With improved management, the business could turn itself around.

The federal *Bankruptcy and Insolvency Act* defines insolvency as: a person or company who is for any reason unable to meet financial obligations as they become due, or whose assets at a fair market value are insufficient to pay all financial obligations. If a creditor wants to petition an individual or company into bankruptcy, the degree of insolvency must exceed $1,000 in total to all creditors.

Proposals

A proposal refers to an arrangement proposed by a debtor and negotiated with the creditors. There are three main categories of proposals—the informal proposal negotiated outside the *Bankruptcy and Insolvency Act*, a consumer proposal and the formal proposal under this Act known as a Division 1 proposal.

1. Informal Proposal Outside the *Bankruptcy and Insolvency Act*

An insolvent debtor may make an informal proposal to creditors to negotiate either a reduction in the amount owed or a change in the terms of payment. It is common for creditors to agree to a settlement based on a percentage of the debt owing and with payment terms excluding interest. An informal proposal is usually only feasible where the creditors are few in number, and believe there is no better financial alternative. The alternative is to possibly get much less in a bankruptcy situation.

An informal proposal cannot be imposed upon a creditor who is not in agreement. In most instances, each creditor will have to be approached individually by the debtor. If the creditors decline the proposal, a bankruptcy will not automatically occur. However, the debtor must be cautious because the approach itself is evidence of insolvency and can be used by the creditor as grounds to petition the debtor into bankruptcy. The advantage of an informal proposal is that the debtor is not bound by the administrative procedures prescribed by the *Bankruptcy and Insolvency Act* and does not incur the costs of a trustee.

If the debtor presents the informal settlement alternatives to creditors, the proposal is successful and the debtor complies, the procedure ends here and business will continue. If, however, the offer is unsuccessful, the debtor may attempt a formal proposal.

If a creditor has a personal guarantee of one of the principals of a corporation, then that could eliminate the desire to accept the informal proposal. However, the personal guarantor may have sold or leveraged all his or her personal assets so that there is no equity left. A personal guarantee makes the creditor an unsecured creditor, ranked at the bottom of the list in receiving funds. Refer to Chapter 12 on Creditor Proofing your Business.

Banks also settle for a percentage of a debt owing and terms without interest. It is not uncommon in the case of a personal guarantor for banks to settle for 25¢ to 35¢ on the dollar, depending on the circumstances. It is better to receive 25¢ on the dollar on an informal proposal than 10¢ on the dollar from a formal proposal, or 1¢ on the dollar from a bankruptcy. Have a lawyer or trustee manage an informal proposal for credibility, expertise and impact. Most business owners are not skilled at negotiating out of their debts because they are too emotionally involved.

Advantages of an Informal Proposal
- Rejection of the informal proposal does not result in automatic bankruptcy
- Cost is reduced
- Same outcome could be achieved
- Opportunity to have different settlement terms for different creditors
- Avoid the stigma of action under the *Bankruptcy and Insolvency Act*.

Disadvantages of an Informal Proposal
- Certain creditors may want to negotiate a better deal or hold out to be paid in full
- No stay of proceedings, in terms of collection, or other legal action by creditors during negotiations
- Requires acceptance by all creditors, otherwise unsatisfied creditors could continue collection action.

2. Consumer Proposal
For most people, deciding between filing a bankruptcy or a consumer proposal is serious and confusing. Consumer proposals under the *Bankruptcy and Insolvency Act* are intended to reduce the number of bankruptcy filings by allowing consumers who owe less than $75,000 (excluding mortgages on their principal residences) to negotiate with their creditors for the reduction of their debt and/or extension of time for payments of their debts. Any executions on judgments, garnishees of income and other collection actions by creditors will be stopped once the consumer proposal is filed. Contact a trustee in bankruptcy for more information. How to obtain a trustee is discussed later in this chapter.

3. Formal Proposals under the *Bankruptcy and Insolvency Act* (Division 1 Proposal)
If an insolvent debtor cannot work out an arrangement with creditors, the only avenue open to an unsecured creditor or the debtor would be bankruptcy. A proposal is actually a contract between the debtor and his or her creditors. A formal proposal, if accepted by the majority of creditors representing 66.6% of the claims, becomes binding on all unsecured creditors. A proposal can be made either before or after bankruptcy. If it is made after bankruptcy, the inspectors of the bankrupt's affairs must approve it before it can be presented to the creditors.

A proposal under the *Bankruptcy and Insolvency Act* cannot bind the secured creditors unless they agree. It must also provide for a full payment of trustee's fees and expenses, as well as specified preferred creditors and certain crown claims. If the offer to unsecured creditors is accepted by special resolution at a creditors' meeting, the proposal becomes binding on all the unsecured creditors. A special resolution is passed by a majority in number and 66.6% in value of the creditors with proven claims present at the meeting or by proxy. Once accepted by the creditors, it must also be approved by the court. If the creditors do not accept the proposal, it is treated as though the debtor made an assignment into bankruptcy.

Advantages of a Formal Proposal
- Unsecured creditors are prevented from continuing lawsuits that might result in the seizure of assets, without the court's consent.
- Debtor's cash flow can be used for current operating expenses without having to pay those funds to suppliers for past debts.
- All creditors are dealt with equitably, as set out in the priority fashion required by law.
- The debtor could attempt a temporary delay in payment (stay of proceedings) of his or her secured creditors. This opportunity is up to the discretion of the court. During this interim, negotiations could take place or new investment funds sourced out. However, if the company is in dire financial shape, the court can refuse to provide a stay.
- Commercial leases are generally exempt.

Disadvantages of a Formal Proposal
- It may be difficult to obtain the required support from all classes of creditors.
- Depending on the degree of creditor involvement or control, the extra costs associated with trustee and related legal fees could be considerable.
- If the proposal is rejected, it will automatically lead to bankruptcy of the business. However, this should encourage a debtor to be realistic.
- If you are an unsecured creditor, you need to evaluate whether the proposal is realistic in the circumstances. If not, there may not be any benefit to supporting it.

Here are the key questions to consider when determining the debtor's chance for success:
- How is the debtor's industry doing?
- How well is the debtor doing in that industry?
- How competent is the management of the debtor business, and what is its level of integrity and commitment?
- How realistic are the forecasts and budgets to support the proposal terms?
- Is there adequate working capital to finance the daily operations of the business?

- What are the underlying problems of the debtor and are those problems solved or effectively being solved?
- Will suppliers only operate on a cash basis?
- Are the secured creditors in agreement with the proposal?
- If a lease exists, would the lease be terminated as a result of the problem?
- Can the proposal be completed in the time allocated?
- Where are the proposal payment funds coming from, and are outside sources of funds being used?
- Does the proposal provide more money than would be available under a bankruptcy?

Types of Formal Proposals

An unlimited variety of proposals under the *Bankruptcy and Insolvency Act* might be presented including:

- **Extension of time.** A proposal for an extension of time for payment will often contain other measures such as reducing the amount of the claim also.
- **Percentage of profits.** The creditors agree to accept a percentage of the debtor's profits over time in satisfaction of their claims. The creditor's acceptance and court approval of this type of proposal will depend largely on whether the debtor's future profitability appears promising.
- **Basket proposal.** This is a request to the creditors to restrict their claims to particular assets, thereby enabling the debtor to carry on business with the remaining assets. The debtor places specific assets in a "basket" held by the trustee. This procedure enables the debtor to carry out the proposal immediately and then the trustee determines the extent and priority of the claims to the assets.
- **Conversion of debt to equity.** The creditors agree to refinance a secured debt by accepting shares of the company instead of payment.
- **Lump sum.** The debtor offers a percentage on the dollar of the amount owing, excluding interest—for example, 10% on the dollar with payment two months after formal acceptance by all the creditors, or over two payments six months apart.
- **Liquidation proposal.** A debtor, who anticipates the eventual closing of the business but who wishes to avoid the consequences of bankruptcy, can submit a proposal to transfer all the assets to the trustee to sell and distribute the proceeds among the creditors. The rationale for a liquidation proposal is that if a company is wound down in an orderly fashion, the assets will realize a higher value than if they were tainted with a receivership or bankruptcy.

Procedures Involved in Bankruptcy Proposals

A business debtor wishing to make a formal proposal asks a trustee to supervise a proposal to be made to the creditors. The trustee assists the debtor in determining the terms of the proposal based on the circumstances. Other than the proposal itself, which must be completed and filed with the superintendent of bankruptcy, the forms are similar to those filed in a bankruptcy. When the trustee forwards the normal proof of claim forms sent to creditors, he or she also includes the proposal and a voting letter. The voting letter permits a creditor to vote on a proposal in writing without attending the creditors' meeting. The trustee calls the creditors' meeting in order to discuss the terms of the proposal. A creditor may suggest amendments and extensive bargaining can take place before the proposal is finally voted upon.

Each party knows that if the proposal is not accepted, a bankruptcy will occur which usually will not benefit either party. Normally a representative of the Superintendent of Bankruptcy office attends the meeting of creditors. If the proposal is not approved, an immediate first meeting of creditors and bankruptcy is called.

Trustee's Duties and Fees

If the debtor is a business, the trustee will normally require guarantees of his or her fees and expenses from the principals of the company or from third parties, or will require an advance retainer. At the first meeting of the creditors, the trustee reports to the creditors on his or her investigation of the affairs of the debtor. The report indicates if there have been any possible fraudulent preferences or conveyances or voidable transactions. The report also indicates if there have been any unreasonable payments to directors or improper payment of dividends, whether the proposal appears viable and that recovery for creditors will be enhanced by the proposal. The trustee may chair the meeting and supervise the voting. Scrutineers can be elected by the creditors to review the proofs of claim filed and tally the votes. If the creditors accept the proposal, the trustee must apply to the court for approval. Normally the court will approve the proposal, although it may impose terms.

The trustee will be responsible for collecting the amounts to be remitted to creditors. The proposal obligations will then have been completed and a certificate of completion will be issued. The trustee will apply to the court for a discharge. Sometimes the trustee is given the responsibility under the proposal to supervise the affairs of the debtor until the proposal is completed. In other cases, the proposal calls for the election of inspectors by the group of creditors to control the affairs of the debtor until completion.

A small business venture will normally proceed by way of an informal proposal, as trustee fees and expenses under a formal proposal can be substantial, thereby making it impractical unless the small business has considerable goodwill.

Bankruptcy

The main purposes of the *Bankruptcy and Insolvency Act* are:
- Control of distribution and equitable division of the insolvent debtor's assets to creditors; a system of priorities for distribution of the assets is established and all creditors of the same class receive equal treatment

- Rehabilitation of debtors, whether corporate or consumer; designed to provide the debtor a means of ending onerous financial obligations and attaining equilibrium and stability
- Punishment of fraudulent debtors; provides a system for investigating and imposing sanctions for deliberate fraud
- Regulation of receiverships, even though the debtor is not bankrupt
- Encouragement of confidence in the credit system and overall economic viability.

In addition to knowing your rights and remedies under the *Bankruptcy and Insolvency Act*, as a creditor or debtor, be aware of the *Companies Creditors Arrangement Act* (federal), and provincial statutes such as the *Winding Up Act, Creditors' Relief Act, Fraudulent Conveyance Act, Fraudulent Preferences Act* or *Orderly Payment of Debts Act*, etc. For further information, speak to a lawyer who is an expert in these areas, in addition to a trustee in bankruptcy.

A Worst Case Scenario

Jan and Dave had been in business for about ten years operating through a corporation. Over time, their business location was becoming less attractive and business was decreasing. They collapsed their RRSPs to keep the business afloat. Then the bank called their loan due to a history of missed or late payments. The bank also exercised on their security, and had a bailiff enter their premises to secure the business inventory and assets. Jan and Dave had signed personal guarantees of all their corporate debts, and had pledged their home as collateral security. The CCRA (formerly Revenue Canada) entered the picture and made a claim against the two directors, Jan and Dave, for employee deductions at source that were not remitted. Jan and Dave had used the money as they were desperate for cash flow. The provincial government then took action against them as directors for arrears of employee salaries. The situation was a mess. Jan and Dave walked away from the business, declared personal bankruptcy and lost their home to a forced sale. All the stress caused immense family tensions and health problems, resulting in marital separation and divorce.

To avoid this gloomy but common scenario, legal advice would have helped. Strategic planning, assessing risk scenarios and setting up approaches to deal with them, could have been done. A lawyer could have negotiated with creditors to buy time, reduce or delay payments or settle for a reduced amount on the dollar over time. Unfortunately, Jan and Dave did not act strategically. Almost all of these sad scenarios could have been avoided through prudent tactical legal planning.

The Bankruptcy Process

The court hears the petition approximately ten days after it has been served on the debtor and the Superintendent of Bankruptcy. Once the court is satisfied that the debtor is insolvent, the debtor has committed an act of bankruptcy and the petitioner is acting in good faith, a receiving order will be issued declaring the debtor to be bankrupt. The effective date of bankruptcy is the date that the receiving order is granted. During this ten-day period, the trustee has no power to act and a number of things might occur which could be prejudicial to the creditors. The *Bankruptcy and Insolvency Act* therefore makes provision for the appointment of a licensed trustee as an interim receiver of the debtor's property. The interim receiver has the power to act immediately and take possession of the debtor's property. To obtain an interim order, the petitioning creditor must demonstrate to the court that such an order is necessary. The creditor must also undertake the responsibility for any damages suffered by the debtor in the event the petition is ultimately dismissed.

Once appointed, the interim receiver assumes the status of a caretaker and cannot unduly interfere with the debtor's business, except as authorized by the court. If necessary, the court will grant the interim receiver power to dispose of any property that is perishable or likely to depreciate rapidly in value. The interim receiver is in the awkward position of acting in the best interest of the creditors, while refraining from interfering in the business of the debtor.

After the date of bankruptcy, unsecured creditors must make their claims through the trustee. Secured creditors' rights are generally restricted to the extent necessary to enable the trustee to ensure that the creditors' security is valid. Preferred creditors generally must await the orderly administration of the debtor's estate by the trustee before they are paid.

Steps Taken by Trustee

The trustee will review the debtor's affairs watching for:

- **Fraudulent preferences.** The trustee may review any payment made to a bona fide creditor within three months from the date of bankruptcy including a gifting of an asset without fair consideration (payment). The bankrupt's intention would be to give the creditor a preference over other creditors. The transaction can be deemed fraudulent and the court will order payment of the monies to the trustee.
- **Fraudulent conveyance.** Transfers of property or other assets at a price that is not a fair market price may have the intent to defraud creditors. Frequently the transfer is to relatives or friends. Any asset transaction within one year prior to the bankruptcy may be reviewed by the court.

Important correspondence will be sent out to all the creditors including:

- **Notice to creditors of first meeting.** This document informs the creditor of the bankruptcy, invites him/her to attend the first meeting of creditors on the date and at the place fixed, and advises that a proof of claim is to be filed.

- **Proof of claim.** This form asks the creditor to verify the amount of the debt and to substantiate the claim. Substantiation includes attaching an invoice, statement of account, or promissory note. The creditor will also be asked to indicate his or her status as a secured, preferred, or unsecured creditor.
- **Proxy.** If the creditor is unable to attend the first meeting of creditors, a proxy form may be completed appointing someone else to act on his/her behalf. It is fairly common for creditors to appoint the trustee as their proxy, especially if the creditors reside outside the geographic area in which the creditors' meeting would be held.

First Meeting of Creditors

The trustees will report on the affairs of the bankrupt at the first meeting of creditors. This preliminary report includes the value of all property, the total liability and the trustee's opinion of the types and validity of creditors' claims. The trustee will also give an opinion on whether the affairs of the bankrupt have been conducted properly.

Normally within three weeks of the trustee's appointment, the first meeting of creditors is held to review the affairs of the bankrupt and either ratify the appointment of the trustee or appoint a new trustee. The creditors also decide whether to appoint inspectors to supervise the estate. A quorum at the creditors' meeting consists of just one creditor who has proven his or her claim. This creditor can be personally present, be represented, or by proxy. Under summary administration (personal bankruptcy), a meeting of creditors is not usually called until requested.

Rights of the Creditor

A creditor who has a valid, supported claim against the bankrupt, may share in the distribution of the debtor's assets providing there is enough money to pay the claims that are ranked before that creditor's. A creditor has additional rights including the right to:

- Examine the proof of claim of other creditors
- Vote on any matters that may arise, such as selection, removal or substitution of the trustee or inspectors
- Object to the discharge of the bankrupt or the trustee
- Appeal to the court if he or she is in disagreement with any act or decision of the trustee
- Take independent action in the recovery of assets, with the permission of the court, if the trustee fails to do so.

Duties of the Bankrupt

Within five days after bankruptcy is filed, the bankrupt is instructed in writing to attend a meeting of creditors. The bankrupt must be present at this meeting unless prevented by sickness or other sufficient cause. Under the *Bankruptcy and Insolvency Act*, a bankrupt must act honestly and cooperate fully with the trustee to facilitate the highest return from the bankrupt's assets for disposition to the creditors.

Following is a list of the bankrupt's duties. He or she must:

- Turn over to the trustee all assets in his or her possession or control, including credit cards
- Deliver to the trustee all records, books and documents relating to his or her assets or affairs
- Attend the office of the official receiver to be examined under oath as to the facts of the bankruptcy
- Submit to other examinations under oath when required
- Provide a statement of affairs, normally prepared by the trustee, listing all the assets and liabilities, including creditors' names, addresses, account numbers, invoices and amounts. If any additional bills or legal documents are received after the list is prepared, they must be forwarded or if any assets or debts have been accidentally omitted, the trustee must be promptly informed
- Disclose to the trustee all property disposed of within one year preceding bankruptcy
- Disclose to the trustee all gifts disposed of by the bankrupt during the five years prior to the bankruptcy, including how they were disposed, to whom, why and for how much
- Attend at first meeting of creditors and other meetings when required, for examination
- Not attempt to obtain new credit until discharged
- Not make any payments to creditors without consulting with trustee
- Help in the realization of his or her property and the distribution of proceeds among creditors
- Execute such forms or other documents as may be required
- Examine the correctness of all proofs of claim submitted to the trustee and disclose any false claims to the trustee by creditors
- Remit to the trustee immediately upon receipt all money received from lotteries, inheritances, or any similar sources
- Keep the trustee advised of any change of address, employment or salary.

The *Bankruptcy and Insolvency Act* outlines the penalties which can be imposed against the bankrupt who has not acted appropriately. If an interested party suspects that an offence under the Act has been committed, the office of the Superintendent of Bankruptcy is informed. If the superintendent feels that an investigation is warranted, the matter is referred to the RCMP. If found guilty, a bankrupt is subject to imprisonment, a fine, or both, where the bankrupt:

- Failed to perform his or her duties as previously described
- Makes a fraudulent disposition of assets before or after bankruptcy
- Refuses or neglects to answer fully and truthfully all questions when examined under oath

- Makes a false declaration regarding assets or liabilities
- Destroys, mutilates, conceals or falsifies a document relating to the bankrupt's property after or within 12 months preceding the bankruptcy
- Obtains credit or property by false representations after or within 12 months preceding the bankruptcy and until the date of discharge
- Fraudulently conceals property of a value of $50 or more after or within 12 months preceding the bankruptcy
- Pawns or pledges property on which credit has been obtained but not paid off within 12 months preceding the bankruptcy
- Engages in a new business occupation or obtains credit in excess of $500, without disclosure of undischarged bankrupt status.

Discharge of the Bankrupt

A discharge by the court will generally provide final relief to the bankrupt. For a first-time bankruptcy, the discharge is automatically set for nine months from the date of bankruptcy. For a second-time bankruptcy, the trustee must apply for the discharge or not less than three and not more than 12 months from the date of the bankruptcy. The trustee completes a report on the affairs and conduct of the bankrupt and the cause of bankruptcy. The trustee advises the creditors that application will be made for the bankrupt's discharge. The hearing, an informal procedure, is held before the District Registrar of the court.

A creditor can oppose a discharge by appearing before the Registrar, after giving written notice of his or her intention to do so. If a discharge is opposed, the Registrar may adjourn the discharge. The bankrupt should, in order to have further applications for discharge made, engage a lawyer who will arrange for the matter to be decided by a judge.

Once the discharge application is in front of the judge, the court may then do one of the following:

- Issue an order of absolute discharge, meaning that the debtor is no longer responsible for his or her debts, except for those listed by the court
- Issue an order of conditional discharge, meaning that the bankrupt is required to pay a sum of money for distribution to creditors, and then obtain absolute discharge
- Issue an order of suspended discharge, essentially the same as an absolute discharge except that the court orders a delay before the discharge is effective
- Postpone the hearing to a later date
- Refuse the discharge; a power rarely exercised by the court and only for serious reasons.

There are certain debts that an order of discharge does not release the bankrupt from paying including:

- Any fine, penalty, restitution order or similar order, imposed by a court in respect of an offence, or any debt arising out of a recognizance or bail

- Any debt or liability for alimony
- Any debt or liability under a maintenance or affiliation order or under an agreement for maintenance and support of a spouse or child living apart from the bankrupt
- Any debt or liability arising out of fraud, embezzlement, or misappropriation while acting in a position of trust
- Any debt or liability for obtaining property by false pretences or fraudulent misrepresentation
- Liability for the dividend that a creditor would have been entitled to receive on any provable claim not disclosed to the trustee, unless such creditor had knowledge of the bankruptcy and failed to take reasonable action to prove his or her claim
- Damage awards for bodily harm, sexual assault or wrongful death
- For student loans, the bankrupt has to have ceased to be a student for ten years prior to the date of bankruptcy.

Receivership

If a debenture or General Security Agreement (GSA) is given by a corporation to a lender, and the debtor does not comply, then a receivership could occur. In this circumstance, a receiver or receiver-manager is appointed either by the terms of the document or by the court. Other forms of security such as mortgages or assignments of inventory could also involve the appointment of receivers. The debenture or GSA are the most common ways that receiverships are triggered.

Debentures

A debenture is similar to a GSA and is a form of security provided by a corporation to a lender. The document describes the nature of the security, the property it encumbers and the steps that will be taken by the lender if the borrower defaults.

Appointment of Receiver

If the debtor defaults under the terms of the security document, the lender has the right to appoint a receiver or receiver-manager to take possession of the debtor's assets. The receiver then controls the assets.

If the directors of the company cannot pay out the security holder, the receiver manager directs actions to be taken, such as sale of the assets or the company as a whole. This latter situation may occur where unsecured creditors are taking steps to collect unpaid accounts, such as garnisheeing, thereby depleting the assets to pay creditors who would otherwise rank behind the debenture or GSA holder.

In other instances, the receiver-manager manages the business to protect its value, including goodwill, so that it can be sold as a going concern at the best price. This tends to occur when a business cannot be operated so as to service its debt load.

A receiver-manager operates much like a trustee in bankruptcy. However, he or she must rely on business law principles and statues rather than the *Bankruptcy and Insolvency Act*. A debtor may have property that is either on loan or is rented. The receiver-manager does not obtain any more right to these goods than the company had. Payments must be kept in good standing or the assets returned. If the receiver-manager inadvertently sells property not owned by the company, he or she may be held liable. In many cases, the receiver-manager operates through a limited liability corporation.

If you have any questions on receivership or bankruptcy, consult a trustee who specializes in these areas. Normally an accountant who is a trustee in bankruptcy also acts as a receiver-manager. Look in the Yellow Pages under "Trustees in Bankruptcy." If you are being asked to sign a debenture or GSA on behalf of your company, obtain competent legal advice from a business lawyer on negotiating the security document or negotiating out of it. Make sure that you also speak to your accountant before signing any security document.

Summary
There are many ways to resolve financial difficulties in your business before they evolve into insolvency, bankruptcy or receivership. It is important to obtain advice from a business lawyer at the first sign of financial problems. With sufficient lead-time, your options are increased, in terms of negotiating settlements, structuring your business affairs and planning your strategy.

Glossary

Administrator The person appointed by the court to administer the estate. This occurs when there is no will, the will did not name an executor, or the named executor has died or is unwilling or unable to act. Sometimes referred to as a "personal representative."

Affidavit A sworn statement in writing, made before an authorized party, such as a lawyer or notary public.

Agent Someone who legally represents someone else, and can act in that person's or company's name.

Agreement for Sale This agreement between the seller and the purchaser is an alternative to a mortgage for financing the purchase of real property. Under this type of arrangement the seller of the property finances the purchase rather than a lending institution. Once the agreement is made the purchaser can possess the property but legal title to the property remains with the seller until the purchaser completes making all payments to the seller.

Agreement of Purchase and Sale A written agreement between the owner and a purchaser for the purchase of real estate on a pre-determined price and terms.

Arbitration The resolution of a dispute between two parties by an impartial third party. Used in commercial disputes when direct negotiations fail. The arbitrator's decision may or may not be final, depending on the nature of your contract. Each province has an *Arbitration Act* setting out procedures.

Arm's Length Refers to a transaction between two or more unrelated companies or individuals.

Articles of Incorporation A legal document filed with the province and/or federally that sets forth the purposes and/or regulations for a corporation. These papers must be approved by the province and/or federally before a corporation legally exists and is allowed to do business.

Assets The valuable resources or property rights owned by an individual or business enterprise. Tangible assets include cash, inventory, land and buildings, and intangible assets include patents and goodwill.

Attribution Rules Under the *Income Tax Act*—the rules that govern attribution of income and/or capital gains in certain situations. For example, where property is transferred, directly or through a trust, for the benefit of a spouse, the income on that property may be deemed to be attributed as income of the transferor rather than the person holding the property.

Bad Debts Money owed to you that you can't collect.

Bankruptcy   The financial and legal position of a person or corporation unable to pay debts. A legal bankrupt must transfer control of any remaining assets to a Trustee in Bankruptcy. Governed by the federal *Bankruptcy and Insolvency Act.*

Basis Point   This is equal to 1/100 of 1%.

Beneficiary   A person who receives a benefit or gift under a will, or a person for whose benefit a trust is created.

Bequest   A disposition in a will concerning property.

Blended Payments   Equal payments consisting of both a principal and an interest component, paid each month during the term of the mortgage. The principal portion increases each month, while the interest portion decreases, but the total monthly payment does not change.

Breakup Value   The estimated value of a business after its operations are stopped and the assets sold and the liabilities paid off. Usually less than the "going concern" value.

Broker   Anyone who brings a potential buyer and a potential seller together, in return for a fee or commission charged to one, the other, or both; e.g., business, franchise, insurance.

Builder's Lien   A lien which can be registered against the title of property as security for the payment of a contractor's bill for work done on, or supplies delivered to, that particular property.

Business Expense   An expense of producing and/or selling a product, which can be deducted from gross income to arrive at net income for taxation purposes.

Buy-Sell Agreement   See Shotgun Agreement.

Capital   The amount of money owner(s) have invested in the business (including profits that are not taken out). Also called equity, owners' equity or shareholders' equity.

Capital Cost Allowance   The amount of tax relief that CCRA allows for depreciation. This would include an asset that has a useful but diminishing life over time, e.g., car, equipment, furniture. Different assets have different amounts of annual depreciation, ranging from 4% to 100%.

Capital Gain   Gain earned on the sale of an asset or gain deemed to be realized on the death of an individual, as if the asset had been sold on the date of death, e.g., deemed disposition. The difference between a capital property's fair market value and its adjusted cost base—essentially, what you've made on the investment.

Capital Loss   Loss experienced on the sale of an asset or loss deemed to be experienced on the death of an individual, as if the asset had been sold on the date of death.

Cash Surrender Value   The money paid out by an insurer upon cancellation of a life insurance policy.

Casualty Insurance   Insurance other than accident and life insurance: fire, theft, general liability.

Charitable Gift Annuity   A life annuity issued by a charitable organization. It is based on an individual paying more than the expected annuity payments. At the time of the recipient's death, any capital remaining in the annuity reverts to the issuer for the benefit of the charity.

Charitable Remainder Trust   In this case, you would transfer property to a trust and name a charity as the capital beneficiary. Until your death you would be the income beneficiary; you can use the property and receive any income it generates.

Chattel Mortgage   A charge over goods or equipment of a movable nature, as opposed to real estate. This document must be registered with the provincial government.

Codicil   Change or addition to a will requiring all the formalities of signing and witnessing needed for a will.

Collection Period   The average number of days it takes a company to collect receivables.

Commissioner for Taking Oaths   An official appointed by law to take affidavits such as a lawyer or notary public or other government appointee.

Common Law   The precedents established by previous court decisions, which have all the force of written statutes unless parliament passes a law to the contrary.

Common Stock   Securities which represent ownership in a corporation and carry voting privileges.

Conditional Sale   A sale made but not final until certain acts or events take place.

Consignment   Sale of goods through a third party whereby ownership of the goods remain in the name of the supplier until the goods have been sold, at which time the seller is indebted to the supplier.

Continuing Power of Attorney   A power of attorney which contains a "continuing" or "enduring" clause so that it will remain effective even if you become mentally incapable.

Contract   An agreement regarding mutual responsibilities between two or more parties. In business law, a contract exists when there has been a meeting of minds, whether the contract is written or oral. However, a contract should be clear and in written form to protect your interests.

Conveyancing   The transfer of property, or title to property, from one party to another.

Copyright   The legal registration and ownership of the product of a writer, painter, singer, musician, choreographer, photographer or other original creator. The owner of a copyright owns all rights to use the copyrighted material. Copyright laws are subject to international treaties.

Corporation   A business comprised of one or more individuals treated by the law as a separate legal entity. Liability is limited to the assets of the corporation. See Limited Company.

Co-Signers   Joint signers of a loan agreement, pledging to meet the obligations in case of default. When you ask someone to co-sign a note, you are asking them to fully assume a debt with you if you can't pay it back. They guarantee the loan will be paid back, and the lender can take legal action against them if they refuse to pay.

Covenant   A promise or legal arrangement you make when getting a loan. You must adhere to these covenants for your loan to remain in good standing.

Credit Bureau   A business whose product is information, which it sells, on the credit transactions and relevant personal information of individual people, as well as companies.

Damages   Money that must be paid to someone who has suffered financial losses or personal injury.

Debenture   A formal legal document provided as security for a loan. It has the practical effect of being a "mortgage" on the corporation. Only a corporation can issue a debenture.

Deemed Realization   A transfer of assets which, for tax purposes, is considered a "sale" by CCRA, although no cash or other consideration may be involved.

Demand Loan   A loan that must be repaid whenever the lender chooses.

Devise   A disposition of land by will.

Disability   The inability, due to illness or injury, to continue to work. Definitions of "disability" vary from contract to contract, and whether or not your policy will pay you benefits may well hinge on how it defines disability.

Discharged Bankrupt   One who has been declared legally bankrupt, and thus has no liability to debtors.

Due Diligence   The conducting of reasonable investigative procedures by the underwriter and other persons to provide a defensible basis for believing that there are no misrepresentations contained in a prospectus.

Easement   A right which allows one person to use the property of another.

Encumbrance   A legal claim registered against a property. The claim does not necessarily prevent the property from being transferred, but may affect the property's value. Examples of encumbrances are liens, judgments, rights of way, easements, leases and restrictive covenants. Mortgages are also considered to be encumbrances.

Enduring Power of Attorney   See Continuing Power of Attorney.

Equity   The difference between the assets and liabilities of a company, often referred to as net worth.

Equity Capital / Financing   All money invested in a business in exchange for ownership (shares). Venture capital is equity provided by outside investors (i.e., not the owner/manager). Equity does not have to be repaid on a specific date and there are no interest charges (although dividends are normally paid from time to time).

Escheat   The process by which the assets of a deceased person pass to the provincial government when he or she dies without a will and without a spouse and next-of-kin.

Escrow   The deferment of an obligation to pay or right of ownership for a stated time or until stated conditions are met.

Estate   The right, title or interest which a person has in any property. Your estate consists of the assets owned by you at death which are governed by your will.

Estate Freeze   A legal procedure which limits the growth in the value of the freezor's estate. This is done by diverting the growth to a subsequent generation.

Executor   The person(s) or institution named under a will to administer, manage and/or transfer an estate, in accordance with the terms of a will.

Fair Market Value   The price a commodity can command on a free market, one in which there is no compulsion on buyer or seller to accept or reject a certain amount.

Fiduciary   An individual or institution under a legal obligation to act for the benefit of another party.

Fiduciary Duty   The level of obligation required of a trustee. A fiduciary duty implies a very high level and standard of care in dealing with assets on behalf of a beneficiary. If this duty and standard is not met, the trustee could be legally liable for the consequences.

Financial Statements   Documents that show your financial situation. Two major statements are needed to cover the information necessary to run a business and get financing (income statement and balance sheet).

Fiscal Year   An accounting cycle of 12 months that could start at any point during a calendar year. The government uses April 1 to March 31.

Foreclose   To sell or cause to be sold, a property, when the owner fails to meet mortgage, tax or other debt payments on it. Must be approved by the courts.

Form of Business Organization   The legal structure that is established and registered and the appropriate level(s) of government in order to carry on a business.

Franchisee   The person (or firm) who has purchased a franchise and is responsible for managing the business.

Franchising   A way of starting a business whereby an already established firm supplies the product, trademark, techniques, materials and expertise, and sets standards in exchange for purchase price and ongoing benefit.

Franchisor   The person (or firm) granting a franchise.

Fraudulent Conveyance   An illegal transfer of ownership from one person to another for the purpose of cheating creditors.

Garnishee   To deduct money from a debtor's wages or receivables to pay a creditor. The creditor obtains a court order directing the person, company or bank to make the deduction and pay it into court.

General Power of Attorney   A document which gives your selected representative broad authority to make decisions relating to your assets.

Generally Accepted Accounting Procedures   GAAP is the term used to describe the basis on which financial statements are normally prepared. This is codified in the *Handbook of the Canadian Institute of Chartered Accountants.*

Going Public   The action of a private corporation in offering its shares for general sale to the public through the stock exchange.

Good Faith   An unspoken attitude of honesty and serious intention between two or more parties.

Goodwill   The value of customer lists, trade reputation, etc., which is assumed to go with a company and its name, particularly when trying to arrive at the sale price for the company. In accounting terms it is the amount a purchaser pays over the book value.

Grant of Probate   A certificate confirming the authority set out in a will to administer a particular estate; issued to an Executor by the court. Also called Grant of Letters Probate and Letters Probate.

Guarantor   A person or company that guarantees to pay the financial obligations of a business or contract.

Holding Company   A company which exists to buy and own a majority of shares in other companies, thus to control them.

Holograph Will   A will written completely in the handwriting of the person making it, having no witnesses to the signature of the testator.

Income Beneficiary   The person or persons entitled to the income generated by the trust property. The income includes dividends and interest. It does not commonly include capital gains, which become part of the capital. See Life Tenant.

Income Splitting   A tax planning device frequently available to business owners where total tax paid by the company and the shareholders can be minimized. Splitting can refer to splitting between salaries and dividends, husband and wife salaries, etc.

Intellectual Property   Knowledge and information which can be legally owned, as defined by laws governing copyright, trademarks, patents, industrial design, royalty obligations, etc.

Inter Vivos Trust   This type of trust document comes into effect during the lifetime of the settlor. Also known as a living trust.

Intestate   The person who dies without a will. A partial intestacy is where a valid will does not deal with all of the estate.

Irrevocable Trust   The person who created the trust cannot revoke it.

Issue   All persons who have descended from a common ancestor. It is a broader term than children which is limited to one generation (e.g., grandchildren, great-grandchildren, etc.)

Joint and Several Liability   Each (general) partner is fully liable for all the debts of the partnership and his personal assets may be required to pay off debts incurred by another partner.

Joint Tenancy   An estate which arises by the purchase of land by two or more persons. This type of tenancy includes the right of survivorship which means that when one owner dies, his or her share passes automatically to the other joint tenant. A joint tenant cannot pass on his or her interest by means of a will.

Joint Venture   A business partnership formed for the sake of a specific project. Joint ventures may be undertaken by two or more companies or individuals, or by the government and private companies.

Key Personnel Insurance   Special insurance available on the lives of the principal active shareholders in a company. Can be used to fund buy-sell agreements as well as to provide funds to continue the company in the event of one manager's death. The name the policies are registered in, as well as who pays the premiums, can have important tax implications.

Lease   A contract in which the owner of a piece of property gives the exclusive use of it to someone else, in exchange for a stated sum of money, for the duration of a specified time.

Leasehold Improvement   Renovation and other improvements made to the business premises. These become the property of the landlord.

Legacy   Personal property or money given by a will. See also Bequest.

Lessee   The tenant (or person) who signs a lease to get temporary use of space.

Lessor   The company (or person) providing temporary use of space in return for rental payments.

Letter of Credit (L/C)   An arrangement whereby an importer arranges with his or her bank to transfer the amount of the transaction to a Canadian bank for payment to the Canadian exporter. This amount is available to the exporter provided the requirements of the L/C are met. When the exporter presents the invoices and shipping documents to the bank, he or she receives immediate payment.

Letters of Administration   The court grant appointing an administrator to administer the estate of an individual dying intestate.

Letters Probate   The court grant confirming the appointment of an executor named in a will and confirming the validity of the will itself.

Leveraged Buy-out   To complete the financing in the purchase of a company, the purchaser borrows against its unused borrowing capacity (usually based on the company's market value of its assets rather than the book value).

Liabilities   All the debts of a business; includes short-term or current liabilities such as accounts payable, income taxes due, the amount of long-term debt that must be paid within 12 months; and long-term liabilities such as long-term debts and deferred income taxes. On a balance sheet, liabilities are subtracted from assets; what remains is the shareholder's equity or ownership in the business.

Lien   A charge placed over an asset by such parties as (1) the seller of that asset or (2) in the case of construction or repairs, by the person (contractor) who carries out the work. The lien holder may take possession until the asset/work is paid for in full. Liens must be registered under the various provincial laws in order to be protected and enforceable.

Life Interest   A benefit given to a beneficiary in a will that permits that beneficiary to enjoy or have the use of some property or some amount of money for the balance of the beneficiary's lifetime only.

Life Tenant   A beneficiary who has an interest in trust property for balance of that beneficiary's life (a life interest). For example, a beneficiary may be entitled to live in a house rent-free for life. On the death of the beneficiary, the trust property reverts to the capital beneficiary.

Limited Company   A separate legal entity that is owned by shareholders for the purpose of carrying on business. Assets and liabilities of owners (shareholders) are separate from the company. Can be private or public, as well as provincial or federal. Also called incorporated company or corporation.

Limited Liability The legal protection accorded shareholders of an incorporated company whereby the owner's financial liability is limited to the amount of his or her share ownership, except where he or she owes money to the company or has assumed additional liabilities (e.g., personally guaranteeing its debts).

Limited Partnership A legal partnership where certain owners assume responsibility only up to the amount of their investment. Investors who put up money for a business venture without being directly involved in its operation are not held responsible for the debts of the other partners beyond the possible loss of money they have invested.

Limited Power of Attorney A power of attorney which limits your attorney to specific transactions, such as banking, the sale of real estate, or negotiating securities.

Line of Credit A negotiated agreement with a bank, subject to periodic review, whereby the borrower is permitted to draw upon additional funds up to a specified limit at a certain rate of interest (e.g., prime rate plus 2%).

Liquidate To settle a debt or to convert to cash.

Liquidity A term used to describe the solvency of a business and which has special reference to the degree of readiness in which assets can be converted into cash without a loss. Also called cash position. If a firm's current assets cannot be converted into cash to meet current liabilities, the firm is said to be illiquid. A frequent measurement of liquidity is the quick or acid test ratio.

Lis Pendens A notice which can be registered on the title of a piece of property and which shows that the property is subject to a forthcoming lawsuit. The property cannot be transferred to another owner while the *lis pendens* is on title.

Living Trust A trust created by a settlor while he or she is alive. See Inter Vivos Trust.

Living Will Also referred to as a "health care directive" or "advance medical care directive." This document explains to family, friends, doctors and other caregivers your personal philosophy regarding medical treatment and health care. It also conveys your wishes with respect to procedures to prolong your life in the event of terminal illness.

Long-Term Liabilities Debts that will not be paid off within one year.

Medium-Term Financing Loans or other credit on which the principal does not have to be repaid for three to five years.

Misleading Advertising Advertising that lies, implicitly or explicitly, about the price, quality, or use of a product. Illegal.

Negative Covenant An undertaking not to do certain things. It is frequently argued that negative covenants are preferable to positive covenants because it is easier to establish if something which was not to have been done has in fact been done, rather than vice versa. The breaking of a covenant usually constitutes a default which in turn gives rise to certain specified remedies which can be taken by the security holder.

Net The amount that is left of a gross amount after deduction of expenses or debts. For example, the net working capital is the total current assets after deductions of the total current liabilities.

Net Lease Signifies a property lease where a lessee/tenant is responsible for all costs such as taxes, heat, light, power, insurance and maintenance.

Offer to Purchase A formal, legal agreement which offers a certain price for a specified real property. The offer may be firm (no conditions attached) or conditional (certain conditions must be fulfilled). Once the offer is accepted it becomes an "agreement of purchase and sale."

Option   The right to buy a property, business, or other asset or right within a certain time. The potential buyer must pay for this right, but the owner of the property may not sell to anyone else until the agreed-upon time has passed.

Order of Sale   Term used in the mortgage document to refer to the mortgagee's (lender's) right to sell the home, in many cases without court approval, in order to recover the full principal and interest outstanding. Generally used in the case of default of payment by the owner. If there is any money left after the property is sold, and after the lender has recovered its principal, interest and costs, the borrower would receive the balance.

Pari Passu   Side by side at an equal rate or in equal instalments or, in terms of security, ranking equally.

Partnership   A legal business relationship of two or more people or companies who share responsibilities, resources, profits, and liabilities. An agreement in writing is essential, detailing the nature of the relationship. Each province has a *Partnership Act* which governs this type of business structure.

Patent   The legal right to ownership of an invention issued in Canada under the *Patent Act*. For a limited period, the inventor can charge a royalty for the use and application of the invention or sell such rights to another person.

Payables   Trade or other liabilities that are due. One of the basic records kept by a bookkeeper is accounts payable.

Personal Guarantee   A personal promise made by an individual on behalf of a personal or corporate borrower to repay a debt if the borrower fails to repay as agreed.

Power of Attorney   A written document by which you grant to someone the authority to act on your behalf on various matters. A power of attorney is different from a will, which provides for the orderly distribution of your estate after your death; a power of attorney terminates on your death. There are different types of powers of attorney dealing with specific or general financial or health issues.

Power of Attorney for Personal Care   A document which gives your stated representative expansive authority to make personal care decisions on your behalf if you become mentally incapacitated. This document may include instructions normally covered in a "living will."

Preferred Creditor   A creditor who must be paid after secured creditors and before unsecured creditors in the event of a business failure under the *Bankruptcy and Insolvency Act*. Usually certain provincial and federal government departments.

Price Fixing   Collusion among competitive businesses to keep prices up. Illegal.

Principal   Property or capital assets as opposed to income; also, one who is directly concerned in a business enterprise.

Pro Forma   A projection or estimate of what may result in the future from actions in the present. A *pro forma* financial statement is one that shows how the actual operations of the business will turn out if certain assumptions are realized.

Probate   Formal proof before the appropriate officer or court that the will presented is the last will of the testator. In addition, the executor(s) named are formally confirmed.

Profit   The excess of the selling price over all costs and expenses incurred in making the sale. Gross profit is the profit before corporate income taxes. Net profit is the final profit of the firm after all deductions have been made.

Proprietorship   Sole ownership of a business. Personal and business assets and liabilities are not considered separate legal entities. Also called sole proprietorship.

Receivables   Money owing to a company from those who were extended credit.

Receivership The control of a business and its assets by a Receiver (usually a chartered accountant). This person is appointed by the creditor under the term of a debenture and remains in control until the debts are paid or the business and/or assets are sold.

Registered Encumbrances Legal claims against real property. Debt for which the property was pledged as security.

Return on Investment (ROI) The determination of the profit to be accrued from a capital investment.

Right of Way A form of easement, usually to allow public passage over private land or to allow municipalities and power companies the right to lay down and maintain sewers, gas lines, etc.

Secured Protected or guaranteed. A secured loan makes the lender better protected, by having the debtor place something of value as collateral as a guarantee of repayment.

Securities Negotiable instruments, such as stocks and bonds.

Security (often called Collateral Security) Assets(s) belonging to the business or to you personally, which are pledged to the bank in support of a loan and which can be sold in the event you do not repay your loan. In the case of term loans, the property (e.g., land, buildings, equipment) being purchased with the loan usually forms the security for the loan.

Shotgun Agreement An agreement between partners that gives either party the right to offer to buy all of the other's shares in the event of a disagreement. The offer states a price, which can be accepted or rejected. If the other party refuses the bid, he/she must buy the offeror's shares at the offeror's offering price.

Small Business A firm with 20 or fewer employees. This is the definition used in Statistics Canada's monthly employment survey. According to the federal or various provincial governments, a small business is any manufacturing firm with fewer than 100 employees or, in any other sector, a firm with fewer than 50 employees. Using either definition, small business accounts for 80% to 90% of all businesses in Canada.

Specific Bequest A gift under a will of a specific term of personal property or a specific amount of cash.

Spousal Trust A trust, under which the spouse is entitled to all of the income for his or her lifetime. Spousal trusts are most commonly created as testamentary trusts, that is, takes effect on death and is part of the will. The major benefit of a spousal trust is that the transfer of property to the trust does not create a capital gain.

Spread Expression used among financial sources to describe the difference between the interest rate paid on money and the interest rate received (e.g., cost is 6%, rate charged is 8%, spread is 2%).

Subject Clauses Conditions that have to be met or escape options in an offer to purchase and sell, allowing the potential buyer or seller to back out if the deal starts to look unsatisfactory.

Subordinated Debt An obligation where one lender has agreed in writing to rank behind another in claiming an asset. The lender will receive his or her capital back only after the other has been fully paid out. A bank will often insist that shareholder loans be subordinated to the obligations to the bank. This is also known as subrogation.

Term Loan A loan intended for medium or long-term financing to supply cash to purchase fixed assets, such as machinery, land or buildings, or to renovate business premises.

Terms of Sale   The conditions concerning payment for a purchase.

Testamentary Trust   A trust which is created under a will.

Testator   A person who makes a will.

Trade Credit   The credit terms offered by suppliers (no interest is charged until after the due date).

Trademark   A name, symbol or other mark that identifies a product to customers, and is legally owned by its manufacturer or inventor.

Trust   A legal arrangement in which one person (the settlor) transfers legal title to a trustee (a fiduciary) to manage the property for the benefit of a person or institution (the beneficiaries). A testamentary trust is set up in a will and takes effect only after death. There are two main types of trust components. A living trust (*inter vivos*) is a trust set up during an individual's lifetime.

Trust Account   The separate account in which a lawyer or real estate broker holds funds until the real estate closing takes place.

Trust Funds   Funds held in trust, either held as a deposit for the purchase of real property or to pay taxes and insurance.

Trustee   A person who acts in a position of trust in administering assets on behalf of someone else. The person or institution who takes legal title to the trust property and who is required to follow the terms of the trust. The trustee may be an individual or trust company or both (co-trustees). Often settlors will name joint or co-trustees with equal authority.

Turnkey Operation   A project such as setting up a business or an office in which all work is done by a contractor and handed over in working order to the owner.

Venture Capital   An individual or institution that provides "high risk" debt or equity capital unavailable from traditional sources for the growth (or in some instances, seed funding) of small businesses at any stage before they go public.

Warrant   A financial instrument which authorizes the holder to purchase securities at a predetermined price until a specified time in the future.

Warranty   This is a minor promise that does not go to the heart of the contract. If there is a breach of warranty, the purchaser cannot cancel but must complete the contract and sue for damages, that is, financial losses that can be shown.

Will   A written document conforming to strict provincial rules relating to form and signing. The purpose is to instruct the executors appointed under the will how the property of a deceased person should be distributed.

Wills Variation Act   The provincial statute permitting a spouse, dependent child or others to obtain benefits from the estate of a deceased if not adequately provided for by the will.

Winding Up   The legal procedures of closing down a limited company.

Index

About the Author

Douglas Gray, LL.B., is a Vancouver-based expert on small business. Formerly a practicing business lawyer, he is now a consultant, speaker, columnist and author or co-author of 19 bestselling business and personal finance books. Among these titles is Canada's most popular and comprehensive business book, *The Complete Canadian Small Business Guide, 3rd edition*. His books include ten titles on small business, six on real estate and three on retirement and estate planning issues. Some of his business books are published in up to nine languages.

Douglas has given seminars to over 250,000 people nationally and internationally in his various areas of expertise. He is a member of the Canadian Bar Association.

He is a regular expert contributor on personal finance issues for various Internet sites and Microsoft and Quicken CD-Roms. He is frequently interviewed by the media as an authority on business and personal finance matters.

Douglas lives with his wife in Vancouver.

READER FEEDBACK AND AUTHOR SEMINARS

If you would like to give the author feedback on the contents of this book or suggestions for future revisions, or would like further information about seminars and consulting services available, please contact the author at:

Douglas Gray, LL.B.
Canadian Enterprise Development Group Inc.
#300—3665 Kingsway
Vancouver, B.C. V5R 5W2
Tel: (604) 436-9311
Fax: (604) 436-9155
Email: **dgray@institute.ca**

McGraw-Hill Ryerson's
SMALL BUSINESS SOLUTIONS SERIES

BIG IDEAS FOR GROWING YOUR SMALL BUSINESS

0-07-087874-9 • $24.99 • paperback

Your business is up and running. Now take it to the next level – make it bigger and better. Learn how to grow your business and still remain successful and profitable.

WIRED FOR SMALL BUSINESS SUCCESS

0-07-087593-6 • $24.99 • paperback

These days, being well connected has little to do with how many people you know. Full of practical advice on making the best technology choices for your business.

SMART MARKETING ON A SMALL BUDGET

0-07-560469-8 • $22.99 • paperback

Customers are the lifeblood of any thriving business. Learn how to prepare effective, professional-looking marketing materials that will attract and keep clients—all on a shoe-string budget!

HIRING, MANAGING AND KEEPING THE BEST

0-07-0864217 • $24.99 • paperback

You have always dreamed of being your own boss... but does the idea of being someone else's boss give you nightmares? Find out all you need to know to handle every aspect of employee matters.

MAKE SURE IT'S DEDUCTIBLE

0-07-560543-0 • $18.99 • paperback

Paying taxes is a certainty in life, but it doesn't have to be a hardship. Learn little-known tips that can save SOHO owners big tax dollars —from Evelyn Jacks, Canada's most trusted tax authority.

WHAT TO SAY WHEN YOUR CUSTOMERS WON'T PAY

0-07-560411-6 • $18.99 • paperback

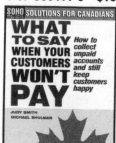

Every business has to deal with accounts receivable. But collections doesn't have to rely on intimidation tactics and threats. Learn the most effective ways to get your due —and keep your customers too.

BOOKS FOR
SMALL
BUSINESS